FEELING GODLY

FEELING GODLY

Religious Affections and Christian Contact in Early North America

EDITED BY

CAROLINE WIGGINTON AND
ABRAM VAN ENGEN

University of Massachusetts Press
Amherst and Boston

Printed in the United States of America

ISBN 978-1-62534-590-5 (paper); 591-2 (hardcover)

Designed by Sally Nichols
Set in Caslon Antique and Adobe Caslon Pro
Printed and bound by Books International, Inc.

Cover design by Frank Gutbrod
Cover by Mahlon Day. Detail from *The New-England Primer, Improved,* pages 12-13. [Books].
Retrieved from https://libwww.freelibrary.org/digital/item/55721

Library of Congress Cataloging-in-Publication Data

Names: Wigginton, Caroline, editor. | Van Engen, Abram C., 1981– editor.
Title: Feeling godly : religious affections and Christian contact in early North America / edited by Caroline Wigginton, Abram Van Engen.
Description: Amherst : University of Massachusetts Press, [2021] | Includes bibliographical references and index.
Identifiers: LCCN 2020053363 (print) | LCCN 2020053364 (ebook) | ISBN 9781625345905 (paperback) | ISBN 9781625345912 (hardcover) | ISBN 9781613768464 (ebook) | ISBN 9781613768471 (ebook)
Subjects: LCSH: North America—Church history. | Conversion—Christianity—History. | Emotions—Religious aspects—Christianity—History.
Classification: LCC BR510 .F44 2021 (print) | LCC BR510 (ebook) | DDC 277.3/07—dc23
LC record available at https://lccn.loc.gov/2020053363
LC ebook record available at https://lccn.loc.gov/2020053364

British Library Cataloguing-in-Publication Data
A catalog record for this book is available from the British Library.

Contents

Acknowledgments

This volume began with a panel organized for the Society of Early Americanists biennial conference in 2013. We thank Craig Atwood, Kathleen Howard, Noeleen McIlvenna, and Ivy Schweitzer for participating in that session. The Huntington Library was instrumental in helping us expand our exploration. We are grateful to Steve Hindle and the Huntington Library for awarding us a grant and helping us gather scholars and public intellectuals for a two-day conference on religious affections in colonial North America in San Marino, California, in 2017. We are also grateful to the conference's presenters: Marilynne Robinson, Emma Anderson, Herman Bennett, Joanna Brooks, Emily Clark, Kathleen Donegan, Sandra Gustafson, Peter Mancall, Barbara Rosenwein, Jon Sensbach, Emily Berquist Soule, Scott Manning Stevens, and Mark Valeri. We thank the University of Massachusetts Press and its generous and thoughtful readers. Finally, as always, we thank our Early American Writing Group—Angie Calcaterra, Travis Foster, Greta LaFleur, Michele Currie Navakas, Wendy Roberts, and Kacy Tillman—for offering their usual invaluable feedback on our introduction. Their excellent scholarship and ways of reading have profoundly influenced this collection and all our work. We dedicate this book to them in thanks for all their insight, encouragement, and aid through the years.

FEELING GODLY

Introduction

CAROLINE WIGGINTON AND
ABRAM VAN ENGEN

Feeling Godly explores the central importance of religious affections in early North America. Ranging across evangelical New England laity and preachers, Haudenosaunee Anglicans, Mohegan missionaries, Nahua and Spanish Catholics in Mexico, Quaker Carolinians, enslaved Barbadian proselytes, and more, the essays in this volume open surprising comparative possibilities that illuminate important distinctions and confluences around theology and experience, mind and body, intellect and feeling.[1] In doing so, the collection suggests a new avenue for explicating the often unruly spiritual and emotional transformations wrought by contact with and between Christian communities.

Two examples from diverse geographies and time periods demonstrate the productive juxtapositions encouraged by a consideration of religious affections. In an 1804 letter, free Black Antiguan Anne Hart Gilbert (1773–1834) employs a biblical verse to convey the spiritual state of her island's population prior to the arrival of Methodist missionaries in the 1760s: "Darkness covered the Land and gross darkness the hearts of the people."[2] Riffing on a quote from Isaiah, she adds a reference to "hearts" and thereby creates an unexpected parallel to "land." To modify scripture, even if attempting only to clarify it, is to interpret it; and here the interpretation focuses our attention not on people but on the people's hearts. Her version suggests that the affections—the disposition and expressions of the heart—should be the true target of conversion and salvation.[3] Christianity converts hearts weighed down by darkness, clearing away the clouds so that they may look up to God. It catalyzes a chain reaction that lightens first the hearts, then the people, then the land.[4]

For Hart Gilbert, the hearts most in need of conversion were those of the enslaved. Slaveholders had kept their hearts dark on purpose through willful refusal to share "Moral and divine truth" with them, "lest by it they should discover" they were "Men, and Brethren" rather than "Beasts, and Reptiles." Their hearts' darkness was evidenced primarily by what she views as "diabolical superstition." She describes funeral processions that included rattles and improvised songs recounting the "heathenish . . . Life & Death of the deceased," and prayers to the spiritual world to maintain "friend[sh]ip" with the dead and avenge unnatural deaths. Prior to conversion, enslaved Antiguans marked Christmas by "strewing" food and "pouring bottles of Rum, upon the graves of their departed friends." She notes that the island's "Obeah men & women of that day were very rich people; possessed of large sums of money," as Black and white Antiguans alike employed their knowledge, rituals, and charms to protect against harm and retaliate against their abusers and foes.[5]

In describing such practices, Hart Gilbert's epistolary history of Antigua foregrounds the affections as a locus for religious conversion.[6] To judge the spiritual state of others—and the spiritual state of an entire land and people—through *feeling* can be done only by observing and commenting on their emotional *expressions*. The inner heart must out. Prior to conversion, enslaved persons' funeral processions were structured around what Hart Gilbert takes to be the wrong emotions or the wrong attachments: mourners felt the loss of a friend or family member, desired ongoing connection, and demanded revenge. They used Obeah remedies and rituals to protect against enslavers' brutality, signaling a religious practice driven by earthly fears and anxieties.[7] "Clouds of sin and error" hid God, leading the unconverted to find joy, fear, and sorrow in their relationships with the people and goods of the world, as their ceremonies and practices made clear. Conversion promised to shift the heart away from both improper emotions and the improper expression of emotions. Methodism, Hart Gilbert claims in her history, attaches hearts to God. Christianity allows enslaved and free Antiguans of all races to understand that they are "Brethren" because they have the capacity to love God with one another rather than simply feel love for one another.

A plethora of differences would seem to separate Hart Gilbert from John Winthrop, the Puritan governor of Massachusetts Bay in 1630. Yet more than a century before Hart Gilbert, he too adjusted scripture ever so slightly to make the pronouncements of Moses emphasize the affections of the heart. In the last paragraph of *A Modell of Christian Charity*, his "city on a hill" sermon, Winthrop invoked and modified Deuteronomy 30:15–20. Moses commanded all his followers "to love the Lord thy God"; Winthrop added that they were also "to love one another." His model religious community required a reciprocal relationship between love of God and love of one another. As he explained throughout his sermon, its success depended thoroughly upon the "affeccions of loue in the hearte."[8] Yet within a few years, Christian affections would become again a major source of contestation and vulnerability. According to Winthrop, Anne Hutchinson and her fellow Antinomians infected Massachusetts Bay with a spiritual "plague" by preying on godly Puritans' avid desire for love: they "would strangely labour to insinuate themselves into their [targets'] affections, by loving salutes, humble carriage, kind invitements, friendly visits, and so they would winne upon men, and steale into their bosomes, before they were aware." By degrees Antinomians "seduce[d]" hearts away from Puritan elders and the colony's "spirituall Fathers," then used those affections of friendship and love to denounce ministers as unsaved and spread what many of those ministers considered false teaching.[9] Despite differences elsewhere, here Hart Gilbert and Winthrop agree: the affections and their expression are a locus for religious judgment, exchange, and transformation, good and bad. The community—land, colony—hinges on religious affections.[10]

Hart Gilbert's and Winthrop's writings point us to considering how a study of the affections may help explain and illumine the transformations wrought by contact with and between Christians in early North America. All people feel emotions, ranging from fear, terror, and hatred to joy, ecstasy, attachment, and love. At the same time, how people name, interpret, value, manage, and express particular emotions—including the pleasurable ones—can vary with individuals and communities, cultures and geographies, spiritual practices and religious beliefs. Shared affections can bridge seemingly intractable differences, and their absence can stymie exchange. They can be conduit and language or barrier and disciplinary technology. Emotions rather than race or status shape Hart Gilbert's history of Antigua and understanding of conversion. Darkness covers the island because most Antiguans feel and express sinful emotions and earthly attachments. Their affections are the wrong ones, and Black followers of Obeah and nominal white Christians who feel improperly are akin. When Christianity changes hearts, Hart Gilbert argues, it changes everything: feelings, beliefs, and actions. Emotions also shape Winthrop's vision and early history of Massachusetts Bay. Realigning the affections to enfold God and fellow Puritans catalyzes the founding of a praiseworthy and glorifying colony, but attachments of love and sympathy with the wrong sort can make the colony prone to unwanted and destructive transformations as well.

Reading Winthrop and Hart Gilbert together helps us reread an older, ingrained trajectory of early American development. In the usual teleology, Protestant Christianity in North America moves away from harsh and hierarchical Puritanism toward liberatory and emotional evangelicalism. It moves from fear and obedience to love and joy, emotions more often associated with the affections. This sort of account often implies a focus that moves from stratification and social control to personalized freedom and application, and it aligns with a common political narrative of the U.S. nation's democratic origins.[11] But observing that "religious affections" pertain throughout, not just to the rise of evangelicalism, disrupts that account. The radical appeal of evangelicalism for many Americans—white and Black, enslaved and free, Native, Caribbean and otherwise—is well known.[12] But time and again Winthrop returns to Puritans' "sweet" and "simple" capacity for love, individual and collective: Puritans too felt a radical appeal to the heart. Hart Gilbert, conversely, used the religious affections to define alternative norms, expectations, and forms of authority; she insisted that all Antiguans must love God with others, rather than feel love for others at the expense of what was for her the one true God. The act of *loving with* would show that all were "Brethren" because all had one holy affection: for God. A revolution in the brutal iniquities of a slave society should follow, but as an effect rather than impetus of conversion.[13]

Through explorations of diverse examples like these, this volume provides a set of conversations about the complex meanings and operations of religious affections. Four essays limn and apply definitions of religious affections within a particular site of Christian contact, and four scholars in turn respond, often reconsidering an essay's definition and approach within an alternative context. We focus on Christianity because it has been central to interdisciplinary scholarship in early North American studies, tied as it is to the continent's political, economic, military, and social colonization. As Susan Juster and Linda Gregerson emphasize, the region's "religious and political narratives of discovery and resettlement" have an "intimate connection": "It is no exaggeration to say that religious passions and conflicts drove" European colonization.[14] Exchanges could be violent or harmonious, with wide-ranging spiritual and secular effects that enfolded everyone, Christian and non-Christian alike. Indeed, as Stephanie Kirk and Sarah Rivett maintain, "The collision of European traditions with American environmental and cultural realities, the reinstitution of religious hierarchy in colonial settings, and the challenge of indigenous [and we would add African] cultures and new population configurations engendered religious reinvention."[15] These reinventions and other changes arose from and gave rise to new and confounding feelings and emotional expressions. We refer to these feelings and expressions as *affections* in order to emphasize that they include not just pain and fear but joy and pleasure. Christians in early North America, including the Caribbean, had to negotiate what it means to love God (and whether or not to love the Christian one) in a shifting environment of unruly human feeling.

We do not claim to offer decisive definitions and conclusions; rather, for us, the concept of religious affections produces a series of questions with variable and provocative answers that can begin a longer and larger conversation. How are the "hearts" in Hart Gilbert related to the "affections" in John Winthrop? What are affections anyway, and when do they become "religious"? How do religious belief and practice shape the expression and interpretation of the emotions and vice versa? How do communities combine theologies, perspectives, experiences, and practices of multiple surrounding groups and cultures, some Christian and others not? How do affections cross religious, cultural, linguistic, and sectarian divides, even when the exchange is unwanted? And when do they build barriers that cannot be crossed? How might a focus on religious affections across different settings and among different kinds of Christians in sites of varied contact help us better understand the many kinds of conversion happening in early North America: conversions to Christianity but also within Christianity itself? And in particular, what difference does that inextricably intercultural context of early North American encounter make? These are some of the guiding questions of this collection.

What Is the Religious? What Are the Affections?

The focus of this collection is the place of religious affections in scenes of contact with and between Christians in early North America. But what are the religious affections, especially in cultures where the religious permeated every part of society in ways that would not necessarily be recognized by that culture *as* "religious"? In that case, it does not make sense to define a religious affection by outlining a certain kind of feeling against some other predetermined nonreligious realm of affection or emotion. The key here and throughout, it seems to us, is to focus on the definitions and understandings offered by particular communities at particular times, trying to determine how they policed, guarded, encouraged, discouraged, recognized, acknowledged, or denied various emotions. Which ones are pleasurable, desirable, proper, or godly? If we ask what constitutes "religious affections" for a given set of people, we find ourselves situated in communities of interpretation—and we also have to recognize when those communities had no such term at all. How to constitute the religious is always an act of interpretation, and that act only gets harder when we ask what constitutes a religious *affection*.

Within the discipline of religious studies, agreeing on what religion is has proved to be a long-standing intractable problem. As Malory Nye points out in his concise textbook *Religion: The Basics*, one can assemble dozens of definitions.[16] Moreover, the tenets and practices of a religion frequently do not align, especially among the laity. Therefore, the discipline has often attempted to gain a comparative understanding of religion through a kind of anthropological approach to communities, observing and examining cultural behavior and expression. Getting into the specifics of what people actually do in their daily lives, rather than (or in addition to) what they say they believe, is part and parcel of what many call "lived religion."[17] Such a method attempts to move beyond doctrines and creeds, asking instead how people embody and inhabit religion in their regular lives—sometimes flowing from their stated beliefs, sometimes in contradiction to them, sometimes giving rise to them or challenging them, but always inhabiting religion beyond a set of statements. This understanding of religion has been bolstered in recent years by the rise of "post-secularism," which, in addition to questioning any firm boundary between the "religious" and the nonreligious or "secular," has also revealed the way that Protestant investments in questions of faith, doctrine, and belief have too often dominated the definition, description, and study of religion—and even of secularism as well.[18]

Religion, then, is at the very least more than a set of propositions to which people give assent, and it often works differently than first having a set of ideas and secondly living them out (though such a relation also exists). Communities of formation and ways of life—including rituals and rites that may go back a long way—give shape and form to beliefs, which can arise secondarily or sometimes never come to full or articulate expression. For this reason, more scholars have begun to call for "broader, richer understandings of religion [that] might embrace habits of thought and intellectual propositions, certainly, but also the structures of practice (spanning ritual and language itself), the horizons and possibilities of belief, the exploration and discipline of virtue, the complexities of ethical relation, the potentialities of exchange, the goodness of faith, love, and hope."[19] We agree with Nye: to contain these approaches in a brief definition of "religion" or the "religious" cannot be easy—if even possible—but a good starting point might be Daniel Philpott's definition of religion as "communities of belief and practice oriented around claims about the ultimate ground of existence."[20]

An important emphasis here for us lies on the concept of "community," which serves as a useful heuristic for understanding "religious affections." Religious affections arise in relation. For many, more than one person or being must be present at the moment of affections—in both the experience and the understanding of that experience. Even when "religious affections" describe a person's inmost private rapture, those affections come about in relation to a spirit or a god or multiple gods or a sense of the sacred. Just as crucially, those particular religious affections come already shaped in the understanding and experience of them by communities of tradition, practice, and belief which distinguish religious affections from the nonreligious, or the properly religious from the improperly religious. Such communities not only help determine the meaning of what has happened to a person but also help produce the very thing that is happening.

Religions prepare the groundwork for religious affections, and they do so through community and tradition.

Because the study of religious affections requires a consideration of communal norms, it is also always a study of authority. Distinguishing one kind of religious feeling from another—while at the same time attempting to prompt and produce those feelings—leads to questions of how those decisions get made or enforced. Who decides what constitutes a proper religious expression? Who draws the boundaries around affections, directing them one way rather than another, and what happens when affections breach those bounds and reach across orthodox lines? Orthodoxy—which comes from the Greek for "straight opinion"—is often all about drawing clear lines, *straight* lines, but affections seldom flow in such ways. They are blurry, hard to capture, difficult to define or describe, often seeping out in multiple directions at once. That is why, for example, it took Jonathan Edwards in his *Treatise Concerning Religious Affections* (1746) so many pages to get straight what counts as a proper religious affection and what does not. Authority and community are both present wherever affections are known or experienced as religious, sometimes comfortably supporting one another, sometimes filled with tension, contradiction, and challenge. Community and authority guide how individuals relate to their communities and assess their own spiritual experiences and also how other overlapping communities—racial, economic, political, cultural—shifted and emerged alongside the experience and expression of emotion.

The study of religions in early North America has much to gain by examining more closely how they shaped or were shaped by community and authority, including how community and authority intersected in the expression, description, disciplining, and undisciplining of religious affections. What role did particular values, ways of feeling, and modes of expression play in configuring particular doctrines or beliefs or practices in those communities? And how did those doctrines, beliefs, and practices in turn come to change the values, feelings, and expressions of a whole host of religious groups? We study religious affections because we are interested in how the individual somatic experience of emotion is embedded and interpreted within and between religious communities, while always extending back out beyond the self and producing relations and transformations, sometimes even unconsciously. Many early North American communities considered themselves to be Christian even as they often differed in regard to what it meant to worship, live, and feel as Christians. Because of these differences, studying religious affections requires understanding contact not just with but also between Christians.

This is no easy task, given the multiplicity of overlapping communities. As suggested earlier, however "bound" people might be to a particular religious community, they belong to far more fellowships than just their "religious" one—and sometimes to more than one religious community itself. Communities come together; norms collide; some people leave one community for another, or integrate one aspect of one community alongside other aspects of others. Religious affections point us to the marked way in which systems and structures of practice, belief, and worship are seldom stable. The boundary lines are porous, always shifting. Hart Gilbert's "History of Methodism," with which we began, serves as a case in point. Her text offers a history of religious affections wherein multiple spiritual traditions uneasily coexist. Many of her fellow Antiguans live, pray, and feel in several communities at once. As narrated in her history, the emotions and practices of eighteenth-century Antiguans belie easy distinctions between the religious and secular, the spiritual and medicinal, ceremony and daily life. Religious affections bridge these divides and connect Antigua and its conversions to a longer and broader cultural history.

While we think there is a great deal still left to explore and many new insights to discover, in some ways this volume joins a process that has been ongoing for ages. The study of religion and emotion is not new. Modern studies of religion and emotion begin by moving, in a sense, outside of religious traditions and trying to account in a more universal way for the relationship between emotional experience and religious belief in any religious tradition. In the nineteenth century, for example, Friedrich Schleiermacher defined religion as the "feeling of absolute dependence" and differentiated that feeling from all others. A certain kind of feeling lay at the heart of all religious traditions. Meanwhile, Rudolf Otto identified an emotional experience he called *mysterium tremendum*—a mysterious, almost mystical feeling he placed at the foundation of any religion. William James's important work added a "descriptive/typological approach," as religious studies scholar John Corrigan has written, which attempted to create "inventories of 'kinds' of religious experiences" that went into the making of religious belief. James furthermore theorized emotions as body-first sensations, physiological responses that generated emotional meaning or explanations after the fact.[21] In *Varieties of Religious Experience* (1902), James came to a more complex view of "religious emotion" in particular, seeing a kind of consciousness impacted by cultural setting and related to bodily sensation. But the thrust of James's work was to categorize and define. Meanwhile, Émile Durkheim, another influential theorist writing at the turn of the twentieth century, took a different approach. As Corrigan explains, his was an "analytical method" that attempted an investigation into the "sources and 'causes' of religion." Whereas James wanted to describe and categorize religious emotion and experience, Durkheim wanted to explain it.[22]

These theorists, working from a variety of disciplines and perspectives, largely assumed a universalist explanation of both religion and emotion. One of the dividing lines in academic studies of emotion has been the difference between such approaches and those that emphasize some form of social or cultural constructedness. More and more, such a distinction has separated scholars by discipline and department. Scientific accounts of emotion often attempt to find something approximating the universal, reaching for what is held in common across human nature and diverse cultures. The humanities, in contrast, have often (not always) emphasized the way that emotions take shape only in context. The meaning of any particular emotion is part of the emotion itself, and meaning arises from the constraints, expectations, norms, and possibilities of a given culture at a particular time. Historians especially have taken up this latter approach, and in the past forty years or more they have begun unfolding "the historically variable ways persons conceive of emotion and the ways emotional life has changed over time because of altered contexts for social life."[23]

This kind of history is known as the history of emotions, and it constitutes a relatively young subfield of historical studies. Recent years have seen a host of new introductions and overviews making sense of this movement, and most of those introductions and overviews date the launch of this particular historical interest to 1985, when Carol Zisowitz Stearns and Peter N. Stearns brought attention to the term "emotionology" and called for the study of changing emotional standards.[24] To conduct such research, Stearns and Stearns studied modern conduct manuals, deciphering appropriate emotional expression from the advice given, and separating that emotional standard from the actual emotional experience of historical actors. In that sense, "emotionology" began the history of emotions with a look at the spoken and unspoken emotional norms a society sets.[25]

This was the first stage, but others soon followed. Barbara Rosenwein and Riccardo Cristiani, in their recent introduction to the field, usefully lay out four stages in the development of the history of emotions. The second stage begins with the work of William Reddy and his twinned concepts of "emotives" and "emotional regimes." The focus, for Reddy, was on power. "Emotional control is the real site of the exercise of power," he wrote, explaining that "politics is just a process of determining who must repress as illegitimate, who must foreground as valuable, the feelings and desires that come up for them in given contexts and relationships."[26] Emotional regimes set the standards for proper and improper feeling and expression, but emotives are always working up through and against that regime, reordering it as they come to fruition. Emotives, in that sense, are the motor of change. They are speech acts expressing the emotion of the speaker that simultaneously produce and perform that emotion, changing both the addressor and the addressee. As Reddy makes clear, emotives are not static descriptions of emotions; they are expressions of emotion that act on the world. If emotional regimes are top-down affairs, the official norms set by those in power, emotives are bottom-up occurrences, individual expressions that always bear some relation to the regime, whether conformity or tension or challenge, or likely some combination of all three.[27]

The concept of "emotional communities" from the work of Barbara Rosenwein—a foremost scholar of the history of the emotions and the author of this book's afterword—afforded a third stage of development. As Rosenwein defines them, "emotional communities are groups—usually but not always social groups—that have their own particular values, modes of feeling, and ways to express those feelings. . . . Emotional communities are not always 'emotional.' They simply share important norms concerning the emotions that they value and deplore and the modes of expressing them. Thus the members of an emotional community will not necessarily express love or affection toward one another if that community values hostile, aggressive, or ambivalent interpersonal relations."[28] Yet as Rosenwein notes, few people belong to only one hermetically sealed community. Most come into contact with several, even through the course of a single day, and each community has its own competing or coordinating set of expectations and rules for feeling and expression. Rosenwein in that sense brought emotions closer to lived experience on a daily basis. A certain kind of elite or politically powerful class might set expectations, but the daily community had far more to do with the expectations guiding one's experiences, behaviors, emotions, and expressions. Thus, "Rosenwein was more interested in the multiple emotional solutions that people created even within a seemingly hegemonic system."[29] As a result, her idea of "emotional communities," which has been so fruitful for so many scholars (including many of the contributors to this volume), has often led especially to microhistorical work on particular communities in particular contexts.[30]

The latest stage in the history of emotions comes with a renewed focus on the body, in the line of William James but with an innovative account of performance. The foundational figure here is Gerd Althoff, whose notion of "performatives" suggests not that people feign their emotions, but rather that emotional expression necessarily involves bodily expression, a performance visible and communicable to others, which might arise from the willed actions of the actor or might arise more from the pressures and influences of the surrounding environment. The emphasis, as Rosenwein and Cristiani make clear, is on the "external effects of emotions as they play out in front of others, and also on the ways in which those effects, whether desired or dreaded, define the self who is emoting."[31] Where the first three stages in the history of emotions (emotionology, emotives and emotional regimes, emotional communities) focused on language and text, the most recent stage has returned the emphasis, above all, to the body.[32]

These concepts from the history of emotions—emotionology, emotional regimes, emotives, emotional communities, and performatives—can help shed light on religious affections, contact, and transformation in early North America. Christians like Hart Gilbert and Winthrop carry with their faiths certain sets of emotional values. These values indicate which emotions are good and where feelings should be directed. They help distinguish between right and wrong hearts, and provide prescriptions for how a true love of God manifests itself. In the case of Hart Gilbert, her standards (emotionology) attempt, in a way, to control expressions (emotional regime), but those active expressions (emotives) influence both her understanding of the affections she witnesses and those who are doing the expressing. These expressions are often behaviors (performatives), ritualized and otherwise, which give the emotions force and allow them to be seen, analyzed, understood, and experienced. Moreover, she applies her standards and assessment to a mix of groups that combine different traditions, different norms, different experiences and expectations (emotional communities). Her history of Antigua thus narrates and speculates how contact between different religions *and* emotional communities can and should produce change.

In early North America, an array of religions and emotional communities came in contact. Their shared capacities to define, practice, and interpret religious affections—even as the tenor and expression of religious affections differed—presented new opportunities for communication, new forms of misapprehension, new configurations of community, and new structures of power. As the history of emotions and the example of Hart Gilbert both make clear, emotions are experienced by everyone, but how they are experienced, which ones are experienced, and ultimately how they are interpreted is neither universal nor essential. Their consequence for both communities and individuals are highly contingent and historically bound. Rosenwein insists upon this point. The most precise definition of emotion that she can give is that "there is a biological and universal human aptitude for feeling and expressing what we now call 'emotions.' But what those emotions are, what they are called, how they are evaluated and felt, and how they are expressed (or not)—all these are shaped by 'emotional communities.'"[33]

This volume is concerned specifically with the way emotional communities defined, regulated, and produced religious affections. And like emotions generally, the subset *affections* is both consequential and contingent. We conclude this section of the introduction, therefore, with a series of registers that we believe, in combination with the essays and responses, can produce new approaches to, and understandings of, how religious affections help us track transformations wrought by contact with and between Christians in early North America.

The first register comes from Jonathan Edwards, as described in *A Treatise Concerning Religious Affections*. As Edwards famously insists, "True Religion, in great Part, consists in holy Affections." In part one of his treatise, he offers a brief definition: "The Affections are no other, than the more vigorous and sensible Exercises of the Inclination and Will of the Soul."[34] As he expounds upon his definition, he provides a series of synonyms for affections, or the soul's vigorous inclinations: liking, pleasedness, joy, approval, hope, gratitude, delight, desire, complacence, and love. The soul's inclinations are endowed by God, and are counterbalanced by the soul's disinclinations: disliking, displeasedness, aversion, rejection, disapproval, grief, fear, anger, sorrow, and hatred.[35] Affections in an Edwardsian context are simply part of the makeup of human nature, being the action of the will; they can be positive or negative, deceptive or true. Godly affections, however, have as their object the essential and transcendent, and to follow the soul's godly inclinations requires individuals to attend to their feelings—those produced by bodily sensation and by reflection—and judge both their intensity and their aim. The vigor stirred up by God or the godly, whether it is a vigorous joy or a vigorous sorrow, can help Christian believers determine not just what affections they hold but (more importantly) for whom or for what causes they hold them. This assessment of the strength and orientation of affections then could become a way to judge one's "heart."[36]

Focusing on an evaluation of the heart, this register of affection could be as determinative of one's social status as one's spiritual status. For to have a great deal of affection for others—to be touched by others, and to be caring and tender toward others—raises (among other things) the eighteenth-century context of moral sense philosophy.[37] "Affection" and the "affections" were not necessarily key words among such philosophers, who focused more on the language of "sensibility" and "sympathy," but all of this vocabulary operated in a similar orbit; all of it indicated a person whose heart could be reached and moved—someone who had replaced a heart of stone with a heart of flesh. According to moral sense philosophers, Christian civil society depended on the presence in all people of some such affection, which was often considered simply a part of human nature. And yet it could also be cultivated and trained, so that the more "sensible" people were, the more refined and civilized they might be thought.

Moral sense philosophy—which deeply influenced theologians like Edwards—points to the widespread use of affection and other performances of emotion to evaluate individuals and their status within a spiritual community. As in our earlier discussion of affections, there is a strong connection between individual experience and communal belonging: the ability to experience and express the right sorts of affections in the right ways at the right times in the right sorts of directions. These norms were in motion, a product of the interplay and reciprocal relation between individual and community that allow for change over time. They shifted as the result of contemporary needs placing pressure on tradition, as in the case of Edwards, who came from a long line of Puritan divines who deeply influenced his thinking, but whose understanding of "religious affections" was also very much of his moment and directed toward the struggles and needs of a particular Christian parish, even as his actual treatise on religious affections seemed most in conversation with philosophers and theologians not in his midst but across the Atlantic.

As Edwards demonstrates almost excessively, the study of either "affections" or "affection" nearly always implies a conscious cognitive element: an interpretation and application of emotion and experience. But there is another register that strips these words of their suffix: "affect" functions extra-cognitively as both noun and verb. For this reason, a theory of affect distinguishes between it and emotion. Brian Massumi, for example, equates affect with intensity and categorizes it as something "irreducibly bodily and autonomic."[38] Similarly, Gregory J. Seigworth and Melissa Gregg explain, "Affect, at its most anthropomorphic, is the name we give to those forces—visceral forces beneath, alongside, or generally *other than* conscious knowing, vital forces insisting beyond emotion—that can serve to drive us toward movement, toward thought and extension, that can likewise suspend us (as if in neutral) across a barely registering accretion of force-relations."[39] In short, emotion follows affect and is its cognitive qualification and narration. Affect is part of the environment, impressing itself on individuals through bodily sensations before a person is aware. Bearing in mind ideas of affect when studying religious affections means asking questions about how those affections produce forces and dynamics—sometimes unwittingly—that are counter to or cross usual theological and sectarian divisions. Affect underscores the messiness of thinking about religious affections and their entanglement with bodily sensation, evaluation and interpretation, performance, and interpersonal relations.[40]

We invoke these registers to foreground that this collection of essays also begins with Edwardsian affections and then expands and layers on questions of disinclinations, uncertainty, performance, intensity, narration, unconscious force, and transformation. Moreover, these registers, loosely following the chapters of this book, track with various developments in the history of emotions from conscious standards and their translatability (or not) to individual experiences within and between multiple sets of communal norms to the investigation of porous bodies affected by their environments pre-cognitively. Along the way, questions arise about how affections advance and encourage religious change, how they emerge through performance and communication, how they are judged, and above all, how they draw lines of authority around not just the meaning of emotional experience but also its proper or improper expression.

Studying religious affections, in other words, offers a new avenue into understanding both tight-knit communities and intercultural relations. "Religious affections" are interpreted experiences. Where and how the experiences arise is one matter; how and why they are interpreted in a certain manner is another; but the latter also ties back to the former, since the interpretations themselves can produce the experiences—can make them come about. In both cases—whether on the level of the manifestation of experience or on the level of its interpretation and evaluation—we will be forced to look from the individual to the emotional communities that surround that individual, which might or might not overlap with the religion the individual overtly professes. In this way, religious affections present a powerful arena for comparative work that purposefully looks across and through in order to understand more fully how seemingly disparate geographic, cultural, and temporal communities relate and transform.[41]

From Theory and Language to Visions and Experience

As we look to the intersection of authority and community in the expression, consequences, and regulation of religious affections, we draw upon theories of the religious and the history of emotions, focusing in particular on the concept of emotional communities. With a comparative approach, we try to draw together microhistorical moments of encounter with and between Christians spread across time and space in early North America to see what can be learned from a broad-ranging conversation about religious affections. At the same time, our four centers of attention pair into two different types of study. The first pairing of chapters (part one, on theory and language) pertains to the Northeast and radiates from Jonathan Edwards's ideas of religious affections. Edwards's *Treatise Concerning Religious Affections* is often considered one of the classic theological and philosophical attempts to make sense of the Great Awakenings in New England, both justifying the conversions and attempting to curtail their excesses. Mark Valeri brings a new context to bear on understanding Edwards's treatise, reading it in conjunction with another hefty tome that Edwards wrote: *A Careful and Strict Enquiry into the Modern Prevailing Notions of that Freedom of the Will*

(1754). At stake in both treatises, Valeri shows, is an understanding of moral freedom that weds Calvinist theology to fresh modes of political discourse through the language of affections. The eighteenth century saw a redefinition of terms such as "will" and "affection" that united religion and politics into new valences and possibilities. While the diaries of more ordinary converts do not reveal Edwards's "careful and strict enquiry" into terms—often ending in a tangle of causes including free will, God's grace, and turned hearts—they together posit a definite shift from seventeenth-century understandings of how the affections relate to conversion, now integrating and elevating a developing discourse of liberty. That shift, Valeri hints, had wide-ranging consequences.

The initial chapter on Jonathan Edwards, therefore, could well be placed within the tradition of "emotionology" that Carol Zisowitz Stearns and Peter N. Stearns first introduced. Here, though, the central question is not primarily how norms and standards change over time (though that is present as well), but rather how the redefinition of emotions in a moment of contact and change creates and transforms the norms that surround those emotions. Edwards is concerned with what religious affections really *are*, and in the process of trying to answer that question he also adapts new terminology and begins to set a new standard for others to judge their own experience. In that sense, we see the work of emotionology not just in the way that expectations around a common term and emotion (such as anger or shame) change over time, but also in how people at various times try to define what counts as that term, that emotion, at all. Edwards's work on "religious affections" is simultaneously an attempt at a definition and the defining of a standard.

In the response of Joanna Brooks, we find an older question in the history of emotions reemerging to contextualize Valeri's account of Edwards and the Great Awakenings: To what extent, Brooks asks, are the experiences of eighteenth-century revivals different from the emotional experience of revival in the twenty-first century? To what extent do they rely on articulated discourses of liberty and free will? Or, she asks, are they better understood as unarticulated responses to the violence and trauma of early North America—a violence and trauma that in many ways continue to resurface? In this sense, her transhistorical work begins to question some of the microhistorical work that underlies the thinking of "emotional communities." In other words, whereas Valeri offers a close analysis of religious affections in Edwards's context and community, Brooks offers a much larger, almost macrohistorical account of radical religious transformation *and continuity* (even almost a sense of *repetition*) over time.

The next chapter shifts the context of Edwards's thinking not temporally but culturally and geographically. If Jonathan Edwards's careful parsing of religious affections and free will had a hard time translating clearly to Anglo-American evangelical audiences in New England (speaking almost more to theologians and philosophers across the sea), it certainly did not translate with any precision beyond them. In chapter 3, Scott Manning Stevens addresses the "radical linguistic alterity" that greeted missionaries throughout the region, especially in the Haudenosaunee homelands. Not only is it difficult to translate a *term* like "religious affections," but also the New Light theology that stood behind this term further engaged all kinds of linguistic, emotional, and doctrinal registers that would be all but impossible to convey in another language without complete fluency. If "emotives" are speech acts that effect an emotion in such a way as to act on the world (in part through their interaction with emotional regimes), then the language of speech—the understanding of it—matters. And fluency was all but impossible to obtain. The language surrounding detailed definitions, norms, and expectations could not be translated from English into the vocabulary and grammar of the various Native nations and peoples around Edwards. Emotives and emotional regimes depend, at the very least, on shared language, and in early North America, radically different emotional communities were also separated by radically different languages.

Linguistic specificity marks one aspect in the history of emotions; cultural specificity marks another. Even if fluency could be obtained by missionaries—and claims to have obtained it should be approached with a great deal of skepticism, Stevens shows—the evangelical theology of affections was extremely hard to translate to a culture that viewed emotions much differently, as the Haudenosaunee Condolence Ceremony reveals. Understanding these different cultural approaches to emotion and affection helps make sense of the misunderstanding that so often resulted from encounters. That misunderstanding is central to Caroline Wigginton's response, where she demonstrates that the colonists' "lack of fluency . . . was at the heart of colonialism." A lack of fluency, a basic illegibility, applied equally to those who converted and those who did not. While structures of power under settler colonialism historically gave colonizers interpretive authority, a Native convert could practice illegibility in many ways, acting as "an agent of unfluency" to create and inhabit forms of religious affection and devotion that would not be determined—could never be *known*—by missionaries.

From theories, definitions, and linguistic barriers, we turn in part two to dreams, visions, and experiences that often grasp at language. The more recent work on studies of the body comes into play here. In accordance with her work on pharmaceuticals and the religious experiences they induced—including conflicts with religious authorities—Melissa Frost's chapter focuses on the body and the way that new experiences, enabled through drugs, produced new understandings of religious affections. In her analysis, the body precedes and prompts religious affections; meaning is made in response. In that sense, her chapter fits within the Jamesian tradition of beginning with the body and its performance, and only secondly turning to the way that the body's sensations are experienced and understood emotionally. Performatives, in that sense, are all-important. Yet Frost also draws this approach together with others in the history of emotions by asking how the newly understood emotional experience was then fitted (or not) into an orthodox and authoritative structure of religious affection. The consumption of pre-Columbian hallucinogens by non-Native and multiracial Catholics signals the ways that religious affections—including those catalyzed by medicinal and herbal practices—could form new emotional communities that crossed racial, class, and sectarian divisions. The Catholic Church policed and punished hallucinogen use even as members of the laity found the range of emotions experienced under the influence of these substances to be wholly consistent with Catholicism and even to intensify their devotion and piety. In her response to Frost, Stephanie Kirk underscores the caution that readers must bring to colonial records, reminding us that most extant documents are structured around a refrain of horror and an insistence on perversion rather than objective or sympathetic observation. Kirk suggests that women—whose Catholicism tended more toward embodiment—were the core members and creators of these emotional communities.

Whereas Frost's chapter focuses on the body and its responses, Jon Sensbach's chapter asks *which* body we are looking at and what difference that makes. Beginning, like Frost, in the world of visions and dreams, Sensbach shows the extent to which emotional meaning arose from the imagination of another kind of body (a Black body in this case). Performatives cannot be separated from the particularities of the bodies involved and the contexts that coded those bodies with meaning. Sensbach's "Working Down a Bad Spirit" examines the history and writings of slaveholding Quakers and homes in a battle occurring at the nexus of transatlantic slavery, religion, and the history of emotions. The nascent antislavery movement emerging in white Quaker circles hinged on both acknowledging existence of an inner Christ in enslaved Africans—who expressed spiritual love and joy—and feeling and then atoning for the self-horror arising from the realization that one has therefore brutalized Jesus himself. Kathleen Donegan, in "Bad Spirits," shifts focus from the Quaker emotions of recognizing an inner Christ to another emotion at this same nexus. For her, the emotion is terror, and the religious beliefs and feelings of a slave society like Barbados heighten that terror and mold its expression.

The model established by these sets of chapters, therefore, can be thought of roughly as moving from language (part one) to body (part two), from theorizing religious affections to experiences that grasp at theory, and in each case and in every history the questions of authority and community—the disciplining and undisciplining of religious affections, the boundaries of belonging and the crossing of those boundaries—come to the fore. The book concludes with Barbara Rosenwein's afterword, "Messy Entanglements," which connects the collection to a longer history. In such a way we hope to both model and contribute to an ongoing and expanding conversation focused on religious affections and all that they might reveal about early North America and beyond.

Notes

1. Here we refer to some of this collection's subjects. Examples of work that touches on emotion and conversion in scenes of Christian contact, which have partly inspired this collection, include Laura Stevens, *The Poor Indians: British Missionaries, Native Americans, and Colonial Sensibility* (Philadelphia: University of Pennsylvania Press, 2006); Emily Clark, *Masterless Mistresses: The New Orleans Ursulines and the Development of a New World Society, 1727–1834* (Chapel Hill: University of North Carolina Press, 2012), esp. 84, 100–101; and Emma Anderson, *The Death and Afterlife of the North American Martyrs* (Cambridge: Harvard University Press, 2013), 54–97. This volume builds on methods of study for emotion, affection, affiliation, and identity at work in books such as Kathleen Donegan, *Seasons of Misery: Catastrophe and Colonial Settlement in Early America* (Philadelphia: University of Pennsylvania Press, 2014); Emily Berquist Soule, *The Bishop's Utopia: Envisioning Improvement in Colonial Peru*

(Philadelphia: University of Pennsylvania, 2014); and Caroline Wigginton, *In the Neighborhood: Women's Publication in Early America* (Amherst: University of Massachusetts Press, 2016). Citations to other important sources can be found throughout.

2. Anne Hart Gilbert, "History of Methodism," in *The Hart Sisters: Early African Caribbean Writers, Evangelicals, and Radicals*, ed. Moira Ferguson (Lincoln: University of Nebraska Press, 1993), 58. Gilbert is writing to Richard Pattison, a Methodist minister and missionary on nearby Nevis. In the 1750s, Moravian missionaries, according to Hart Gilbert, had begun the work of "dispers[ing]" the "clouds of sin and error," but this work did not truly move forward until white Methodists Nathaniel and Francis Gilbert arrived in 1760 (Hart Gilbert, "History of Methodism," 58). Anne Hart married Nathaniel Gilbert in 1798.
3. Isaiah 60:2: "For, behold, the darkness shall cover the earth, and gross darkness the people" (KJV).
4. The use of the adjective "gross" was fairly common in Anglo-Christian poetry of the long eighteenth century, whereby sin is understood to transform the soul from something ethereal to something heavy and material. See the *OED*, s.v. "gross," 8b and 8c, which includes an example from John Milton's *Paradise Lost* 6.661: "Spirits of purest light, Purest at first, now gross by sinning grown."
5. Hart Gilbert, "History of Methodism," 58–59.
6. For a discussion of affect in Hart Gilbert's writings, especially those related to her work as an agent of the Female Refuge Society, see Sue Thomas, "Affective Dynamics of Colonial Reform and Modernisation in Antigua, 1815–1835," *Feminist Review* 104, no. 1 (2013): 24–41. For an account of another Black Caribbean Christian woman missionary, see Jon Sensbach, *Rebecca's Revival: Creating Black Christianity in the Atlantic World* (Cambridge: Harvard University Press, 2006).
7. Hart Gilbert's examples suggest that Obeah is akin to a religion, but it is also a medical system. As Kelly Wisecup and Toni Wall Jaudon explain: "'Obeah' refers to a set of practices employed by Africans for ends that enslaved peoples perceived as socially useful, from healing and revenge, to protection and rebellion. These practices were constituted by what we would now designate as separate medical and religious components: the knowledge and application of herbal remedies; singing or chanting prayers or powerful words; a diagnosis of physical ailments; and mediation with nonhuman powers. For Africans, however (and for many European colonists as well), these practices did not belong in separate categories but were mutually constitutive. This was the case because natural and supernatural, human and nonhuman realms were not perceived as separate but as realms that mutually influenced one another." See Kelly Wisecup and Toni Wall Jaudon, "On Knowing and Not Knowing about Obeah," *Atlantic Studies* 12, no. 2 (2015): 130. Because most of our knowledge about eighteenth-century Obeah comes from colonialist sources, it is difficult to pinpoint where (or even if), for example, Obeah practitioners would locate love or fear in the body. They may not have associated the heart with emotions.
8. John Winthrop, *A Modell of Christian Charity*, in *The Winthrop Papers*, 7 vols. (Boston: Massachusetts Historical Society, 1929–), 2:288.
9. John Winthrop, *A Short Story of the Rise, Reign, and Ruin of the Antinomians, Familists & Libertines, that Infected the Churches of New-England* (London: Ralph Smith, 1644), unpaginated.
10. For more on the definition of "affections" in Puritanism and the role of such affections in the Antinomian Controversy, see Abram Van Engen, *Sympathetic Puritans:*

Calvinist Fellow Feeling in Early New England (New York: Oxford University Press, 2015). For links between Puritanism and later evangelicalism, see Baird Tipson, *Hartford Puritanism: Thomas Hooker, Samuel Stone, and Their Terrifying God* (New York: Oxford University Press, 2015).

11. The trajectory of British evangelicalism, especially Methodism, has been different, at least until the last decade or so. Tracing a line from eighteenth-century engraver William Hogarth to Marxist historian E. P. Thompson and beyond, Phyllis Mack identifies two main strands in the historiography of British Methodism, both of which "promoted an image of the ordinary Methodist as a person without autonomy or agency: terrified of damnation, mesmerized by charismatic preachers, hysterical in public worship, imitative of conservative bourgeois values, enslaved to an inflated work ethic, emotionally repressed in intimate relationships." See Phyllis Mack, *Heart Religion in the British Enlightenment: Gender and Emotion in Early Methodism* (Cambridge: Cambridge University Press, 2008), 5.
12. See, for example, Joanna Brooks, *American Lazarus: Religion and the Rise of African-American and Native American Literatures* (New York: Oxford University Press, 2003). Douglas Winiarski argues that "the primary agents" of New England's evangelical Great Awakenings were the laity, "whose burgeoning fascination with the drama of conversion and the charismatic gifts of the Holy Spirit drove them out of the churches of the Congregational standing order." See Douglas L. Winiarski, *Darkness Falls on the Land of Light: Experiencing Religious Awakenings in Eighteenth-Century New England* (Chapel Hill: University of North Carolina Press, 2017), 9.
13. Hart Gilbert's sister Elizabeth held similar religious views but was more outspoken against slavery. See Elizabeth Hart Thwaites, "Letter from Elizabeth Hart to a Friend (1794)," in *Transatlantic Feminisms in the Age of Revolutions*, ed. Lisa L. Moore, Joanna Brooks, and Caroline Wigginton (New York: Oxford University Press, 2012), 300–308. For more on the complex relationship between submission to God and earthly righteousness, see Mack, *Heart Religion*, 10–18. Methodists often drew a distinction between spiritual and earthly liberation. For example, George Whitefield, one of Methodism's early celebrity leaders, tied his spiritual mission in Georgia to the expansion of slavery. See Jessica Parr, *Inventing George Whitefield: Race, Revivalism, and the Making of a Religious Icon* (Jackson: University of Mississippi Press, 2015), 61–80.
14. Susan Juster and Linda Gregerson, introduction to *Empires of God: Religious Encounters in the Early Modern Atlantic*, ed. Linda Gregerson and Susan Juster (Philadelphia: University of Pennsylvania Press, 2011), 1.
15. Stephanie Kirk and Sarah Rivett, introduction to *Religious Transformations in the Early Modern Americas*, ed. Stephanie Kirk and Sarah Rivett (Philadelphia: University of Pennsylvania Press, 2014), 1.
16. "The term 'religion' means many different things, and so there are many different ways in which we can say something is 'religious.'" Malory Nye, *Religion: The Basics*, 2nd ed. (London: Routledge, 2008), 17.
17. For some examples from the vast body of scholarship on "lived religion" in North America, see Robert Orsi, *The Madonna of 115th Street: Faith and Community in Italian Harlem, 1880–1950*, 3rd ed. (New Haven: Yale University Press, 2010); David D. Hall, *Worlds of Wonder, Days of Judgment: Popular Religious Belief in Early New England* (Cambridge: Harvard University Press, 1990); David D. Hall, ed.,

Lived Religion in America: Toward a History of Practice (Princeton: Princeton University Press, 2020); and Wendy Raphael Roberts, *Awakening Verse: The Poetics of Early American Evangelicalism* (Oxford: Oxford University Press, 2020). Religious records also provide a useful archive to reveal the daily lives of a variety of early Americans. See, for example, Herman L. Bennett, *Colonial Blackness: A History of Afro-Mexico* (Bloomington: Indiana University Press, 2009).

18. For key scholarship that questions the boundary between the "religious" and the "secular," see Talal Asad, *Formations of the Secular: Christianity, Islam, Modernity* (Palo Alto: Stanford University Press, 2003); Tracy Fessenden, *Culture and Redemption: Religion, the Secular, and American Literature* (Princeton: Princeton University Press, 2007); and John Lardas Modern, *Secularism in Antebellum America* (Chicago: University of Chicago Press, 2011). See also the essays in the special issue "After the Postsecular," *American Literature* 86, no. 4 (2014), ed. Peter Coviello and Jared Hickman.
19. Susannah Brietz Monta, "Introduction: Religion, Literature, and the Academy," *Religion and Literature* 46, no. 2–3 (2014): 3.
20. Daniel Philpott quoted in Susan Felch, introduction to *The Cambridge Companion to Literature and Religion*, ed. Susan Felch (New York: Cambridge University Press, 2016), 3. In the definitions of "religion" and the "religious" offered by the *Oxford English Dictionary*, this sense of community also comes to the fore. One potential etymology for the word "religion" links it to the concept of being "bound" or "tied," either to a tradition or to others within a regulated, set-apart community. The "religious," according to one definition, are those "bound by vows" and "belonging to or connected with" a specific order. But the word "religious" can also identify particular individuals, or their desires and drives, by highlighting motivation and personal attachment within a broader community: the religious are those "devoted to religion," or those "exhibiting the spiritual or practical effects of religion"—those who, in another phrase, are "following the requirements of religion." Even when that relation goes mostly missing from a definition, it still shows up implicitly. The final definitions of "religious" offered by the *OED* yield a kind of word association game of synonyms, and each term gestures toward differing kinds of emotional communities. The "religious" identifies those things, practices, beliefs, or feelings that are holy, sacred, scrupulous, exact, strict, conscientious, or solemn. In this final list of adjectives we see again—in the background, as it were—the shaping power of community and its affective norms. How something comes to be understood as holy or sacred or solemn—how a person comes to be scrupulous, exact, strict, or conscientious—depends on interpretative communities. To be "exact" requires a rule, and a rule requires a system, a sense of order, a set of standards and norms produced outside of oneself and learned through engagement in community.
21. Since another scholar, Carl George Lange, was coming to the same conclusion at roughly the same time, this view of emotions has come to be known as the James-Lange theory of emotions, and its legacy can be found, much later, in the studies that claim a bodily posture or disturbance can produce emotions after the fact. As the body moves, so the mind responds. Emotions are a matter of meaning-making arising from physical sensations.
22. John Corrigan is a central figure in the study of religion and emotion. His many works offer excellent starting points for the study. This paragraph draws on John Corrigan, "Introduction: Emotions Research and the Academic Study of

Religion," in *Religion and Emotion: Approaches and Interpretations*, ed. John Corrigan (New York: Oxford University Press, 2004), 3–31 (quotes on 5, 9). For individual essays on Schleiermacher, Otto, James, and Durkheim, see John Corrigan, ed., *The Oxford Handbook of Religion and Emotion* (New York: Oxford University Press, 2007). See also John Corrigan, Eric Clump, and John Kloos, *Emotions and Religion: A Critical Assessment and Annotated Bibliography* (Westport, CT: Greenwood Press, 2000); and John Corrigan, "History, Religion, and Emotion: An Historiographical Survey," in *Business of the Heart: Religion and Emotion in the Nineteenth Century* (Berkeley: University of California Press, 2002), 269–80.

23. John Corrigan, "Introduction: Emotions Research and the Academic Study of Religion," in *Business of the Heart*, 12.
24. See Carol Zisowitz Stearns and Peter N. Stearns, "Emotionology: Clarifying the History of Emotions and Emotional Standards," *American Historical Review* 90, no. 4 (1985): 813–36. Elsewhere Stearns and Stearns explain emotionology through a study of anger: "We call the conventions and standards by which Americans evaluated anger, and the institutions they developed to reflect and encourage these standards, *emotionology*. Emotionology is not the same thing as emotional experience. A society may organize courtship to discourage love, but that does not prove that love does not exist or even flourish. A family may discountenance anger, but there may be much anger in that family's operations." See Carol Zisowitz Stearns and Peter N. Stearns, *Anger: The Struggle for Emotional Control in America's History* (Chicago: University of Chicago Press, 1986), 14.
25. This paragraph and the next few draw from Barbara H. Rosenwein and Riccardo Cristiani, *What Is the History of Emotions?* (Medford, MA: Polity, 2018), which is one of the most useful recent introductions to the history of emotions. For others, see Susan Matt and Peter N. Stearns, eds., *Doing Emotions History* (Urbana: University of Illinois Press, 2014); Jan Plamper, *The History of Emotions: An Introduction*, trans. Keith Tribe (Oxford: Oxford University Press, 2015); Ute Frevert, "The History of Emotions," in *Handbook of Emotions*, ed. Lisa Feldman Barrett, Michael Lewis, and Jeannette M. Haviland-Jones, 4th ed. (New York: Guilford, 2016), 49–65; and Jan Plamper et al., "The History of Emotions: An Interview with William Reddy, Barbara Rosenwein, and Peter Stearns," *History and Theory* 49, no. 2 (May 2010): 237–65.
26. Quoted in Rosenwein and Cristiani, *What Is the History of Emotions?*, 36.
27. The key article here is William M. Reddy, "Against Constructionism: The Historical Ethnography of Emotions," *Current Anthropology* 38 (1997): 327–51. See also William M. Reddy, *The Navigation of Feeling: A Framework for the History of Emotions* (Cambridge: Cambridge University Press, 2001).
28. Barbara H. Rosenwein, *Generations of Feeling: A History of Emotions, 600–1700* (Cambridge: Cambridge University Press, 2016), 3.
29. Rosenwein and Cristiani, *What Is the History of Emotions?*, 40.
30. For more on emotional communities, see Barbara H. Rosenwein, *Emotional Communities in the Early Middle Ages* (Ithaca: Cornell University Press, 2006), 23–25.
31. Rosenwein and Cristiani, *What Is the History of Emotions?*, 49.
32. See, for example, Dolores Martín-Moruno and Beatriz Pichel, eds., *Emotional Bodies: The Historical Performativity of Emotions* (Urbana: University of Illinois Press, 2019).

33. Rosenwein, *Generations of Feeling*, 3.
34. Jonathan Edwards, *A Treatise Concerning Religious Affections, in Three Parts* (Boston: S. Kneeland and T. Green, 1746), 4.
35. Edwards, *A Treatise Concerning Religious Affections*, 4–6.
36. Edwards's sermons attempted to stir up these vigorous feelings. As Sandra Gustafson explains, what "Edwards hoped to achieve with his own sermonic language, his 'rhetoric of sensation' [was] a sense of abstractions as transcendent realities evoking clear emotional responses." See Sandra Gustafson, *Eloquence Is Power: Oratory and Performance in Early America* (Chapel Hill: University of North Carolina Press, 2000), 57.
37. The key text, of course, is Adam Smith, *The Theory of Moral Sentiments* (1759), but Smith culminated a tradition extending back at least to Anthony Ashley Cooper, the third Earl of Shaftesbury, in *Characteristics of Men, Manners, Opinions, Times* (1711).
38. Brian Massumi, "The Autonomy of Affect," *Cultural Critique* 31 (1995): 6.
39. Gregory J. Seigworth and Melissa Gregg, "An Inventory of Shimmers," in *The Affect Theory Reader*, ed. Gregory J. Seigworth and Melissa Gregg (Durham: Duke University Press, 2010), 1.
40 For more on affect and methodological messiness, see Ben Highmore, "Bitter after Taste: Affect, Food, and Social Aesthetics" in Seigworth and Gregg, *The Affect Theory Reader*, 118–37.
41. Here we follow the comparative method of Indigenous studies scholar Chadwick Allen, who writes: "The point is not to displace the necessary, invigorating study of specific traditions and contexts but rather to complement these by augmenting and expanding broader, globally Indigenous fields of inquiry. The point is to invite specific studies into different kinds of conversation, and to acknowledge the mobility and multiple interactions of Indigenous peoples, cultures, histories, and texts." Much the same could be said about comparing religious affections in the long eighteenth century and beyond. See Chadwick Allen, *Trans-Indigenous: Methodologies for Global Native Literary Studies* (Minneapolis: University of Minnesota Press, 2012), xiv.

Part I

Theory and Language

CHAPTER 1

Conversion, Free Will, and the Affections in Eighteenth-Century New England

MARK VALERI

New England Protestants during the eighteenth century held no single definition of "religious affections." They contested the term because to them the word "religious" conveyed a theological judgment: "religious" in the sense of true to the right religion, or divine revelation as interpreted in Protestant tradition. For many New Englanders, the term raised questions about the effusion of emotions, the weeping for sin and crying for the joy of salvation, that attended some of the revivals that we have come to know as the Great Awakening. Critics of the revival, and some defenders such as Jonathan Edwards, warned that pure emotion in such terms might be an expression of mundane passion, something quite apart from true religion. He and many of his contemporaries spoke of religious affections as the result of an experience of divine realities such as the Holy Spirit or grace: more sobering and edifying, in their view, than passion or enthusiasm. Arguments about the revivals, however, raised a further set of questions about the meaning of "affection" itself and its relationship to moral choice. In this sense, "affection" was often used interchangeably with disposition, inclination, taste, or simply the heart. As a central term in the moral philosophy of the day, it was associated with moral judgment or conscience.[1]

Disputes about affections in this sense—as components of moral consciousness—shadowed religious controversy throughout the century. In the most general terms, New Englanders considered affections to be mental sensations that attended one's relationship with another—love, say, or hate. Affections also marked one's perception of oneself, as in the pleasure of doing good or the pain of doing bad. As perceptions of the goodness or badness of some act or some thing under consideration, they amounted to moral judgments. And as moral judgments, they at least informed and at most determined one's moral choices or the will. New Englanders debated how to conceive of the power of affections, but they agreed on this: they were crucial to religious choice, especially conversion.

Scholars of Puritanism have maintained that affections had long stood in Reformed teaching for a realm of experience outside of individuals' self-determination.[2] Puritans used the term to refute competing Protestant and Catholic theologies that emphasized faith as a choice by a free will and love as an act of moral volition. Protestants often gave the name Arminian, after the Dutch theologian Jacobus Arminius, to those who defined faith as a choice. Calvinists contended that one could not choose one's affections. They were subject to disorder and corruption and equally subject to an infusion of divine grace, all matters beyond conscious control. If one construed faith or love for God as the central act of conversion, and faith or love as affections, then conversion was involuntary. Although this claim created no small amount of anxiety among Puritans who wondered if they had undergone conversion, it sustained a Protestant emphasis on divine sovereignty and the role of the godly community in helping individuals to fathom their spiritual conditions.[3]

An eighteenth-century imperative to script the idioms of moral reasonableness, liberty of conscience, and religious choice onto conversion shaped the evangelical movement in ways that diverged from Puritanism. Political and philosophical affairs in the Anglo-American world had, by the time of the revivals, pushed Protestants to legitimate the language of human liberty, free will, moral choice, and uncoerced conscience. Revivalists such as George Whitefield, Gilbert Tennent, David Brainerd, and Jonathan Edwards claimed that zeal for the absolute sovereignty of God and denial of human moral capability defined the very soul of Christianity, yet they called on people to select the way of salvation, close with Christ, and choose heaven. Evangelistic preaching was premised on the idea of religious choice, as were the missions to Native Americans that followed in its wake. New approaches to the evangelization of Native peoples during the mid-eighteenth century, foreshadowed by Cotton Mather's desire for less cultural critique and more mutual exchange of sentiments among missionaries and Native Americans, assumed the potency of voluntary religious affiliation.[4]

Evangelicals proposed that conversion, as well as post-conversion attempts to obey God, were concurrently acts of choice and changes of affections. We often think of preachers such as Edwards as apologists for the Calvinist doctrine of predestination. True enough in a way, but we must also consider how their defense of Calvinism rested on a redefinition of terms such as will and affection—a redefinition that allowed them to align the doctrines of grace with the ideals of liberty.

This line of argument cuts against the grain of an older historiography, exemplified by Garry Wills's *Head and Heart*, that limns evangelicalism as a religion of emotion in contrast to Enlightenment reason. It also offers a different perspective from more recent interpretations, such as Douglas Winiarski's *Darkness Falls on the Land of Light*, that emphasize the ecstatic experiences and social divisiveness of the early revival movement. Emotion, affections, ecstasies, and social schism certainly characterized much of the eighteenth-century revivals, but so too did the efforts of leaders such as Edwards to align so-called experimental (or evangelical) Calvinism with contemporary ideas about moral virtue, religious sincerity, and political liberty. Evangelicals' acceptance of the social and philosophical mandates of these ideas helps to explain, among other developments, their agreement with other Americans who promoted independence as a matter of deep moral conscience.[5]

In its emphasis on eighteenth-century innovations among New Englanders, this argument also diverges from scholarly interpretations that focus on seventeenth-century precedents. Historians such as Mark Noll, Bruce Hindmarsh, and W. R. Ward have argued that evangelicalism can best be understood as a confluence of Enlightenment epistemologies of sensation and seventeenth-century religious streams such as Puritan doctrines of divine grace and Pietist teachings about devotion.[6] There is something to this historical explanation. Pious eighteenth-century New Englanders read plenty of Puritan literature, which confirmed the salience of introspection and affection in the experience of conversion. Divines such as Edwards frequently engaged the writings of his Puritan predecessors. Yet these interpretations tend to obscure important differences between Puritan and evangelical Calvinist accounts. Edwards, Whitefield, and their followers engaged a new moral vocabulary and confronted new social and political demands. Rearticulating conversion accordingly, they accepted a discourse of liberty that Puritans would have found incredible.

The eighteenth-century push for freedom and its impact on the evangelical notion of conversion clarifies one aspect of the role of affections in New England and suggests its revolutionary political implications. The following account describes how political and philosophical developments in England after the Glorious Revolution pressured English Protestants to embrace the idea of moral freedom. New England divines during the first three decades of the eighteenth century stumbled to articulate the relationship between affections—which theologians had associated with uncontrolled power over one's volition—and the will, using new Lockean vocabularies in contradictory ways. This confusion came to the surface especially during the revivals, when converts such as the laywoman Sarah Osborn blended older Puritan notions of the affections with newer understandings of religious choice. In the aftermath of the revivals, Edwards especially applied himself to the task of clarifying how the experience of grace and the social mandate for moral freedom were compatible. Edwards represented, in a particularly influential fashion, how evangelical Calvinists adopted a language that sustained republican social and political agendas. By the mid-1770s, in fact, that language conveyed the legitimacy of independence from Britain as a free moral choice, a corollary to the choices made in religious conversion.

The relationship between divinely infused grace and human choice in conversion—or, more simply, the problem of free will—had long occupied Protestants and especially Calvinists, but had taken on new meaning by the time of the Awakening. At the time of the Glorious Revolution, English Protestants with Whig sentiments touted the idioms of moral freedom or liberty as integral to social virtue. Many moralists during the last decade of the seventeenth century and the first three decades of the eighteenth—from Locke through Tillotson, to the Scottish moral sense school of Shaftesbury and Hutcheson—along with many of their New England admirers, argued that the very notion of virtue assumed moral responsibility and, thus, an assertion of free will. Only with such an assertion, they argued, could individuals be said to act in a moral manner, deserving of praise or blame.

That argument sustained liberal perspectives on England's commonwealth. Whig politics, with its republican insistence on self-determination, rested on the language of free choice in religious, social, and moral matters. In contrast, the moral determinism of writers such as Thomas Hobbes stood for political authoritarianism. A good Whig, progressive, republican, opponent of absolute tyranny—what have you—used a moral discourse grounded in the assumption of human moral freedom.[7] In this context, "free will" came to be associated less with Reformation-era and seventeenth-century controversies about the efficacy of moral effort in obtaining divine grace—debates between Erasmus and Luther or Dutch Arminians and Dortian Calvinists—and more with philosophical and political agendas to confirm individual moral liberty whatever one's theological doctrines.[8]

Parsing conversion in the terms of liberty also highlighted, for English moralists, the superiority of Protestantism to other religious traditions. Toward the end of the seventeenth century, for example, New Englanders eagerly consumed accounts of Protestants who were forced to "convert" to a different religion: Huguenots faced with either enslavement on galleys or the Mass in post–Edict of Nantes France and New England mariners compelled to adopt Islam when captured by Algerian pirates. Conversion without moral freedom, without liberty of conscience, appeared in this literature as tyranny; Cotton Mather often criticized the deployment of forced conversions in Catholic and Islamic territories. Such tales did not directly address the meaning of free will, but they drove home with vivid illustration the dangers, from a Protestant perspective, of separating conversion from free moral choice. Coercion, whether describing the policies of a Catholic monarch or the saving operations of grace, sounded dangerous to many Anglo-Protestant ears.[9]

Patriotic admirers of England's constitutional monarchy during the first three decades of the eighteenth century, New England Calvinists struggled to find a vocabulary to express the doctrine of irresistible grace within a social and political culture shaped by assertions of human moral liberty. They drew especially on Locke, whose *Essay Concerning Human Understanding* (1690) suggested definitions of the will that had the potential to harmonize Protestant ideas about conversion with moral freedom. Locke argued that it was nonsense to speak of volition or the will as "free" in the sense of free to choose. The will was the choice. To assert that the will was free in the sense of free to choose was a tautology, merely to say that the will wills. Rather, Locke maintained, the "will" amounted to the conclusion of a complex mental process of self-reflection that determined whether certain objects were good or bad. That determination could be, and most often in common parlance was, expressed as affections: to love, hate, esteem, despise, and the like.[10]

New England Calvinists tinkered with a Lockean vocabulary of mental self-perception, action, power, and choice. Yet they were wary of Arminianism and its varied challenges to Reformed theology, from an emphasis on moral effort in the pursuit of salvation to a denial of the doctrine of original sin. As a result, they tended to deploy the rhetoric of freedom without clearly or fully harmonizing Calvinism and free will. They did not come to a coherent account of the relationship between the affections, grace, and free choice or will in ways that satisfied the social and political mandate to assert moral liberty.

Take, for example, the 1719 lecture by Solomon Stoddard (Edwards's grandfather), published as *A Treatise Concerning Conversion*. Stoddard began his account by distinguishing conversion from pious disciplines and works of preparation. He did so by using a diction that conveyed passive subjects and divine causation: "Conversion is wrought at once." He proceeded to layer onto his analysis the language of choice. Conversion was "an Act of Faith," and as such "performed" by "accepting Jesus Christ." Again, in stronger terms: "The accepting of Christ is always an act of great freedom: when they [believers] do it, they do it out of choice." Yet, Stoddard argued as he tacked back to Calvinism for most of the second half of his discourse, these choices followed from changes in understanding. The intellect moved the will. So the mind became "convinced of the Gloriousness of God" and then moved the will "to accept of Christ." God, in other words, made people "capable to know" and of "seeing with clearness" divine truths when he gave them "Light." In this sense, "God is the Author of Conversion" because "when God makes an Understanding he makes a Will." Stoddard left unexplained the definition of will and the meaning of understanding, but gave the overall impression that the will was free in no real way.[11]

Five years later, Cotton Mather gave an even more befuddling definition of conversion in *The Converted Sinner* (an especially unfortunate confusion given the fact that Mather delivered this sermon as a last bit of advice for some pirates just before their execution). The "Nature, the Meaning, the Intention of a Conversion," he warned, lay outside of human control because it implied "a Change of the Heart, with a New Disposition," and such matters could not be willfully selected; "you must be Turned." One could not choose one's affections, and conversion meant above all else affections toward God and self. To be sure, he exhorted his hearers to pray, and rather cleverly suggested that the mere "asking of Him to Turn you, is the Turning Point," intimating that something that people could do (ask God to turn them) was to effect a turning that only God could do. Yet again, Mather's rhetoric of God's sovereignty, rather than of moral liberty, dominated the sermon with the central refrain "NO man will Turn unto GOD, until GOD shall please to Turn him."[12]

The experiences of New Englanders during the revivals demonstrated the unsettledness—one might even say incoherence—of common perceptions about the affections and free choice in matters of conversion. Evangelical conversions in fact highlighted the odd state of Calvinist teaching: intent on asserting the unbidden change of heart effected by divine grace and insisting at the same time on the individual's search, decision, and choice for Christ. Most conversion narratives put the emphasis on affections and therefore an individual's lack of self-determination. Recounting a succession of sensations from despair and mistrust of God to joy and love toward Christ, spiritual diaries of the period focused on divine intervention rather than rational moral freedom, despite the language of choice that sometimes entered the script. Critics charged revivalists with violation of the common standards of moral reasonableness that sustained a free social order in the British colonies.[13]

The conundrums of the affections and free will, in other words, beset common New Englanders as much as they did evangelical divines. The memoir of the Newport, Rhode Island, schoolteacher Sarah Osborn offers one example. Osborn underwent conversion in 1737, when she was twenty-three years old. By that time she already had suffered through the death of her husband, impoverishment, and a debilitating illness. The physical and economic pains of life in Newport, as she recalled, were matched by intense spiritual discomfort. The sermons of the local Congregationalist pastor Thomas Clap had got her thinking about her unwillingness to trust Christ. She saw "before her [own] eyes" that she "resisted all the kind invitations of a compassionate Saviour." She reiterated such observations: how "it was now strongly impressed on [her] mind" that she had rejected God's mercy, much to her "distress." She was "alarmed with these thoughts" even as there "seemed to be conveyed" to her "mind" the possibility that she "may yet obtain mercy."[14]

Osborn continued to use the image of "seeing" or perceiving her own mind at work as she narrated her eventual conversion. Although she could not fathom how God was "willing to receive so vile a wretch," she felt "those powerful influences of the spirit of God" when she read 1 Corinthians 10:13 ("God is faithful, who will not suffer you to be tempted above that you are able; but will . . . make a way for your escape"). This "excited" in her "a sense of the excellence glory and truth of God," and she "had a pleasing confidence and rest in the divine faithfulness, and embraced the promises." As she experienced such glory, her mental sensations changed from misery to pleasure. Then she did what she had been unable to do before this moment. She chose Christ. She "embraced the promises." New perceptions, pleasures, and the sense of freedom went together. "And [as] it is not possible for me to express," she wrote, "the greatness of the distress, in which I was before; so it [is] as much impossible for me to make any one sensible of the joy with which I was instantly filled." Thus "seeing"—once again—that Christ was "willing to receive" her, she "could freely trust [her] soul in his hands." It had been "impossible," she explained, for "me of myself to believe" before this experience. In this sense, she demurred about her ability to make a godly choice: "Whatever others may boast of a free will, I have none of my own." Yet her conversion culminated in a series of quite willful choices: to "plead," "embrace," "own the covenant" and "give" herself "up." She was "brought to lay down" her "arms of rebellion," a willful act even if she claimed to have had no free will.[15]

Throughout her account, Osborn used a language of self-perception that, however much it resonated with a long tradition of Christian introspection, sounded particularly contemporary in its vocabulary: the mind, mental impressions, seeing, sensation, and pleasure. It echoed popular versions of British moral philosophy, including Lockean theories of knowledge, that had inflected common parlance. Such notes of her memoir aside, Osborn wrote without philosophical precision. Like many of her contemporaries, she did not clarify the relationship among her affections, the intrusion of divine grace, and her choices in conversion. Influenced by Calvinism, she admitted her inability to believe of her own power, her complete lack of free will, and the overwhelming power of divine grace to "excite" in her a "sense" of divine things beyond her control. Yet she also described her experience as a sequence of active choices: she resisted and rejected, then embraced and "freely" trusted, the promises of God in Christ. Osborn's memoir gave expression to the changing—and sometimes tangled—meanings of conversion among evangelical New Englanders.[16]

The diary of Hannah Heaton, a woman from rural North Haven, Connecticut, and Southampton, Long Island, further exemplified the perplexity around affections and will for evangelical Calvinists. After hearing George Whitefield preach in 1741 in New Haven, she began to regret that she was unconverted, a state evidenced by the fact that "worldly concerns" occupied her "mind" more than did the worship of God. Yet she could not bring herself to change her feelings. As a result, she resented God; her "heart would quarrel with god thus," she wrote, that "he knows i cant convert myself." She "had no sence of the justice of god" but instead "felt a hatred" of religious activities.[17]

Her succession of unpleasant feelings—numbness, sadness, bitterness, and depression—continued until she realized that conversion was not a hyper-ecstatic experience, what she called a "trance," but a change of will. She had a vision of Jesus, she recounted, who told her that he "had been willing all this while to save me but i was not willing" to trust him. "All that kept me from him" was her "will." At that point, Heaton claimed with no further explanation that she was converted: her "heart went out with love and thankfulness and admiration." Heaton's use of "heart" implied volition and affection together without a clear distinction. She moved toward Christ as she sensed "the love of god in christ." Her post-conversion admission, "I felt a stubborn will," likewise involved a confusion of terms, as though her will had a moral disposition—stubborn disbelief—apart from what she wanted. Heaton continued to vacillate between the sense that she was subject to overwhelming affections such as serenity, love for God, and "grief" at her impiety, and her conviction that she had indeed chosen to place her "interest in Christ." She believed, as she put it, in the "liberty of conscience" that belonged to all subjects of the English monarchy, a phrase that implied not only tolerance in a political sense but also volition in a philosophical sense.[18]

Heaton never untangled the knot of unbidden affections, self-conscious volitions, and religious beliefs, although it appeared that she often felt to be at the mercy of her affections. She once expressed her bewilderment in a remarkable turn of phrase: "I felt an absent god."[19] The same could be said of Daniel Rogers, a Harvard graduate who longed to have "an experimental knowledge of Jesus" after he heard Whitefield preach in 1740. Rogers's diary shows that he underwent conversion a few weeks after his encounter with Whitefield: "It pleased God of his free and sovereign grace to come into my poor soul" and "fill me with Peace" and "Joy." He began itinerating as well, preaching throughout Massachusetts and Maine over the next two years. Rogers did not understand his own experience in terms of will or choice. He wrote about affections that overwhelmed him apart from any volition: bouts of despondence and dullness, and periods of joy and assurance. He nonetheless admired preachers such as Nathaniel Appleton, who "exhorted and invited . . . sinners to come" to Christ and "venture themselves upon Him." Rogers judged that urging other people to convert was effective, despite the inability to move his own will.[20]

The revivals that became known as the Great Awakening produced dozens of such stories, which recounted conversions in what we might think of as a confusion of causes, divine and human: overwhelming affections, divine visitations, outpourings of grace, and willful, self-conscious acts of faith. These stories prompted evangelical pastors such as Edwards to give some order to the jumble of impressions that attended conversion, and to do so in a way that corresponded with contemporary demands to valorize moral and political liberty more thoroughly than had previous Calvinists such as Stoddard.

Edwards provides a particularly enduring theological example of how evangelical Calvinists came to terms with free will. He did so by adopting the vocabularies and arguments of a post-Lockean generation of British moral philosophers. It was not that Edwards rejected Locke completely. In his miscellaneous reflections from the mid-1720s through the early 1730s, he adopted many of Locke's definitions and arguments in the *Essay* on agency, power, and the will. He eventually criticized Locke, however, for contending that a separate mental faculty, which Locke called the understanding, had power over the will. This so-called "intellectualist" stance of Locke, which Edwards's grandfather Stoddard had taken, led to the troublesome conclusion that the will was subordinate to the direction of rational understanding apart from moral sensation or affection. From Edwards's position, this appeared to push affections too far out of the picture. He concluded early on that it was best to speak of the whole person—affection, understanding, moral determination, and volition all bound together—as free to do as one willed. That, he came to argue, was the commonsense meaning of will.[21]

As Norman Fiering has shown, Edwards found a more useful set of philosophical idioms and explanations in the writing of Francis Hutcheson, a Scottish moral philosopher of deist bent whose 1725 *Inquiry into the Original of our Ideas of Beauty and Virtue* became standard reading among divines and philosophers in Scotland, England, and New England. Hutcheson attempted to improve on the ideas of the third Earl of Shaftesbury, a student of Locke who argued that Locke had overestimated the power of the understanding over the will and underestimated the role of moral sentiments or affections. According to Shaftesbury, common people did not make moral judgments in the ways that Locke described, that is, through the understanding. They had immediate mental impressions or affections that guided their moral judgments and therefore their wills. They felt contentment at virtue and unease at vice, and chose accordingly.[22]

Shaftesbury's ideas appeared to many moralists to have reduced moral judgment to base instinct or a pleasure principle. Hutcheson determined to defend Shaftesbury by showing how people's innate moral sensibilities led them not to vicious self-interest but to social affections such as benevolence. He argued from common experience. We sense the feeling of approval in our minds when we see others behave charitably, read a play whose hero sacrifices self for others, or recognize our own decision to speak honestly. Conversely, we sense disapproval when we observe other people behave in a mean manner, read of treachery, or realize that we have just placed our own interests above the needs of others. As Hutcheson explained, the feeling that attended approval was pleasure, so that it brought happiness to observe—in others or in ourselves—virtues such as benevolence and unhappiness to observe vice. In the long run, then, acting sociably or having love toward other people was, quite remarkably, completely congruent with happiness and therefore self-interest.[23]

Hutcheson had subsumed Locke's idea of a separate faculty of understanding into a broad category of sensation, contended that the affections derived from moral sensations, and concluded that those affections drove the will. Edwards repeatedly drew from this paradigm. In his first major post-Awakening publication, his 1746 *Treatise Concerning Religious Affections*, he attempted an analysis of the various affections that indicated true conversion. In this treatise he made an important adjustment to his formulations. The affections that a person had were themselves dependent on one's "inclination," tastes, or moral dispositions of the self, or the "soul" as he often put it. This explained how people could have different affections in response to the same encounter, such as hearing the gospel. One person might have affections of love toward God, for instance, while another might have affections of dislike or repulsion.[24]

Edwards signaled his new approach to the relationship among affection, disposition, and volition in the very title to his major treatise on the subject. In contrast to the classic Protestant assault on free will, Martin Luther's 1525 *On the Bondage of the Will*, Edwards published his work under a title that sounded more nuanced: *A Careful and Strict Enquiry into . . . Freedom of the Will.* This was not to be an uncompromising denial of moral liberty but an explanation of how Calvinism was congruent with modern ideas of freedom.

Much of the argument of *Freedom of the Will*, like Edwards's early "Miscellanies" on the will and his *Religious Affections*, gives an initial impression that Edwards was determined to deny moral freedom—and as a corollary legitimate Calvinist teaching on conversion—by focusing on the determination of the will by sensations outside of voluntary control. The treatise begins with the assertion that most people hold that will is the "power or principle of mind by which it is capable of choosing." Its choice, however, is merely a recognition of what the mind perceives to be the most agreeable option under consideration, so much so that one could say that the will was the same thing "as the greatest apparent good is." One could not say properly that will was determined by anything external to it, because that would merely raise the question: "determined" to do what? To like or dislike? Like and dislike meant the same thing as to will for or against something. There was no robbing the will of its action. A person always willed as he or she pleased because what one pleased was the will.[25]

This led to the role of affections. Using the vocabulary of contemporary moral philosophers such as Hutcheson, Edwards explained that the very term "will" meant to be inclined toward or have a sense of the goodness or badness of things, to be pleased or pained. Whence, Edwards then asked, came that sense of things—the affections? The answer could not be that the will chose such affections out of nothing or pure indifference. People did not understand their choices in that way. Even if they did, to say that the will chose from a position of indifference was merely to shift the issue to the reason for *that* choice. One could argue that one chose such things from one's tastes, inclinations, dispositions, or the heart. True enough in a way, Edwards maintained, but then asked, whence those dispositions? There had to be a cause somewhere at the end of the chain. The end of the chain, of course, lay outside one's will or choice because to say that one chose the end of the chain was merely to jump back into the circle of questions about the source of that choice. Edwards appeared to give an unrelenting argument for a cause that lay outside the will. In such terms, the evangelical revivals could be read in this manner: the "cause" of so many conversions, including Osborn's, Heaton's, and Rogers's, was divine grace. Outpourings of Christ's mercy and infusions of the Spirit changed people's dispositions, transformed their affections, and moved their wills.

Yet, Edwards insisted repeatedly throughout his treatise, there was nothing in this argument that contradicted common notions of freedom. By his account, the will still could be said to be free to dictate people's actions. There was no physical constraint to or coercion of the will. One was free to "do as one willed," or act according to one's choice. Most people spoke of free will in just such terms. The term "is never used in vulgar speech in that sense which Arminian divines use it in, namely for the self-determinate exercise of the will . . . without any necessary connection with anything foregoing." Instead, the term "voluntarily" is "originally and commonly" used to mean "as the effect of his choice," whether "that choice or volition be self-determined, or no." No one thought that free will meant a disconnection with "habitual bias," "the stronger motive," or other such terms for moral tastes over which the person had no control. In common parlance such as in the accounts of evangelical converts, "the man is fully and perfectly free," and at "liberty" to "do and conduct as he will, or according to his choice." Edwards here gave a full endorsement of the moral-philosophical and political mandates to assert the moral competence and freedom of ordinary people.[26]

In the most fulsome, and sometimes humorous, parts of his treatise, Edwards even claimed that experimental Calvinists better sustained the idea of moral liberty than did proponents of free will, such as the rationalist or skeptical critics of the revival, who failed to give affections and disposition their due. These critics—we can call them Arminians for short—had argued that Calvinists echoed Hobbesian determinism, and such determinism contradicted the idea that individuals made willful moral choices and were therefore accountable for them. In order to be called truly free, the Arminians argued, the will had to be seen as indifferent: uncaused by previous affections and dispositions. Freedom meant freedom from overwhelming affection. Only someone who chose the good out of indifference could be called genuinely free and therefore worthy of moral commendation. Moral approbation and disapprobation, and with them the whole idea of moral responsibility, depended on such a definition of freedom.

This, Edwards scoffed, amounted to the absurd claim that someone who made a choice for no good reason, out of no sense of right and wrong, under the sway of blind chance or in a state of insensitivity and obliviousness, ought to receive more praise than someone who chose the good out of deep moral conviction and inclination. Or to raise another problem, as Edwards explained, the Arminian attempt to sever moral freedom from moral necessity—the power of affections—allowed people to excuse themselves for their wicked hearts. They refused to see themselves as sinners because they could not choose their affections. Heaton had claimed that this was the very state of mind before her conversion: she hated God because, she said, "I cant convert myself." As Edwards put it, "conscience does not condemn them for those things, because *they cannot love God of themselves, they cannot believe of themselves*, and the like." It was much better instead to realize that the power of affections cohered with the real nature of free will and therefore moral culpability: one was all the more guilty, not less, for one's "wickedness."[27]

Edwards's critique rose to the level of sarcasm. Arminians by their logic ought not to induce or motivate people to resist evil or pursue the good because to do so would be to move them off their indifference, which would be to take away their freedom and therefore rob them of any chance of being called good or evil. This perverse notion of liberty implied that preaching, moral education and training, efforts to reform, and political persuasion were all immoral. Edwards again observed that no common person thought this way. People thought more highly of a deed motivated by a sense of virtue than of a deed motivated by arbitrary and amoral choice.[28] As Edwards informed his Scottish correspondent John Erskine, he wanted to demonstrate that experimental Calvinism accorded perfectly with the "nature of that freedom of moral agents which makes them proper subjects of moral governments, moral precepts, councils, calls, motives, persuasions, promises and threatenings." The "late great objections and outcries against Calvinistic divinity" by those who claimed that "Calvinistic notions of God's moral government are contrary to the common sense of mankind," in other words, amounted to sheer nonsense.[29]

Although Edwards aimed to disprove Arminianism and validate affection-laden revivals as a work of God, he also provided a rather powerful example of how evangelicals could use the language of freedom and choice. "All that men do in religion," he wrote in *Freedom of the Will*, "is their own act" or "an exertion of their own power" according to "the ordinary use of language." He did not deny the validity of that language. He inscribed it onto the evangelical narrative. It took some fairly clever arguments—and some that were vulnerable to further critique—for Edwards to make that point. Yet he insisted. However one came by one's will, he concluded, "man is fully and perfectly free, according to the primary and common notion of freedom."[30]

This meant that the accounts of conversion by people such as Osborn, Heaton, and Rogers could indeed be considered reasonable and responsible. Many evangelical converts did not put it as logically or precisely as did Edwards—tucked away in Stockbridge with his books—but they could rest assured. It was true that they were overcome with divine affections and at the same time freely chose Christ. That was how the will worked. They could deny that they were free in an Arminian sense, as did Heaton, and also, like Heaton, reflect on their "liberty" to choose. As Edwards said, they could "do and conduct" as they "will."[31] There was no need to choose, as it were, between grace and freedom, no either-or.

Speaking for much of New England's religious establishment, Ezra Stiles, a Newport pastor and later president of Yale, reflected on the legacy of Edwards and his generation in such terms. Stiles told a clerical convention in 1760 that old disputes between "*calvinism* and *arminianism*" had faded away. All good New England ministers, he hoped, had agreed to affirm both divine grace and "the moral liberty and free agency of man" as essential tenets of New England Protestantism.[32]

Edwards had another point, and here experimental Calvinism converged with more widespread moral and political convictions. His arguments implied that if one wanted a philosophy of the will and affections to authenticate the moral judgments of most people and, by extension, to legitimate the politics of Britain's constitutional, semi-republican monarchy, then one had better be a Calvinist than an Arminian. Moral sense philosophy, which became widespread in Edwards's time, gave Calvinists a language to express the power of the human will and credence in divine sovereignty together. It was no surprise that they gained this from the likes of Hutcheson. The Scottish moralist drew out the political implications of his moral sense thought in explicitly republican terms. The moral sense operated reliably—sociably, benevolently, responsibly—among all people regardless of political status and learning. He derived a theory of universal human rights from his moral treatises, and became a favorite of Whig and republican critics of absolutism and imperial tyranny.[33]

We can also surmise that evangelical notions of conversion—moral affections and free will acting in concert—partly shaped political sentiments in America. A decade after Edwards's death, New Englanders' reverence for the monarchy had soured into discontent with the British Empire. As that restiveness sharpened into designs for independence, evangelicals, rationalists, and middle-of-the-road establishment types alike deployed the language of liberty, as Christopher Clark put it, to express the religious reasons for political rebellion. To cite two examples of many, Stephen Johnson, a Connecticut patriot and devotee of Edwards's theology, and Stephen West, a Massachusetts Old Light who opposed Edwards on many theological points, equally linked the cause of American independence to careful expositions of moral freedom. The moral philosophy used by Edwards to explain conversion and solve the dilemma of free will informed New Englanders that they were at liberty to enact their most solemn affections. They were free to choose according to their sentiments—whether the choice concerned God or king.[34]

To put this in slightly different terms, Edwards's argument that moral dispositions shaped the will, as Gordon Wood once suggested, provided a potent rationale for revolution against—not merely resistance to—British rule in North America. Commentators who interpreted events in an Edwardsean fashion—whether they were evangelicals or not—attributed bad moral choices to bad dispositions and vicious affections. This led to accusations during the 1770s that rulers in London were not merely incompetent or financially strapped but evil. Even policy decisions that, on the face of it, deserved a good riot at most and a shrug of the shoulders at least—such as a tax on tea, arrest of smugglers, quartering of soldiers, or toleration of Catholicism in Quebec—provoked declamations against king and Parliament, accusations of betrayal and enmity, and declarations of independence.[35]

We can also focus, however, on the freedom side of Edwards's argument rather than the power of depraved affections, and the widespread use of the idioms of free will and moral liberty across the Protestant landscape in New England. Evangelical conversion conveyed the necessity of self-reflection to moral judgment. It also validated the idea that affections amplified rather than overcame free will. This language confirmed the conviction that choice was essential to moral life and therefore to one's social identity. People ought to realize that they freely chose their religious community. If that were the case, then they were certainly morally free to choose their politically loyalties, even if they were physically constrained by the power of sovereigns. The language of liberty suffused not only the sermons of evangelical patriot preachers but also, once again, the diaries of Osborn and Heaton during the Revolution, long after their conversions.

It might have seemed to eighteenth-century evangelicals such as Osborn, Heaton, and Rogers, not to mention Edwards, that an interpretation such as this overemphasizes freedom language in evangelical New England. (Heaton, who joined a separate congregation in order to escape theologians like Edwards, might actually have said that neither she nor I knew what I was talking about.) They might have protested that they were exalting divine sovereignty and the gift of godly affections rather than their choices. Edwards was saying nonetheless that such affections and new dispositions or tastes did not coerce people's wills but rather were the same thing as their wills, choices, and moral determinations. In common parlance, they were free to will and do as they willed. It is that part of the equation that marked the real innovations of evangelical New Englanders.

Notes

1. For essential definitions and the relationship between affection and conversion in Reformed teaching, see Abram C. Van Engen, *Sympathetic Puritans: Calvinist Fellow Feeling in Early New England* (New York: Oxford University Press, 2015); Abram Van Engen, "Eliza's Disposition: Freedom, Pleasure, and Sentimental Fiction," *Early American Literature* 51 (2016): 297–331; and Norman Fiering, *Jonathan Edwards's Moral Thought and Its British Context* (Chapel Hill: University of North Carolina Press, 1981). See also note 3.
2. See especially the relevant scholarship cited in Van Engen, "Eliza's Disposition."

3. For many English Puritans, conversion implied an individual's genuine, heartfelt—that is to say, sincere—adherence to the tenets of Protestantism, especially trust in Christ. Outside of conversion to or from Catholicism, it rarely had to do with freely choosing between one religious tradition and another; it more often concerned the mandate to conform to the creed that sustained the English state. The fundamental beliefs of that creed were assumed to be true. Puritan diarists circled around the issue of their own conversion time and again, struggling to determine whether they had experienced regeneration: had submissive wills, charitable hearts, and a sense of divine favor. Puritan divines such as William Ames attempted a resolution to the dilemma by instructing individuals to submit to the direction of the godly. The church informed an individual's conscience about such matters. Its teaching, and the confession of one's religious experiences before Christian elders, illuminated one's self-judgments. See Jerald C. Brauer, "Conversion: From Puritanism to Revivalism" *Journal of Religion* 58 (1978): 227–43; Charles Lloyd Cohen, *God's Caress: The Psychology of Puritan Religious Experience* (New York: Oxford University Press, 1986); and Michael C. Questier, *Conversion, Politics, and Religion in England, 1580–1625* (New York: Cambridge University Press, 1996).
4. Cotton Mather, *India Christiana* (Boston, 1721). This new approach was also evidenced in Edwards's diary of David Brainerd, which highlights Brainerd's willingness to converse in an amiable manner, with a sense of mutuality and respect, with the Lenape Delaware people. Jonathan Edwards, *The Life of David Brainerd*, ed. Norman Pettit, vol. 7 of *The Works of Jonathan Edwards* (New Haven: Yale University Press, 1985) (hereafter *WJE*).
5. Garry Wills, *Head and Heart: American Christianities* (New York: Penguin, 2007); Douglas L. Winiarski, *Darkness Falls on the Land of Light: Experiencing Religious Awakenings in Eighteenth-Century New England* (Chapel Hill: University of North Carolina Press, 2017).
6. Mark A. Noll, *The Rise of Evangelicalism: The Age of Edwards, Whitefield and the Wesleys* (Downers Grove, IL: InterVarsity Press, 2003); D. Bruce Hindmarsh, *The Evangelical Conversion Narrative: Spiritual Autobiography in Early Modern England* (New York: Oxford University Press, 2005); and W. R. Ward, *The Protestant Evangelical Awakening* (New York: Cambridge University Press, 1992).
7. Caroline Robbins, *The Eighteenth-Century Commonwealthman* (Cambridge: Harvard University Press, 1959).
8. Much of this background is admirably summarized in Allen C. Guelzo, *Edwards on the Will: A Century of American Theological Debate* (Middletown: Wesleyan University Press, 1989).
9. English Protestant tales of the fate of Huguenots who remained in France after 1685, replete with condemnations of forced conversions to Catholicism, appeared frequently; see, e.g., [A. D. Aubon], *The French Convert* (Boston, 1725). Cotton Mather wrote several accounts of New England captives in North Africa in this period, e.g., in *The Converted Sinner: The Nature of Conversion to Real and Vital Piety* (Boston, 1724), 20.
10. Paul Ramsey, "Editor's Introduction," in Jonathan Edwards, *Freedom of the Will* (hereafter *FW*), *WJE*, vol. 1, 1–128, esp. 47–65.
11. Solomon Stoddard, *A Treatise Concerning Conversion* (Boston, 1719), 2, 4, 14, 19 (quotations on choice); 43, 48, 57 (on God's disclosure to the mind and the knowledge of God).

12. Mather, *Converted Sinner*, 5–6, 14–15.
13. On disputes over the revivals, see newspaper accounts and debates, as well as well-known texts by Charles Chauncy, Experience Mayhew, and other critics. See Guelzo, *Edwards on the Will*, 26.
14. Sarah Osborn, *Memoirs of the life of Mrs. Sarah Osborn . . .* (Worcester, MA, 1799), 21–24. Osborn's biography and memoirs are discussed in Catherine A. Brekus, *Sarah Osborn's World: The Rise of Evangelical Christianity in Early America* (New Haven: Yale University Press, 2013), esp. 93–118 on conversion. The interpretation here follows Brekus's biography of Osborn but suggests a different account of her conversion.
15. Osborn, *Memoirs*, 24, 26–30.
16. In her study *In the Neighborhood: Women's Publication in Early America* (Amherst: University of Massachusetts Press, 2016), 62–83, Caroline Wigginton gives a compelling reading of how multiple meanings of conversion and affection intersected in Osborn's life and particularly in her vexed relationship with an enslaved woman.
17. Hannah Heaton, *The World of Hannah Heaton: The Diary of an Eighteenth-Century New England Farm Woman*, ed. Barbara E. Lacey (DeKalb: Northern Illinois University Press, 2003), 6–8.
18. Heaton, *The World of Hannah Heaton*, 8–10, 12, 14, 17, 138.
19. Heaton, *The World of Hannah Heaton*, 26.
20. Daniel Rogers, diary, 1740–175[3], Rogers Family Papers, 1614–1950, ser. 2, box 5B, New-York Historical Society.
21. Ramsey, "Editor's Introduction," 47–65.
22. Norman Fiering, *Jonathan Edwards's Moral Thought and Its British Context* (Chapel Hill: University of North Carolina Press for the Institute of Early American History and Culture, 1981). For overviews of Locke, Shaftesbury, and Hutcheson, see Daniel Carey, *Locke, Shaftesbury, and Hutcheson: Contesting Diversity in the Enlightenment and Beyond* (New York: Cambridge University Press, 2006); and Stanley Grean, *Shaftesbury's Philosophy of Religion and Ethics: A Study in Enthusiasm* (Athens: Ohio University Press, 1967). Shaftesbury maintained the following, to be more precise: Locke was right that the mind observed itself as it adjudicated among virtues and social behaviors and came to an understanding of the good or right choice. But Locke had not explained whence the mind came to an impression of the virtues themselves. Instead, he argues in a circle: a complex set of rational reflections on the mind determines the virtues. The understanding, in other words, controls every step in shaping the will. This was not the way that ordinary people made moral choices. Instead, they merely sensed, immediately, pleasure at certain objects or actions and pain at others, and those sensations or affections push the will.
23. Francis Hutcheson, *An Inquiry into the Original of Our Ideas of Beauty and Virtue* (1725), ed. with intro. by Wolfgang Leidhold (Indianapolis: Liberty Fund, 2004), 112, 121–22.
24. Jonathan Edwards, *Treatise Concerning Religious Affections* (Boston, 1746), in *WJE*, vol. 2, *Religious Affections*, ed. John E. Smith (1959), 96.
25. Edwards, *FW*, 137, 144. The explication of Edwards in the text relies heavily on Ramsey, "Editor's Introduction"; and Guelzo, *Edwards on the Will.*
26. Edwards, *FW*, 162, 164, 346–47; Guelzo, *Edwards on the Will*, 39 (quotation from Edwards's "Miscellanies"); Edwards, *FW*, 351.

27. Edwards, quoted in Ramsey, "Editor's Introduction," 72.
28. Edwards, *FW*, 326; Guelzo, *Edwards on the Will*, 26, 51.
29. Guelzo, *Edwards on the Will*, 38.
30. Edwards, *FW*, 162, 164.
31. Edwards, "Miscellanies," quoted in Guelzo, *Edwards on the Will*, 48.
32. Ezra Stiles, *A Discourse on the Christian Union* (1761; repr., Brookfield, MA, 1799), 65–66.
33. The best study of Hutcheson, the moral sense school, and Hutcheson's influence is David Daiches Raphael, *The Moral Sense* (London: Oxford University Press, 1947). For Hutcheson's political views, see Robbins, *Eighteenth-Century Commonwealthman*, 172–93.
34. J. C. D. Clark, *The Language of Liberty, 1660–1832: Political Discourse and Social Dynamics in the Anglo-American World* (Cambridge: Cambridge University Press, 1994). Clark says little about liberty or freedom in a philosophical or theological sense. [Stephen Johnson], *New London Gazette*, September 6 and 20, October 4 and 11, and November 1, 1765, reprinted in Bernard Bailyn, "Religion and Revolution: Three Biographical Studies," *Perspectives in American History* 4 (1970): 85–169, Appendix B (144–69); and Stephen Johnson, *Some Important Observations* (Newport, 1766). Samuel West, *A Sermon Preached before the Honorable Council* (1776), reprinted in *The Pulpit of the American Revolution: Political Sermons of the Period of 1776*, ed. John Wingate Thornton (Boston, 1860), 267–322. As Sarah Knott has shown, ideas of sensibility, linked to common ideas about virtue, were integral to confidence in democratic politics and a republican social order in a more general sense as well. Sarah Knott, *Sensibility and the American Revolution* (Chapel Hill: University of North Carolina Press, 2009).
35. Gordon S. Wood, "Conspiracy and the Paranoid Style: Causality and Deceit in the Eighteenth Century," *William and Mary Quarterly*, 3rd ser., 39 (1982): 401–44.

CHAPTER 2

The Affections

What's Love Got to Do with It?
A Response to Mark Valeri

JOANNA BROOKS

Jonathan Edwards continues to epitomize for me the intellectual discipline and stewardship a life of faith can inculcate, and I marvel at what he was able to accomplish in his rural study in both the volume and the complexity of his work. Mark Valeri's careful, precise work on the intersections between intellectual and political dispositions and theology demonstrates the kind of intellectual discipline and scholarly care Edwards's legacy requires and inspires. Valeri helps us see the intricacy and intentionality of a copious and robustly available American religious archive. The doctrine of religious affections articulated by Edwards, Valeri argues, was shaped by idioms of moral reasonableness, uncoerced consciences, and religious choice that were aligned with the political ideal of liberty and, later, with the movement for political independence, and the affections constituted a "new moral vocabulary" substantially evolved from an earlier, perhaps more pietistic definition of morality. He offers this view as a corrective to historians (eighteenth-century and contemporary) who have taken the affectionate quality of the revivals as a sign of disorderliness, divisiveness, anti-reasonableness, and to those who have mistaken conversion theology as an abdication of will rather than its realignment or even reorganization through the infusion of grace.[1] On both counts, I like Valeri's reading, especially for the space it opens up for thinking of Edwards as a proto-revolutionary thinker. In my response, I ask, using a more personal and affectionate tone than is customary for scholarship, *The affections and revolutions: What's love got to do with it?*[2] For me, this question registers the energies of popular movements that form and re-form in American history—from the religious revivals of Edwards's New England, to Pentecostalism's interracial efflorescence in early twentieth-century Los Angeles, to the massive Black Lives Matter demonstrations of our own time.

Something spiritual (if not overtly religious) has been at work in all human revolutions. Valeri's essay focuses on how individual economies of sensation, cognition, and volition structured through the "affections" engendered specific political dispositions. I would ask two questions beyond the domain of the individual: First, how did the *social* quality of the affections align with or inform revolutionary era politics? How did the idea and manifestation of religious affections make available new or reorganize old social relations? How did they reorganize or renew performance culture or the experience of common space? What were the limits of this new vocabulary of fellow feeling? Certainly these limits become visible when we trace evangelical Christianity forward from the mid-eighteenth to the mid-nineteenth century, in sentimentalism and its complicated and contradictory political implications, especially in regard to race, as Lauren Berlant and so many others have shown.[3] Second, what assumptions about the quality of *history* and God's expression in history were folded in with this view of the will moved by affections through an infusion of grace? Inevitability? A foreordained teleological arc toward redemption, or order? Valeri presents Edwards as one trying to untangle "the knot of unbidden affections, self-conscious volitions, and religious beliefs" and give "some order." Contemplating Valeri's postulation of this hunger for "order," I thought of something I wrote a few years back in *The Book of Mormon Girl*, my own effort to narrate religious affections and their trajectories in the life of a people and a girl. This is what I wrote:

> For I had been born of goodly parents, who in the wilderness of the late twentieth century, saw the wreckage of empires, markets, and civilizations, but did not know how to disentangle effects from causes, nor had the vocabulary to name the strands of these knotted histories, nor their place in them, nor the mundane and disastrous traumas of their own common American upbringings, nor the mundane and disastrous traumas lived by a millennium's worth of their poor and common ancestors, and who heard all around them mocking crowds like faceless laugh tracks of sitcom television threatening oblivion.

> Every night in my second-story room in the tract house in Orange County the year before I was baptized, my father and I read the Book of Mormon, the stories of ancient Israelite peoples led by God to the Americas, and their wars, visions, and wanderings. No one else in the world believed in the Book of Mormon but Mormons like us. So we huddled together, my nursing father and me, safe in tender longing, as the currents and the garbage and the television laugh tracks ran down the streets and fell into the storm drains and rushed along the concreted river channels alongside the freeways past abandoned orange groves out to the black and trackless sea.[4]

No doubt one of the appeals of religious life is adopting or cultivating tools for wresting meaning from chaos. Edwards's adoption of a Lockean outlook centered on a subject at liberty exercising free choice may have been premised on his theological assumption that history was teleologically determined to move toward a meaningful, redemptive end.

But I would posit a third view of the revivals and the affections to take place alongside views of the revivals as disorderly, dark, and schismatic, or events replete with Lockean clarity. This third view reflects the preoccupations guiding my own work in early American religion, which has been an effort to envision the full intricacy implied in a more fragmentary archive: in the writings of Edwards's contemporaries who were denied by the circumstances of birth and imperial histories the privilege to compile so full and continuous a body of work as the one compiled by Edwards. I would propose that the affectionate quality of the revivals was a commentary on the arbitrary violence of the colonial world. That violence was disruptive and interruptive. It interrupted personal and collective histories and sometimes shattered them. Its capriciousness was visited on and within bodies. And it was specifically destructive to Black and Indigenous lives. Being able to revisit, reenact, resignify that trauma and its affective dimensions was an act of freedom. It was a claiming of freedom from the materials of unfreedom. It was a theorizing of freedom not as a teleological state—political, geographical, etcetera—but as a moment wrested out of time and defined by its transcendental interpersonal intimacy. *The affections: What's love got to do, got to do with it?* Freedom, this body of commentary suggests, is something we can have only with other people, people similarly caught up in the mix of human complexity.

This view of the affections and their motility I have traced in an essay tracking not Edwards to Emerson but Edwards to James Baldwin and the legacy of the threshing floor, the scene of crisis conversion as a key alt-American intellectual trope.[5] If we take it a step further even, we can see it in Baldwin's most important contemporary heir, Ta-Nehisi Coates. If Edwards's notion of affections as rational was coupled with a view of history as arcing toward justice, Coates gives us a view of history as a series of discontinuous and capriciously disordered eras, mutually inflected but animated by a seeping inertia. His view of the American political system is that of a "Dream" subsidized by the appropriation of Black bodies, and as freedom and revolution to be found in the warmth of affection. In a letter to his son about how to live as a Black man in the threat of radical discontinuity and violence, he recalls his own experience as a student at Howard, caught up in the mix of an exuberant homecoming dance party, with fellow students of African descent, as a scene of extraordinary energy, affection, and significance: "I felt myself disappearing into all of their bodies. . . . That was a moment, a joyous moment, beyond the Dream—a moment imbued by a power more gorgeous than any voting rights bill. This power, this black power, originates in a view of the American galaxy taken from a dark and essential planet."[6] Are we a long way from Edwards's New England? Perhaps. Are we a long way from the revivals? Or are we in the same space—Coates calls it cosmic—that revival-goers have yearned for and prayed, breathed, and danced their way into across the American centuries, from ring shouts and hush arbors, to George Whitefield's celebrity tour of the eastern seaboard, to the transgressively if momentarily integrated spaces of worship from the Second Great Awakening on the Ohio frontier to the outburst of Pentecostalism in early twentieth-century Los Angeles. Is religious transcendence about this fullness and unity of being, about being in a place where one can experience without danger and even with pleasure in the company of other human beings the arbitrary quality of history and find the courage to strip away the excuses for what Coates calls "the Dream," the version of American history that innocently pretends it is not about violence?[7] I see from where I stand, but this is what I see in the streets of the United States this summer of 2020. I find yet another manifestation of Black genius, a spiritual disposition toward entering the complicated and tangled, and find it redeemed not through disentangling and ordering but through the dissolution of boundaries that individuate being.

This for me begs the question: What if another political legacy of the affections is not only liberty but solidarity and love? *What's love got to do, got to do with it?* Perhaps freedom is something one can only have with other people caught up in the mix of the struggle for life over death. I turned back to my thick bound volumes of Edwards with this question in mind, spent some quality time with the *Religious Affections* in hand and on my nightstand, looking for evidence of that solidarity in the text. I did not find it there in the *Religious Affections*. I did find it, however, in his earlier narrative accounts of the Awakening, in the more historical and social writings. See, for example, his classic *Faithful Narrative of the Surprising Work of God* (1737), a report on the "remarkable conversions" taking place during 1734–35 among the members of his Northampton, Massachusetts, congregation. Edwards specifically observed, "There are several Negroes, that from what was seen in them then, and what is discernable in them since, appear to have been truly born again in the late remarkable season." A few years later, in his more extensive *Some Thoughts Concerning the Present Revival of Religion* (1742), he remarked that, as with African Americans, the minds of "the poor Indians" had "now been strangely opened to receive instruction, and have been deeply affected with the concerns of their precious souls, and have reformed their lives." According to Edwards, these conversions made more "visible" and "conspicuous" in unexpected ways the power of God. But as controversies concerning the trustworthy signs of the New Birth and the validity of the revivals themselves mounted, Edwards adopted a cooler and more critical approach in writings like *The Distinguishing Marks* (1741).[8]

Do we see a movement in Edwards over time from a more affectionate to a less affectionate view of the religious affections? Was Edwards just a senior scholar moving from history to theory? Did he fall out of love with the affections and their various forms of unruly humanity, or did he just choose to express that love in a new way? Does revolutionary ideology rationally conceived entail a retreat from history? Is the tension between rationality, the categorical, the timeless, the universalized subjective—liberty, fraternity, égalité—and the uneven and contradictory textures of lived experience the fatal flaw of revolutions? Or perhaps this frisson and its capacity for generating vulnerability, breakthrough, and the unexpected is where revolution finds its energy and where life finds its fullest valuation. My heart likes to think that Edwards would agree.

Notes

1. See Joseph Tracy, *The Great Awakening: A History of the Revival of Religion in the Time of Edwards and Whitefield* (Boston: Tappan and Dennet, 1842); J. M. Bumsted, *What Must I Do to Be Saved? The Great Awakening in Colonial America* (Hinsdale, IL: Dryden, 1976); Richard Bushman, ed., *The Great Awakening: Documents on the Revival of Religion, 1740–1745* (New York: Atheneum, 1970); Cedric B. Cowing, *The Great Awakening and the American Revolution* (Chicago: Rand McNally, 1971); Edwin Gausted, *The Great Awakening in New England* (New York: Harper and Brothers, 1957); Wesley Gewehr, *The Great Awakening in Virginia, 1740–1790* (Durham: Duke University Press, 1930); C. C. Goen, *Revivalism and Separatism in New England, 1740–1800: Strict Congregationalists and Separate Baptists in the Great Awakening* (New Haven: Yale University Press, 1972); Timothy Hall, *Contested Boundaries: Itinerancy and the Reshaping of the Colonial American Religious World* (Durham: Duke University Press, 1994); Alan Heimert, *Religion and the American Mind: From the Great Awakening to the Revolution* (Cambridge: Harvard University Press, 1966); Alan Heimert and Perry Miller, eds., *The Great Awakening: Documents Illustrating the Crisis and Its Consequences* (Indianapolis: Indiana University Press, 1967); Rhys Isaac, *The Transformation of Virginia, 1740–1790* (Chapel Hill: University of North Carolina Press, 1982); Frank Lambert, *Inventing the Great Awakening* (Princeton: Princeton University Press, 1999); Perry Miller, *Errand into the Wilderness* (Cambridge: Harvard University Press, 1956); Perry Miller, *Jonathan Edwards* (New York: Meridian Books, 1949); Harry Stout, *The New England Soul: Preaching and Religious Culture in Colonial New England* (Oxford: Oxford University Press, 1986); and Marilyn Westerkamp, *Triumph of the Laity: Scots-Irish Piety and the Great Awakening, 1625–1760* (New York: Oxford University Press, 1988). Allen Guelzo provides a graceful review of Great Awakening historiography in "God's Designs: The Literature of the Colonial Revivals of Religion, 1735–1760," in *New Directions in American Religious History*, ed. Harry Stout and D. G. Hart (Oxford: Oxford University Press, 1997), 141–72; while Jonathan Butler presents an alternate and critical view in "Enthusiasm Described and Decried: The Great Awakening as Interpretive Fiction," *Journal of American History* 69 (1982–83): 305–25.
2. My tone and my frank recognition of the role of love and affection in our work and in the work of revolution may not be customary in literary-historical scholarship, but it is a recognized methodology of feminist scholarship from Jane Tompkins, "Me and My Shadow," *New Literary History* 19, no. 1 (Autumn 1987): 169–78, through Chela Sandoval, *Methodology of the Oppressed* (Minneapolis: University of Minnesota Press, 2000), and beyond.
3. See especially James Baldwin, "Everybody's Protest Novel," in *Collected Essays of James Baldwin* (New York: Library of America, 1998), 11–18; Lauren Berlant, "Poor Eliza," *American Literature* 70 (September 1998): 635–66; Lori Merish, *Sentimental Materialism: Gender, Commodity Culture, and Nineteenth-Century American Literature* (Durham: Duke University Press, 2000), 1–87; Karen Sánchez-Eppler, *Dependent States: The Child's Part in Nineteenth-Century American Culture* (Chicago: University of Chicago Press, 2005), 101–48.
4. Joanna Brooks, *The Book of Mormon Girl: A Memoir of an American Faith* (New York: Simon & Schuster/Free Press, 2012), 5–6.

5. See Joanna Brooks, "From Edwards to Baldwin: Heterodoxy, Discontinuity, and New Narratives of American Religious-Literary History," *American Literary History* 22, no. 2 (2010): 439–53.
6. Ta-Nehisi Coates, *Between the World and Me* (New York: Spiegel & Grau, 2015), 149–50.
7. On the willed "innocence" of white American culture, see especially James Baldwin, "My Dungeon Shook: A Letter to My Nephew" (1962), in *The Fire Next Time* (New York: Vintage, 1993), 1–10.
8. The quotations are from Jonathan Edwards, *The Great Awakening*, vol. 4 of *The Works of Jonathan Edwards* (New Haven: Yale University Press, 1972), 159, 346.

CHAPTER 3

The Language of Belief

Religious Conversion in Eighteenth-Century Iroquoia

SCOTT MANNING STEVENS

> Besides the tribe of the Cauneengcheys, or proper Mohawks, there are some appearances among some of the tribe of the Oneidas. . . . Abraham told me of others, considerable men, of the nation of the Oneidas, in other places, and also some of the Tuscororas, that are religiously disposed. God in his providence seems now to be opening the door for introducing the light of the gospel among these nations, more than ever [he] has done before. And if we, the English, don't fail in our [part], there is a prospect of great things being done. And probably this present season is our *now* or *never*.
>
> —Jonathan Edwards to Thomas Hubbard, August 31, 1751

Jonathan Edwards's "now or never" moment for the Reformed English church to evangelize among the Haudenosaunee (aka the Iroquois or Six Nations) came well over a century after French missionary efforts had begun among them under the auspices of the Récollets and the Jesuits. While it is standard to note the piecemeal and belated missionary work of the Church of England among the Indigenous peoples of North America, the Puritans of New England had been active missionaries among Algonquin-speaking nations along the Atlantic seaboard since John Eliot's missions of the 1640s. The Haudenosaunee homelands, in what is now upstate New York, by contrast were just beyond the English colonial frontier until well into the eighteenth century, and Anglican attempts at missionary activity among them were cautious in the extreme.[1]

To be sure, the martial reputation and autonomy of the Six Nations made the type of evangelism that was possible among New England tribes impossible in Iroquoia. Neither the French, Dutch, nor British could claim to have conquered the Six Nations Confederacy during the colonial period, though they all sought its alliance or skirmished with it, in turns, during their almost two centuries of mutual interaction. But I wish to consider the other impediments to the missionaries during this same long period and revisit the notion of radical linguistic alterity that has preoccupied my considerations of European and Haudenosaunee interactions for over a decade. I must first contextualize my linguistic fascination with some autobiographical information. I am the son of a Mohawk mother and a Welsh American father, raised speaking English but in close familiarity with my Mohawk-speaking relatives including grandparents, aunts, uncles, and cousins. Not only was I familiar with the vocabulary and phonology of spoken Mohawk, but also I was keenly aware of its difficulty and differences when compared with European languages. It would require a deep level of fluency for any non-Iroquoian speaker to convey the central message of the Christian faith. The Jesuits had struggles with this fact in the seventeenth century, as had Dutch clergy in New Netherland, such as Johannes Megapolensis. Structural differences in the six Iroquoian languages of the Haudenosaunee Confederacy baffled even those with considerable European and classical language training. The French Jesuit Jean de Brébeuf wondered how the concept of the Trinity was to be understood when Iroquoian pronominal prefixes, which also mandate kinship markers, made the concept especially difficult to translate, and the Dutch minister Megapolensis noted that among Europeans who had lived among the Mohawks for many years, some could use a kind of jargon for trade, but "they do not understand the fundamentals of the language."[2]

I have studied Latin, Anglo-Saxon, French, and German in school and university and have some proficiency in the modern languages, and so I am keenly aware of how structurally different Iroquoian languages are in comparison with Romance or Germanic languages. Because of this awareness I have always taken assertions of fluency in a Native American language with considerable skepticism, and yet the historical record is full of such assertions. These claims are virtually impossible to verify with any certainty, and just as often they are taken on faith. A historical narrative punctuated with meaningful intercultural dialogues is so much more appealing than one of halting misunderstandings due to profound issues of translation or linguistic misprision, but I fear many historical interactions were marked precisely by the latter. If this is the case, it would show in no area more quickly than in that of Christian evangelism. The long history of the Christian religion is a history of making leaps across linguistic and cultural divides—leaps that would bring the message of an Aramaic-speaking Jewish prophet to the far reaches of Ethiopia, India, and Scandinavia in the first, sixth, and eighth centuries, respectively. But that same religion found considerable resistance among the Indigenous nations of North America, and not least among the Haudenosaunee. What can the language of "religious affections"—as Edwards carefully understood the term or as anyone else might have used it at the time—possibly mean when it attempts to cross this border? It would presume a missionary's ability to find workable conceptual cognates in a dramatically different Indigenous language and then introduce the spiritual values espoused by Edwards, such as "evangelical humiliation," meekness, and forgiveness, to a more martial society. This would be even more challenging when it came to extremities of emotional expression in the context of religious practice, which would likely seem repellent to many Haudenosaunee people, one of whose key spiritual practices, the Condolence Ceremony, meant to assuage the emotions rather than stir enthusiasm. Few Protestant missionaries would possess the linguistic acumen necessary to comprehend this ceremony or its centrality, which I discuss further on, to the people to whom they preached.

Geographic distances aside, the European encounter with the Americas is an encounter of extreme linguistic alterity. The Indigenous languages spoken in the Western Hemisphere differed from one another almost as dramatically as they did from the languages of Europe. Besides the staggering number of languages and dialects in the Americas, we must consider the effects of a general lack of alphabetic writing for attempting to learn one of these languages where no single common language existed. Early modern philology, for all its growing sophistication, still lacked a cohesive linguistic theory and very often predicated notions of linguistic difference on the story of the Tower of Babel in the book of Genesis.[3] Knowledge of Latin, Greek, and Hebrew would not be enough to extrapolate the structures in Amerindian languages, and learning these languages as an adult would prove extremely difficult.

If we take the Iroquoian language group as an example, it may be illustrative of the magnitude of such problems. This language group includes not only the languages of the Six Nations (Mohawk, Oneida, Onondaga, Cayuga, Seneca, and Tuscarora) but also Huron (aka Wyandot),

Susquehannock, Nottaway, and Cherokee (which, like Tuscarora, is a branch of southern Iroquoian languages). As a language group, it is as distinct from the other large language group of eastern North America, Algonquin, as Romance languages are from Germanic ones. Iroquoian grammar and syntax do not resemble European languages structurally, and the phonology uses only thirteen of the European alphabetic letters when written, lacking the labial and fricative consonants *m*, *p*, *b*, *f*, and *v*. There are also a number of tonal aspects that affect the meaning of words and phrases, as well as a variety of guttural intonations. Most problematic for language learners is the complex system of pronominal prefixes that govern the grammar of these languages; Mohawk has fifty-eight of these, which, besides the categories familiar with English pronouns, can also indicate number, gender, and animate or inanimate qualities. Whole phrases or sentences can be written as a single word with a verb and noun forming its root.

Of course, the writing of these Native languages was itself a tremendous challenge. Lacking an Indigenous alphabetic system, European auditors had to record what they heard phonetically, which in turn produced highly idiosyncratic versions of Native languages where the orthography was in constant flux. Take, for example, Edwards's use of the word *Cauneengcheys* to mean Mohawks. How is a modern reader, with no knowledge of Iroquoian languages, to make sense of this seemingly random denomination of the Mohawk? First, we must acknowledge that *Mohawk* is not the name of my people in our language, in the same way that in English we use *German* to refer to *Deutsch*. *Mohawk*, a word derived from the Narragansett term related to cannibalism, is an exonym for *Kanien'kéhaka*, or People of the Flint, while *Iroquois* is a Franco-Algonkian denomination used for the *Haudenosaunee*, or People of the Long House. I take Edwards's *Cauneengcheys* to be a very rough attempt at a phonetic spelling of *Kanien'kéha* (which would refer to the language, not the people) if we read his version as beginning with a hard *c* or *k* sound and the *ch* as a *kh* sound. Reading early modern European renderings of Iroquoian words is a bit of an exercise in cryptography. The Mohawk community of Kahnawake, established in the seventeenth century just south of Montreal, has long been rendered as *Caughnawaga* on English-language maps.

This very general consideration of some of the salient differences between Iroquoian languages and European languages is an attempt to alert us to the actual challenges of learning those languages, absent writing or known grammars, before we revisit the issues that surely impacted missionary efforts among the Haudenosaunee in the early modern period, from the beginning of the seventeenth and throughout the eighteenth centuries. We cannot begin to assess the impact of a notion such as Jonathan Edwards's "religious affections" on the missionizing of Native Americans if we fail to acknowledge the enormity of the linguistic challenge before him. In the case of Edwards, his missionary work came late in his career, after being dismissed from his pastoral position in Northampton in 1750. Upon arriving in Stockbridge in 1751, Edwards was in many ways ill-equipped to play the role of a missionary to the Indians.[4] His preaching style relied on the power of his rhetorical skills and his ability to move his audience, while his theology was thoroughly intellectual and sophisticated. Such skills were not readily translatable into the language and idioms of a Native American congregation. Edwards knew no Native language when he arrived in Stockbridge in his late forties and at his age was unlikely to learn one; add to this that in his day the Natives gathered at the Stockbridge Mission came from several different nations and spoke different languages. As the scholar Sarah Rivett has recently noted, Edwards explains his notion to a correspondent that "the 'barbarous tongues' of the American Indians are 'exceeding barren and very unfit to express moral or divine things.'"[5] Edwards's preaching there would be relegated to English speakers in the Stockbridge community or those Native congregants dependent on translators. Because of these deficiencies, many scholars have assumed his time in Stockbridge was largely a kind of exile and that it served primarily as a period in which he could concentrate on his writing.[6] In a typically high-handed manner, the literary scholar Perry Miller described Edwards's removal this way: "He had no choice but to escape to the frontier, as did so many misfits in American history. He went to Stockbridge, where he eked out his last years as a missionary to a lot of moth-eaten Indians."[7]

I find myself very interested in those "moth-eaten Indians." We can presume Miller refers to them as "moth-eaten" because he takes their cultures to be in decline at this point in colonial New England. He unquestioningly buys into the declension narrative that has become a feature of the United States' master narrative, which includes such other elements as Manifest Destiny and American exceptionalism. Acknowledging my contempt for those notions, I wish to consider the Native peoples who would have been present at the Stockbridge Mission in 1751. The community had come into being in the 1730s as a new version of the old praying towns first created by John Eliot's missionary efforts in the Bay Colony almost a century before.[8] Stockbridge was a place of ethnogenesis, amalgamating members of the majority Mahican community with others including members of the Schaghticoke, Tunxis, and Nipmuck nations. Close linguistic and cultural ties between these groups allowed them to form what would become the Stockbridge Indians. For most of their tenure at Stockbridge they had been led by the Reverend John Sergeant, who had learned the Mahican language well enough to translate Isaac Watts's *First Catechism* in 1736.[9]

It was also just around that time when some Mohawk and Oneida leaders decided to accept the invitation to have their sons educated at English mission schools, where they would become more fluent in English and learn to read and write; being proselytized was the price of admission. We should likewise keep in mind Linford Fisher's reminder that "by the 1720s, various Indian communities across southern New England were beginning to see the advantages to literacy and a wider selective English cultural appropriation in service of their own communities."[10] Britain's superintendent of Indian affairs in the northern colonies, Sir William Johnson, had close ties with the Mohawks and encouraged families to give their children an English education in hopes that it would cement the bond between their respective peoples.[11] This was especially the case in the early 1750s as the prospect of war between Britain and France loomed and the Six Nations were important allies to the British. Jonathan Edwards would finally have his "now or never" moment with the Haudenosaunee.

Before we consider the significance, or lack thereof, of this moment in the history of evangelizing the Haudenosaunee, I want to reconsider the French efforts to convert them in the seventeenth century and the historiography depicting that effort. Protestant missionaries motivated by the affective preaching style of the Great Awakening were not the first to see the conversion of the Haudenosaunee as an important milestone in the conversion of Native America. As mentioned earlier, French missionary efforts began with the arrival of the Récollets, a reformed branch of the Franciscans, in Quebec in 1615. It would be the Récollets who would lay the groundwork for the Jesuit missionaries who would arrive in 1625 and supersede them in the field of missionary work among the Natives. Scholars have long credited the Jesuits' scholastic training for their diligence and supposed success at learning Indigenous languages, but this largely rests on Jesuits' claims of fluency in their promotional accounts collectively known as the *Jesuit Relations.* As with many linguistic claims regarding obscure languages, these avowals of fluency are extremely difficult to verify. Only a first-language speaker of Huron or Montagnais who interacted with a given missionary could support or refute such a claim, and we lack such accounts or testimonials.

Ever since the publication of Victor Hanzeli's *Missionary Linguistics in New France: A Study of Seventeenth- and Eighteenth-Century Descriptions of Amerindian Languages* in 1969, scholars have held up Jesuit linguistic work as exemplary without really questioning Hanzeli's conclusions. Though Hanzeli's work is arguably an obscure publication for many readers, its thesis has been cited, invoked, and internalized by numerous influential scholars. Historians such as James Axtell drew on Hanzeli in his important collection of essays *After Columbus: Essays in the Ethnohistory of Colonial North America*, where he uses Hanzeli's thesis to explain why French missionaries so far outperformed the English.[12] Likewise, the internalizing of Hanzeli's work might also explain the assertion by the historian Allan Greer in a selection of Jesuit writings titled *The Jesuit Relations: Natives and Missionaries in Seventeenth-Century North America* of Father Brébeuf's fluency in Huron. Greer notes: "Training in Latin and Greek was part of the education of every Jesuit, but Brébeuf was particularly adept at languages, acquiring a basic knowledge of several North American dialects to go with his fluency in Huron. (In spite of modest disclaimers to the contrary, he spoke Huron well, though not perfectly as of 1636)."[13]

The historian Margaret Leahey has argued that Hanzeli's claims on behalf of the Jesuits in his 1969 monograph were much more modest. "The missionaries had discovered a good deal more about the thorny issues of syntax and morphology than previous historians of linguistics had thought." But given the scope of the difference and challenges of learning these languages, she judges it "very unlikely that missionaries were able to speak fluent Huron, Montagnais, Micmac, or any other language of New France after only a few months or even a few years in the country."[14] Axtell and Greer both acknowledge that the *Relations* are full of admissions about the difficulty Europeans, including the Jesuits, had in learning Indigenous languages but then choose to favor the notion of fluency. While I do not doubt that figures like Brébeuf could speak Huron,

I query how effective it could have been in expressing Christian doctrine. The Jesuit scholar Joseph François Lafitau noted in 1724: "Every barbarous language is extremely difficult to teach a man who speaks another with a totally different structure. He would not be able to succeed by himself without extreme application and several years of practice."[15] It should be noted that only a few missionaries were ever granted the circumstances of safety and good health that allowed them years of practice.

I greatly appreciate the work of Micah True on the *Jesuit Relations* precisely because he does take seriously the linguistic limitations that shaped every aspect of the missionary project in New France. He takes a more pragmatic look at the linguistic information found in the *Relations*, writing: "The glaring differences between the Jesuits' manuscript dictionaries and the published *Relations* on the subject of Amerindian languages provide a clue about the relationship between Jesuit knowledge of Amerindian cultures more generally and the representation thereof that they prepared for readers. . . . Despite the considerable time and ink they devoted to the project, [Jesuit missionary Paul] Le Jeune and his colleagues tended to emphasize their efforts rather than display their results in detail."[16] By no means do I disregard the tremendous advances in comparative linguistics achieved by the Jesuits in New France *avant la lettre*, but I would argue that for scholars to better assess the impact of their linguistic understanding of Indigenous cultures, some serious linguistic work would have to be undertaken in concert with fluent speakers, whenever possible, of the languages in question. Though the Jesuits proclaimed to spread the faith via ear and understanding rather than images, we might better understand the efficacy of the sacraments in the act of conversion over catechizing and preaching. Allan Greer's analysis of Kateri Tekakwitha's conversion and the missionizing work of the Jesuits is instructive; he notes that recent converts' faith was assessed in a way that "was largely behavioral rather than intellectual." Their instruction in the faith relied on learning terminology, the use of images to illustrate the pleasure of heaven and the torments of hell or to illustrate key moments in the life of Christ. Emphasis was also placed on behavioral prohibitions, rote prayers, and making the sign of the cross.[17] This is quite different from the Protestant emphasis on the study of scripture and the rigorous self-examination demanded for admission into the faith. For many Native peoples familiar with their community's traditional ritual actions and behavioral codes, the Jesuit message may have been more accessible—different to be sure, but ultimately comprehensible at the level of behavior. Such notions as Edwards's "evangelical humiliation" would be considerably harder to convey adequately for even the most fluent of speakers.

This essay is an attempt to refocus us on linguistic and cultural issues and discover the depth of the challenges involved while considering a means of bettering our analysis of these problems. I attend to language here because it strikes me that Edwards's focus on the affections faced profound linguistic and cultural challenges that went beyond the issue of fluency. Finding the appropriate Indigenous vocabulary would not guarantee a transparency of meaning. In many cases we could point to a certain level of incommensurability between the European Christian and Haudenosaunee habits of thought. I am thinking along the lines of what Pierre Bourdieu termed the *habitus*: "the way society becomes deposited in persons in the form of lasting dispositions, or trained capacities and structured propensities to think, feel and act in determinant ways, which then guide them."[18] The profound differences separating the worldviews of the Haudenosaunee and the European missionaries were unlikely to be bridged by mere linguistic translation—though that was challenging enough. Allan Greer notes that beyond differing notions of the cosmos and the soul, there were "great chasms of mutual incomprehension" between the missionaries and the Indigenous peoples they sought to convert; "there was a more basic incommensurability in areas such as the division between the natural and supernatural, the nature of the human self, the concept of truth."[19] Such challenges frequently defeated missionary aims.

For the sake of brevity, I wish to pass from the Jesuits and their efforts among the Haudenosaunee, famous for producing almost as many martyrs as converts, to the efforts of the English among the Mohawks and Oneidas almost a century after the French in the eighteenth century. We should also note that French missionaries could claim a considerable harvest of souls beyond their martyred converts. The mixed Haudenosaunee community, though heavily Mohawk-identified, at Kahnawake, just south of Montreal, was made up largely of Haudenosaunee converts who left Iroquoia for a variety of reasons and settled on a reserve granted by the French crown to the Jesuits at Sault-Saint-Louis along the Saint Lawrence in 1680. It would be from that denominationally Catholic reserve that Iroquois warriors joined their French allies in the Deerfield raid of 1704.[20]

It was in that same year that the Society for the Propagation of the Gospel in Foreign Parts would begin their modest efforts among the Mohawk and Oneida communities of eastern Iroquoia. The Church of England poised itself to compete with both the Catholics and Calvinists in the quest for Haudenosaunee converts. The goals of the crown were dependent on alliances created by trade, kinship (actual or figurative), and faith. Religion, though not the sole means of cultural conversion, became the primary justification for the assimilationist policies that began in the colonial period and continue through the twenty-first century. Historically less attention has been given to the Anglican evangelical efforts of the British encounter with the Indigenous peoples of North America when we compare it to scholarship on the Puritan and French missionary enterprises. Because of the comparative successes of the Catholic Church in the Americas overall (especially among the Jesuit missions), the influence of Protestant missionaries has been largely downplayed or treated as secondary to the larger settler colonial project. I argue that the evangelism of British North America went well beyond the missionary work of the English colonizers to a much deeper level of cultural conversion that amounts ultimately to assimilation. Through the overwhelming pressures of settler colonial societies, wherein the Indigenous population becomes a disenfranchised minority and is pressured to accept European cultural norms through religious conversion and education, Native communities were expected to internalize Protestant notions of sin, natural depravity, and damnation and to experience intense and distressing feelings as a result. Many Christians judged the sincerity of belief on the emotions of deep contrition that led to the acceptance of grace. The impact of such notions on the psychological health of Native communities is almost impossible to gauge in the historical record but must have been a large part of the trauma of colonialism. This line of reasoning means to challenge the current revisionist emphasis on a supposed symmetry of influence during the Encounter.

Ever since the publication of Richard White's *Middle Ground*, arguing for the mutuality of cultural encounter, scholars have been drawn to the appealing notion of the influence of Native American cultures on the cultural lives of the colonizers.[21] Unwittingly, this position obscures the overwhelming pressures placed on Native communities to convert or assimilate to European cultural norms, including emotional ones, in the period of conquest as well as the continuation of these pressures down to this day. Conversion as a cultural imperative ultimately left little room for a middle ground. Lifeways that differed dramatically from those of the Europeans would not be tolerated in the end. While it is indeed important to recognize the contributions that Aboriginal cultures made to Euro-American life and the appropriation of a variety of culturally symbolic capital from the Native Americans, we must not presume that this interaction empowered Native peoples. Similarly, in the case of linguistic exchanges, David Murray cautions that although some Europeans did indeed learn Native languages, "it is important to remember . . . that the great *bulk* of language learning and translation was being carried out by Indians, this reflecting, of course the wider situation, in which Indians were also the ones involved, willingly or otherwise, in *cultural* translation."[22] The English literary tradition of seventeenth- and eighteenth-century writings on the figure of the savage, noble or otherwise, makes abundantly clear the enduring power of the discourse of conversion and translation.

It is surprising, then, that relatively few cultural and ethnohistorians have attended to the belated efforts of missionaries from England to the League of Six Nations.[23] Anglican missionary work has been overlooked or noted only as a footnote in the complex relations between the Iroquois, the British, and the French in their respective contests for power. The majority of scholarship concerned with the impact of missionary projects in North America has focused on the more polarized comparisons of the Jesuit missions in New France and New Spain with the seemingly much less successful missionary work of the Puritans of New England—and that predominantly of John Eliot. Because of the profound crisis that wracked the Church of England for much of the seventeenth century, missionary work was left largely in the hands of these dissenting churchmen who had fled to New England. Not until the reign of Queen Anne at the beginning of the eighteenth century was an organized effort made by the Church of England and the crown to establish an English Episcopal Church in the New World.

Once the Society for the Propagation of the Gospel in Foreign Parts was established in 1701 as the officially sanctioned missionary organization of the Church of England, we begin to see clearly the union of British imperial policy with that of the church. From its very inception, the SPG was alert to the strategic importance of Christian converts among Britain's

Aboriginal allies. British colonial values could be said to focus on fur, flag, and faith. This trinity of trade, national expansion, and evangelizing was long in coming compared to Spanish and French efforts in the same arenas. It is commonplace to note early modern Britain's hesitant and piecemeal approach to empire. Because of the competing economic interests of London monopolies and other investment organizations, there was no unified plan advanced by a monolithic state policy. The cause of religious expansion was even more fragmentary because of the crisis facing the Church of England during the course of the seventeenth century. Unlike the Spanish or French, the English lacked anything like a unified state church. Though Protestantism was the official faith of the land from Elizabeth I onward, the very nature of that Protestantism was bitterly contested. Thus the first real efforts at evangelizing the Indians fell to the Congregationalists of New England. Even the episcopal structure of the Church of England in early Virginia was largely Calvinist in theology. It would not be until the beginning of the eighteenth century that Church of England missionaries began to make inroads in Iroquoia by establishing an Anglican mission at Fort Hunter, near the Mohawk village of Tiononderoge, in 1712. Those efforts would cease in a formal manner by 1720, and over the next decades a small group of Mohawk Protestants would maintain their own highly syncretic version of Anglicanism.[24] Elsewhere I have analyzed some of the linguistic challenges that faced English attempts to translate the gospels into Mohawk.[25] At least up until the American Revolution, the majority in Haudenosaunee communities were not substantially Christian.

Arguably, the most serious and sustained Protestant engagement with Native North Americans was undertaken by Congregationalists and Presbyterians in New England and New Jersey and the Moravians in Pennsylvania and, later, North Carolina. In New England, the legacy of the praying towns' founding through John Eliot's missionary work had largely been soured in the aftermath of King Philip's War, when most of these towns were either destroyed or disbanded. Native communities that persisted throughout the eighteenth century now found themselves surrounded and encroached upon by an ever-growing number of white settlers hungry for land. It became increasingly clear to many Native people that, because colonists saw Christianity and civilization as indivisibly linked, the only way Natives might hope to retain something of their original territories and rights was to accept this new religion.[26] This attitude might be more comprehensible in light of the catastrophe of settler colonialism, which had brought devastating epidemics, war, land dispossession, and the blight of alcohol to countless Native communities along the Atlantic coast. Certainly generations born into this world of radical instability and cultural upheaval would have reason to consider religious alternatives, especially as their communities became ever more acculturated to settler beliefs and society. Even so, many colonists recognized they had failed to spread their faith to Native communities after a century of interaction with them. In 1723 Solomon Stoddard would publish a sermon titled "Question Whether God Is Not Angry with the Country for Doing So Little toward the Conversion of the Indians." He warned that settlers would face continued warfare and Indian raids if they did not answer the call to convert and civilize their Indigenous neighbors.[27]

Such a call might have gone largely ignored had it not been for the broad religious revival known as the Great Awakening beginning in the 1730s–1740s and the continued need for Indigenous allies in the contest between the imperial competitors Britain and France. The renewal of religious commitment and convictions became a social phenomenon and affected Christian settlers and Natives alike. It was during this period, in the summer of 1741, that Samson Occom would declare he had been "awakened and converted" at a revival led by James Davenport in New London.[28] Significantly, for my interests, the language of Davenport's preaching was English. We likely hear accounts of the "fire and brimstone" sermons of the period with a sense of recognition of that era's religious zeal, but I suspect few of us can really imagine scenes in which "great numbers cried aloud in the anguish of their souls. Several stout men fell as though a cannon had been discharged, and a ball had made its way through their hearts. Some young women were thrown into hysteric fits."[29] Such preaching could be so affecting only if one knew both the language in which it was delivered and had a deep familiarity with the concepts of sin and eternal damnation. These sermons were after all a means of awakening the slumbering Christian soul as much as, or more than, they might have been expected to convert the nonbeliever. Occom, though he professed to have been raised in heathenism, could not have easily avoided the religious idioms and mores of early eighteenth-century New England.

I ask only that we focus on the notion of the *language* of religious belief. How was one to explain the place of the affections on the path toward true belief if one could not do this through language? To be sure, some evangelists and missionaries used translators to convey their message to Native audiences, but we can know very little about the experience of this type of preaching done in a radically different language; so much depended on the skill and accuracy of the translator. Elsewhere I have discussed what I call "linguistic despair," that is, the notion that no matter how fluent a missionary may become in an Indigenous language, those languages were themselves considered a hindrance to conveying the gospel message.[30] This might strike us as akin to the early twentieth-century notion of linguistic relativity or the so-called "Sapir-Whorf hypothesis," which posited a level of linguistic determinism whereby linguistic structures play a key part in a people's perception of the world. As James Axtell points out in his reading of the *Jesuit Relations*: "It thus appeared to some Jesuits that 'neither the Gospel nor the holy Scripture has been composed for them [the Indians].' Even mundane parables to symbolize the Christian mysteries were nearly untranslatable for lack of vocabulary. 'Their ignorance of the things of the earth,' lamented the worldly priests, 'seem to close for them the way to heaven.'"[31] Similarly, Jane Merritt points out that Moravian missionaries, who earnestly set about learning Indigenous languages, still insisted Natives learn to speak and write in German or English—"because their own languages would never convey the intricacies of Christianity."[32] This presumption about the inherent inadequacies of Indigenous languages constitutes a type of despair that ultimately necessitated the eradication of Indigenous languages. The cold logic of the Indian boarding school was not far off once such a presumption becomes regarded as fact. What schools like the New Light preacher Eleazar Wheelock's would offer, then, is the promise of social advancement through skills in the English language and literacy. This was fundamental to the cultural conversion I mentioned earlier.

But Samson Occom's conversion, though it made him determined to become literate so as to read the Bible in English, was not simply a cultural conversion. He was arguably fairly acculturated already simply by having grown up among the settlers who dominated society in southern New England, but acculturation is not the same as assimilation. As scholars such as Joanna Brooks and Julius Rubin have both persuasively argued, Occom presented a new category in the ethnic and social composition of New England, the Christian Indian.[33] In order to pursue his education,

Occom sought out instruction from Wheelock, whose success in teaching Occom would lead him to found Moor's Indian Charity School and later Dartmouth College. But Wheelock's "Grand Design," as he termed it, was to educate Native missionaries in a mode not unlike that of their English counterparts. Native students would perfect their reading and writing skills in English and then go on to study Latin and Greek. Wheelock's aim was to prepare Indigenous ministers to serve as missionaries and leaders of Native congregations throughout North America. Among his priorities was a mission to the peoples of the Six Nations, whom he considered "a much better breed."[34]

Ironically, Wheelock may have entertained a positive regard for the Haudenosaunee precisely for our resistance to European hegemony, which had left us more independent and more culturally intact than most of the New England nations. But what we had in sovereignty we lacked in religion—at least in the eyes of Christian colonists and colonial administrators. This is not to say that there were not Haudenosaunee Christians. The problem for the English was that the majority of converts from the Six Nations were Catholic and lived outside of Iroquoia in the sphere of the French near Montreal. The tumultuous Beaver Wars of the seventeenth century had created conditions that allowed French Jesuits to make headway in their evangelism among the Haudenosaunee. Many Six Nations communities were already multiethnic, being composed of captives, refugees, and adoptees produced by decades of warfare. This meant that some Huron Christians were now part of Iroquois village life, as were Erie, Neutral, and other peoples that had been incorporated during this period. With a break in the violence in 1665, the Jesuits renewed their evangelism and produced an impressive number of converts among the Mohawk and Oneida, and even some Onondaga. The presence of the aforementioned adoptees may have contributed to this wave of conversions. But as Daniel Richter has shown, tensions between Christian and Iroquois traditionalists soon became violent, and an ever-growing number of Iroquois Christians chose to emigrate to the new Native Christian communities being founded near Montreal.[35]

The emigration of Christian factions meant that Iroquoia remained largely the domain of the traditional followers of the ancient Haudenosaunee religion. The factionalism that had come with the arrival of Christianity made communities remaining in the Haudenosaunee homelands deeply suspicious of further missionary activities, which they generally rejected as anathema to their lifeways and identity. But because of their continued political and strategic relevance in colonial North America, the conversion of the Haudenosaunee would remain a goal—even if an unlikely one. Both Wheelock and Edwards recruited students from among the Mohawk and Oneida nations, and both found some families open to their invitation. It may be that like the Natives of New England, they began to see a variety of benefits in an English education; clearly literacy had power in the settler world. Figures like Sir William Johnson encouraged Mohawks to send their children to Wheelock's school, and Edwards would meet with a Haudenosaunee delegation in Albany to invite them to send students to Stockbridge. In both cases Mohawk and Oneida students did venture into New England, including the young Thayendanegea, or Joseph Brant, who went to Wheelock's school with encouragement from Johnson, while Edwards would send his ten-year-old son Jonathan Jr. with his protégé Gideon Hawley to the mixed Haudenosaunee Christian community of Oquaga in order to learn the rudiments of their languages. Certainly Edwards recognized that learning Indigenous languages was necessary for evangelization, but his goal remained steadfastly one of teaching Native pupils to become fluent in English.

My interest all along has been with the need for one to have fluency in another language when attempting to proselytize the Other, including through emotional appeals about proper and improper feelings. As I discussed earlier, the Haudenosaunee languages presented some daunting structural challenges for non-Native speakers, especially in the absence of grammars and regularized orthography in their written versions. Given the Protestant insistence on the written word and personal exegetical practice as a part of devotional life, the prospects of a truly Indigenized Protestantism seemed dim.[36] One other key issue to consider in attempting to understand the work of New Light missionaries to the Six Nations would be the place of the so-called religious affections in the spiritual lives of the Haudenosaunee. The central ethos of Haudenosaunee spiritual life can be summed up in our concept of *skä•ñonh*, which means peace, but in the sense of harmony or balance. It has often struck me in reading various missionary accounts that very little attention is devoted to trying to understand the belief systems that the missionaries were attempting to displace. It is one thing to convey the message of the gospels in a Haudenosaunee language and another to understand our spiritual practices when explained to outsiders in our own tongue. Had Protestant New Lights investigated the ethos of the Haudenosaunee religion, they would have discovered one potentially at odds with the complex emotions that marked the spiritual regeneration of the redeemed Christian.

Among the few aspects of Haudenosaunee religious and ceremonial life that had wide recognition within the colonial world was the Condolence Ceremony. This ceremony was central for assuaging the individual and community traumas that resulted from warfare, epidemics, and individual deaths. Condolence among the Haudenosaunee has been described in European records, with varying levels of accuracy, at least since the *Jesuit Relations*.[37] The Condolence Ceremony is indivisibly linked to the Peacemaker Epic and the Great Law of Peace, which together recount the founding of the original League of Five Nations and the principles of law that bind us together.[38] Since there was essentially no distinction between religious and secular law, the Great Law was at the center of Haudenosaunee spiritual and civic life. Likewise, the goals of the ceremonial life of the Longhouse are health, balance, and the maintenance of the Good Mind. Central to achieving this state is a life of attentive gratitude to the Creator for the many gifts we enjoy in our world and a relinquishing of jealousy, vengeance, intemperance, anger, and other emotions associated with antisocial behaviors that would divide and sow conflict in the community. Powerful emotions like these play a potentially disruptive part in our lives, and the Condolence Ceremony focuses on removing their ill effects. The symbolic wiping away of tears is a key part at the beginning of the ceremony and should be read not as suppressing the emotions but as encouraging and allowing us to move on from them and recover our balance or Good Mind.

When comparing this ethos of balance achieved both through the catharsis of mourning and the social reintegration made possible through the community's condolence protocols, the spiritual drama of religious struggle experienced by New England Native converts such as Samson Occom and Joseph Johnson seems anathema to the Haudenosaunee way.[39] When one reads of the continued anxiety attendant on working out one's state of grace, the self-abjection for our depraved natures, bouts of religious melancholy that mark the spiritual journeys of the Native converts of the Great Awakening, one wonders how this might ever be translated into a linguistic or experiential idiom consistent with the message of the Good Mind or able to supplant the ceremonial cycles of the Longhouse used to maintain the balance and health of our communities. The dramatic sermons that risked engendering enthusiasm (in its negative sense) within settler congregations might just as likely fall flat altogether when mediated by a translator to a Native audience. But we know the doctrinaire stance of some Great Awakening preachers found receptive listeners among the much more acculturated Indigenous nations of southern New England than among the Haudenosaunee.[40] Even among Indigenous Christian communities that we may associate with the Great Awakening, such as Stockbridge, it needs to be recognized that that community initially flourished because of the Reverend John Sergeant's toleration of a level of cultural syncretism, which allowed for certain traditional dances and seasonal celebrations.[41] If Stockbridge ultimately failed, it was because of its singular focus on its civilizing mission, through an English education, as a means of effecting true conversion.

Decades ago, James Axtell recognized that a great portion of the success ascribed to the Jesuits' missionary efforts could be attributed to their ability to tolerate a level of syncretism with cultural issues they deemed indifferent to the faith.[42] The New England model had revolved steadfastly around the notion that Indigenous peoples need to be "civilized" first and then brought to Christianity. But exceptions did exist among the Haudenosaunee: there were converts to Anglicanism at the Mohawk town of Tiononderoge who had been proselytized by SPG missionary William Andrews between 1712 and 1719 and a mixed Haudenosaunee Protestant community at Oquaga seemingly established by Native Christians near the border of Iroquoia and Pennsylvania in the mid-eighteenth century. The Mohawk converts seem to have persisted because their practice was closer to the Jesuit model but with a Protestant foundation. As Daniel Richter concluded, "The result was a syncretic faith that survived independently of European proselytization and indeed resisted the effects of missionaries to modify it."[43] Whereas Oquaga was much more closely related to the spiritual revivalism of the Great Awakening a generation later, unlike the mission at Stockbridge, it permitted a fair amount of traditional cultural practices as well and did not embrace the rhetoric of the Calvinist penitential life that so disquieted the minds of Occom and Johnson. As Daniel Mandell points out of Oquaga, "It reflected Iroquoian norms of decorous ritual and, at the beginning, shared the powerful spirituality of contemporary Native 'prophets' rather than the radical New Light emotional pietism embraced by the Natives of Connecticut, Rhode Island and eastern Long Island."[44] Such Native prophets called for renewal to heal their communities that had been fractured by alcohol, colonial policies, and disease. Both the syncretism of Tiononderoge and rejection of the New Light religious affections at Oquaga are manifestations of the continued spiritual autonomy of the Haudenosaunee, even among their Christian populations.

Investigations of any missionary work among the Haudenosaunee need to take account of the core religious values, such as that of *skä•ñonh* or the Condolence Ceremony, which have defined Haudenosaunee culture for centuries and would remain at the center of the Longhouse after the revival of that religion by Handsome Lake.[45] How well did non-Haudenosaunee people know these concepts without dependence on Native speakers fluent in English? It is impossible to imagine the influential work of the nineteenth-century white anthropologist Lewis Henry Morgan without Haudenosaunee "informants" such as Ely and Caroline Parker, or later anthropological insights by Haudenosaunee linguists such as J. N. B. Hewitt (Tuscarora), who learned key traditional religious principles from the Onondaga chief Dayodekane, aka Seth Newhouse.[46] These collaborations, noteworthy for their linguistic elements, represent the most significant expansion of knowledge concerning Haudenosaunee religious beliefs in English; we have no comparable insights from three centuries of missionary work.

The most serious Haudenosaunee engagement with New Light theology occurred with the missionary work of Samuel Kirkland among the Oneida at Kanowalohale. Almost two decades after Oquaga became a Christian community, Kirkland arrived in Oneida country to begin his missionary work there. Those intervening years had seen increased pressure placed on the Oneida by the ever-increasing settler hunger for Native land and the development of divisions among the nation between the allies of the traditional chiefs and those of the warriors in their society. In 1751 Edwards had invited the Oneida at Oquaga to send students to Stockbridge, which resulted in Gideon Hawley returning to the Oneida as their minister in 1753, and in 1761 Samson Occom would make missionary contacts among the Oneida near Kanowalohale that would prepare the way for Kirkland six years later. Like Occom, Kirkland had been a student of Wheelock's. But as a white New Englander he was more legible to colonial society than Occom would ever be. As Dean Snow explains of Kirkland, "He unwittingly served as a provider of an alternative belief system for members of a faction that already had reasons to split from others in the community."[47] Kirkland was very much a New Light Calvinist and was shocked to see the continuation of traditional feasts and dances at Oquaga. He prevailed upon the Oneidas under his influence to support the rebel cause during the American Revolution and was a key factor in the rift that divided the Oneida and Tuscarora communities and eventually the League itself. Even with the relative success of Kirkland as a New Light missionary to the Oneida, he sometimes despaired at his modest progress among them, and a visitor to Kirkland's mission in 1784 noted that barely half of the community could be counted as Christians.[48]

It would seem that for many Haudenosaunee people, the traumatic experiences of disease, alcohol, war, and continued settler dispossession had made them open to considering the promises held out by the religion practiced among the ascendant colonial society. It offered the hope of social stability, access to literacy, and potential political autonomy, as well as the possibility of renewed health, or at least the rewards of the afterlife. But in practicing this religion, they were mindful of the core values of Haudenosaunee culture: gratitude, balance, and the importance of the Good Mind. The drama of the so-called religious affections seems deeply out of place in the Haudenosaunee spiritual world. Those faith communities that permitted a level of syncretism seemed destined to last longer among our people because they recognized that something of tremendous value was already in place. With the rise of Handsome Lake's revived Longhouse Religion in the early nineteenth century, some Christian converts doubtless returned to the old ways. Tellingly, the Longhouse remains a vital element of all Haudenosaunee reservation communities today, whereas many church congregations have dwindled to a handful of elders. Younger generations may have decided for themselves that given the state of things, the original path was probably the right one.

Notes

1. Following the establishment of the Province of New York in 1664, after the Dutch relinquished their colony of New Netherland, the English had considerably more contact with the Haudenosaunee, but no significant missionary attempts were

made among them for the remainder of the seventeenth century. Between 1704 and 1742 the Society for the Propagation of the Gospel in Foreign Parts oversaw modest English efforts in the region west of Albany in Mohawk territory, but these were stymied by the Mohawk language. See William Hart, "Mohawk Schoolmasters and Catechists in Mid-Eighteenth-Century Iroquoia: An Experiment in Fostering Literacy and Religious Change," in *The Language Encounter in the Americas, 1492–1800: A Collection of Essays*, ed. Edward Gray and Norman Fiering (New York: Berghahn Books, 2000), 230–57.

2. Marianne Methune, *The Languages of Native North America* (Cambridge: Cambridge University Press, 2001), 5; and Johannes Megapolensis, "Account of the Mohawk Indians" (1644), in *In Mohawk Country: Early Narratives about a Native People*, ed. Dean Snow, Charles Gehring, and William Starna (Syracuse: Syracuse University Press, 1996), 41.
3. For a telling example of this theory among Jesuit scholars of the period, see Joseph François Lafitau, *Customs of the American Indians Compared with the Customs of Primitive Times* (Paris, 1724), ed. and trans. William Fenton and Elizabeth Moore (Toronto: Champlain Society, 1977), 253–56.
4. See Jonathan Gibson, "Jonathan Edwards: A Missionary?," *Themelios* 36, no. 3 (2011): 380–402.
5. See Sarah Rivett, *Unscripted America: Indigenous America and the Origins of Literary Nation* (Oxford: Oxford University Press, 2017), 172.
6. See David Levin, ed., *Jonathan Edwards: A Profile* (New York: Hill and Wang, 1969), xx. Similarly, see Alexander V. G. Allen, *Life and Writings of Jonathan Edwards* (Edinburgh: T&T Clark, 1889), 273–74; Henry Bamford Parkes, *Jonathan Edwards: The Fiery Puritan* (New York: Minton, Balch & Company, 1930), 189–248; Arthur Cushman McGiffert Jr., *Jonathan Edwards* (New York: Harper & Brothers, 1932), 139; Andrew F. Walls, "Missions and Historical Memory: Jonathan Edwards and David Brainerd," in *Jonathan Edwards at Home and Abroad: Historical Memories, Cultural Movements, Global Horizons*, ed. David W. Kling and Douglas A. Sweeney (Columbia: University of South Carolina Press, 2003), 250; and Patricia J. Tracey, *Jonathan Edwards, Pastor: Religion and Society in Eighteenth-Century Northampton* (New York: Hill and Wang, 1980), 180.
7. Perry Miller, *Errand into the Wilderness* (Cambridge: Harvard University Press, 1956), 155.
8. For proselytizing in the earlier period, see Kristina Bross, *Dry Bones and Indian Sermons: Praying Indians in Colonial America* (Ithaca: Cornell University Press, 2004); for a contemporary study of the Stockbridge Mission, see Rachel Wheeler, *To Live upon Hope: Mohicans and Missionaries in the Eighteenth-Century Northeast* (Ithaca: Cornell University Press, 2008).
9. See Julius Rubin, *Tears of Repentance: Christian Indian Identity and Community in Southern New England* (Lincoln: University of Nebraska Press, 2013), 170.
10. Linford Fisher, *The Indian Great Awakening: Religion and the Shaping of Native Cultures in Early America* (Oxford: Oxford University Press, 2012), 43.
11. See James T. Flexner, *Mohawk Baronet: A Biography of Sir William Johnson* (Syracuse: Syracuse University Press, 1990), 290–93.
12. James Axtell, *After Columbus: Essays in the Ethnohistory of Colonial North America* (Oxford: Oxford University Press, 1988), 85.

13. Allan Greer, ed., *The Jesuit Relations: Natives and Missionaries in Seventeenth-Century North America* (New York: Bedford/St. Martin's, 2000), 38.
14. Margaret J. Leahey, "Iconic Discourse: The Language of Images in Seventeenth-Century New France," in Gray and Fiering, *The Language Encounter in the Americas*, 108.
15. Lafitau, *Customs of the American Indians*, 261.
16. Micah True, *Masters and Students: Jesuit Mission Ethnography in Seventeenth-Century New France* (Montreal: McGill University Press, 2013), 61.
17. Allan Greer, *Mohawk Saint: Catherine Tekakwitha and the Jesuits* (Oxford: Oxford University Press, 2005), 51–52.
18. See Loïc Wacquant, "Habitus," in *International Encyclopedia of Economic Sociology*, ed. Jens Beckert and Milan Zafirovski (London: Routledge, 2005), 316.
19. Greer, *Mohawk Saint*, 124.
20. See Evan Haefeli and Kevin Sweeney, *Captors and Captives: The 1704 French and Indian Raid on Deerfield* (Amherst: University of Massachusetts Press, 2003).
21. Richard White, *The Middle Ground: Indians, Empires, and Republics in the Great Lakes Region, 1650–1815*, 20th anniversary ed. (Cambridge: Cambridge University Press, 2011).
22. David Murray, *Forked Tongues: Speech, Writing, and Representation in North American Indian Texts* (Bloomington: Indiana University Press, 1991), 5.
23. Important exceptions to this are to be found in works by Daniel Richter, William Hart, and Laura Stevens, who have all contributed invaluable work concerning Anglican missions among the Haudenosaunee. See Daniel Richter, "'Some of Them . . . Would Always Have a Minister with Them': Mohawk Protestantism, 1683–1719," *American Indian Quarterly* 16, no. 4 (Autumn 1992): 471–84; William Hart, "Mohawk Schoolmasters and Catechists in Mid-Century Iroquoia: An Experiment in Fostering Literacy and Religious Change," in Gray and Fiering, *The Language Encounter in the Americas*, 230–57; Laura Stevens, *The Poor Indians: British Missionaries, Native Americans, and Colonial Sensibility* (Philadelphia: University of Pennsylvania Press, 2004).
24. See Richter, "'Some of Them," 480–81.
25. See Scott Manning Stevens, "'The Voice of One Crying in the Wilderness': The KJV and Ethno-exegesis in Iroquoia," in *The King James Bible across Borders and Centuries*, ed. Angelica Duran (Pittsburgh: Duquesne University Press, 2014), 125–50.
26. See Rubin, *Tears of Repentance*; and Daniel Mandell, "'Turned Their Minds to Religion': Oquaga and the First Iroquois Church, 1748–1776," *Early American Studies: An Interdisciplinary Journal* 11, no. 2 (Spring 2013): 211–42.
27. For Stoddard's sermon, see Rubin, *Tears of Repentance*, 163; and Stevens, *The Poor Indians*, 180.
28. Samson Occom, "A Short Narrative of My Life," in *The Elders Wrote: An Anthology of Early Prose by North American Indians, 1768–1931*, ed. Bernd Peyer (Berlin: Reimer, 1982), 13.
29. Leon Burr Richardson, *An Indian Preacher in New England* (Hanover: Dartmouth College Publications, 1933), 222.
30. Scott Manning Stevens, "Mother Tongues and Native Voices: Linguistic Fantasies in the Age of the Encounter," in *Telling the Stories: Essays on American Indian*

Literatures and Cultures, ed. Elizabeth Hoffman Nelson and Malcolm Nelson (New York: Peter Lang, 2001), 5–19.

31. James Axtell, "The Invasion Within: The Contest of Cultures in Colonial North America," in *The European and the Indian: Essays in the Ethnohistory of Colonial North America* (Oxford: Oxford University Press, 1981), 77.
32. Jane T. Merritt, "Metaphor, Meaning, and Misunderstanding: Language and Power on the Pennsylvania Frontier," in *Contact Points: American Frontiers from the Mohawk Valley to the Mississippi, 1750–1830*, ed. Andrew Cayton and Fredrika Teute (Chapel Hill: University of North Carolina Press, 1998), 67.
33. See Joanna Brooks, *American Lazarus: Religion and the Rise of African-American and Native American Literatures* (Oxford: Oxford University Press, 2003); and Rubin, *Tears of Repentance*, esp. chap. 4, "Samson Occom and Christian Indian Identity."
34. Joseph Johnson, *To Do Good to My Indian Brethren: The Writings of Joseph Johnson, 1751–1776*, ed. Laura Murray (Amherst: University of Massachusetts Press, 1998), 54.
35. Daniel Richter, *The Ordeal of the Longhouse: The Peoples of the Iroquois League in the Era of European Colonization* (Chapel Hill: University of North Carolina Press, 1992), 116–20.
36. On early linguistic anxieties among New England missionaries, see Joshua David Bellin, "'A Little I Shall Say': Translation and Interculturalism in the John Eliot Tracts," in *Reinterpreting New England Indians and the Colonial Experience*, ed. Colin G. Calloway and Neal Salisbury (Boston: Colonial Society of Massachusetts, 2003), 52–83.
37. See Matthew Dennis, *Cultivating a Landscape of Peace: Iroquois-European Encounters in Seventeenth-Century America* (Ithaca: Cornell University Press, 1993), 76–79. Haudenosaunee ethnologists, anthropologists, and faith keepers, including, respectively, J. N. B. Hewitt, Arthur C. Parker, and Oren Lyons, have all related versions of the ceremony, as have non-Native anthropologists working with Native informants such as Lewis Henry Morgan, Paul A. W. Wallace, and William Fenton.
38. See Arthur C. Parker, *The Constitution of the Five Nations, or the Iroquois Book of the Great Law* (1916; repr., Oshwekan, ON: Iroqrafts Iroquois Reprints, 1991), originally published in *New York State Museum Bulletin*, no. 184 (1916).
39. See Tammy Schneider, "'This Once Savage Heart of Mine': Joseph Johnson, Wheelock's 'Indians,' and the Construction of a Christian/Indian Identity, 1764–1776," in Calloway and Salisbury, *Reinterpreting New England Indians*, 232–63.
40. See Rubin, *Tears of Repentance*; and Fisher, *The Indian Great Awakening*.
41. Rubin, *Tears of Repentance*, 169–70.
42. James Axtell, *The Invasion Within: The Contest of Cultures in Colonial North America* (Oxford: Oxford University Press, 1985), 43–126.
43. Richter, "Some of Them," 472.
44. Mandell, "Turned Their Minds to Religion," 214.
45. Sganyodaiyo, aka Handsome Lake (ca. 1735–1815), was the Seneca religious leader of the revival of the Longhouse Religion among Haudenosaunee. In 1799 Sganyodaiyo had a series of visions calling on him to reform his life and return to the traditional forms of Haudenosaunee spirituality. His teaching of the *gaiwiyo* or "good word" is sometimes referred to as the Code of Handsome Lake. Many

contemporary Haudenosaunee people still follow this religion. See Arthur C. Parker, *The Code of Handsome Lake, the Seneca Prophet* (Albany: University of the State New York, 1913).

46. See Lewis Henry Morgan, *The League of the Ho-dé-no-sau-nee, or Iroquois* (Rochester, NY: Sage & Brother Publishers, 1851); and J. N. B. Hewitt, "Iroquoian Cosmology: First Part," in *Annual Report of the Bureau of American Ethnology for the Years 1899–1900*, vol. 21 (Washington, DC: Smithsonian, 1903), 127–339.
47. Dean Snow, *The Iroquois* (Oxford: Blackwell Publishers, 1994), 149.
48. Axtell, *The Invasion Within*, 272.

CHAPTER 4

The Tongue Is Only an Interpreter of the Heart

Translating Religious Affections
A Response to Scott Manning Stevens

CAROLINE WIGGINTON

One of my first times teaching a general education survey of American literatures to the U.S. Civil War, I had two student volunteers reenact an imaginary initial encounter between Christopher Columbus and the Taíno peoples in the Caribbean.[1] I gave each student separate, secret instructions, but neither was allowed to speak. One student, posing as a Taíno islander in this scenario, was to find out where this stranger had come from and if he was dangerous. The student playing Columbus needed to find gold, get the Taíno peoples to yield to the authority of the Spanish crown, and determine if the Taíno were amenable to Catholic conversion. A silent pantomime ensued. When the Taíno-portraying student quizzically pointed toward the horizon, so too did the Columbus-portraying student, while nodding enthusiastically. When the Columbus student placed their hands together in prayer and then made the sign of the cross, the Taíno student mirrored those same gestures. As a class, we then examined the following moment from Columbus's writings about his first voyage:

> I have observed . . . that these people have no religion, neither are they idolaters, but are a very gentle race, without the knowledge of any iniquity. . . . They have a knowledge that there is a God above, and are firmly persuaded that we have come from heaven. They very quickly learn such prayers as

> we repeat to them, and also to make the sign of the cross. Your Highnesses [King Ferdinand and Queen Isabella] should therefore adopt the resolution of converting them to Christianity, in which enterprise I am of opinion that a very short space of time would suffice to gain to our holy faith multitudes of people, and to Spain great riches and immense dominions, with all their inhabitants; there being, without doubt, in these countries vast quantities of gold, for the Indians would not without cause give us such descriptions of places where the inhabitants dug it from the earth, and wore it in massy bracelets at their necks, ears, legs, and arms.[2]

What seemed a straightforward report to students reading Columbus's journal at home now resembled a crafted and fantastic tale. In the absence of a shared language, how does one determine if another has "knowledge of iniquity"? How does one tell another that they must be "from heaven"? How can one give "such descriptions" of where and how to acquire gold? How does one know that a simple gesture over the heart is not self-referential but instead recalls the cross upon which the son of God, in an act of sacrificial love, was crucified prior to his resurrection almost fifteen hundred years before?[3]

It is precisely such suspicions that Scott Manning Stevens brings to the colonial records of eighteenth-century Euro-American missionaries. In "The Language of Belief" in this volume, Stevens highlights the haphazard and fragmentary translation of Christian religious affections in Native contexts. As with Taíno-Spanish interactions, French Catholic and English Protestant missions in the Native Northeast occurred in an environment of what Stevens terms "radical linguistic alterity." Because language enfolds and reflects cultural values, including emotional ones, this alterity impacted the understanding of religious affections and the potency of missionary efforts. Stevens asks, "How was one to explain the place of the affections on the path toward true belief if one could not do this through language?" This explanation was especially fraught in scenes of not just radical linguistic but radical emotional alterity. Reflecting on "the central ethos of Haudenosaunee spiritual life"—which he sums up through the "concept of *skä•ñonh*, which means peace, but in the sense of harmony or balance"—he intimates that the Jesuits experienced relative success in converting the Haudenosaunee because the confederacy viewed Catholicism as conducive to producing balance and consolation through ritual. They did not need fluency in profoundly unfamiliar Iroquoian languages. In contrast, Protestantism and its attendant complex emotions that marked the spiritual regeneration of the redeemed Christian failed to make inroads: "The drama of the so-called religious affections seems deeply out of place in the Haudenosaunee spiritual world." Its greatest successes were with the Native nations living alongside English colonists farther east, who had become habituated to Protestant emotional values and, by the Great Awakening, were more receptive to the cycles of agony and doubt so important to evangelical conversion. The history of missionization in the Northeast therefore requires an accounting of language misunderstanding and emotional values.

Stevens's essay underscores that, when it comes to the contexts of Native-European interaction in early North America, religious affections were always subject to translation, often in the absence of shared language and emotional values. As a result, we might posit that emotional mistranslation was as common as, if not more so than, accurate interpretation. Columbus helped inaugurate a pattern wherein colonists repeatedly observed gestural and linguistic communications that they were not fluent in as expressions of submission, fondness, reverence, and gratitude to the colonizer, to the missionary, and to the Christian God. In the absence of fluency, colonizers witnessed acts of Indigenous bodies that they translated as expressions of Indigenous feeling. And because they presumed they could read love and affection in some hearts, they presumed they could read hate for goodness and love for sin and Satan in others, thus justifying colonization itself. If they could have understood Native peoples, they might have found Native peoples to be instead saying hello, who are you, where did you come from, are you peaceful, you can stay for a little bit, we already have what you call a religion, that sounds interesting, go away, no. Colonists' lack of fluency was not a barrier; rather it was at the heart of colonialism. Noting that their claims to interpretive authority were made regardless of actual understanding—claims that are still echoed by scholars today—exposes the asymmetry of power and influence in early North America and the enormous pressures placed on Native peoples to convert, or at least perform conversion.

In this response to Stevens's essay, I complement his insightful reminder about radical and emotional linguistic alterities and consider the potentials and importance of *un*fluency, not on the part of settler colonists but on the part of Native peoples in the Northeast. I begin with an example from the 1640s—the case of Wequash, a Pequot man and possible Christian—in order to figure the long history of tactical Indigenous unfluency in this period. I then turn to two late eighteenth-century examples, a famous sermon by Mohegan minister Samson Occom and a Mohawk translation of the book of Mark by Thayendanegea (Joseph Brant). I speculate that these men are all agents of uncertainty surrounding religious affections. Their refusals of fluent linguistic and affective translation are moments of survival and resistance to the authoritative colonialist counterclaims regarding their spiritual and emotional legibility. If mistranslation is structural to settler colonialism, perhaps it is structural to Native Christianity as well.

The first example involves Wequash, a seventeenth-century Pequot leader who allied with the English and Narragansetts against his own nation in the Pequot War (1636–1638), during which the colonists massacred hundreds of Pequot women, children, and elderly at Fort Mystic.[4] The interpretation of his Christian conversion has been a subject of fascination since his death in 1642 and subsequent back-to-back publication of two accounts of his deathbed conversion, the first in the anonymous pamphlet *New Englands First Fruits* and the second in banished Puritan Roger Williams's *Key into the Language of America*.[5]

Like *First Fruits*, Williams presents Wequash as a last-minute Christian convert. Wequash's story prefaces *Key*, which is a linguistic and cultural guide for helping English colonists spread "*civilitie*" and "*Christianitie*" to the Narragansetts and other Algonquin-speaking peoples of the Northeast.[6] Williams describes his deathbed conversation with Wequash: "Hee told me that some two or three yeare before he had lodged at my House, where I had acquainted him with the *Condition* of *all Mankind*, & his *Own* in particular, how *God* created *Man* and *Allthings*: how *Man* fell from *God*, and of his present *Enmity* against *God*, and the *wrath of God* against *Him* untill *Repentance*: said he your *words . . . were never out of my heart to this present*; and said hee *me much pray to Jesus Christ*." One might expect some subtle self-congratulation from Williams: he was Wequash's first and it seems only teacher in Christian principles. Instead, Williams refuses to ascribe any benefit to that first conversation. He challenges Wequash: "I told him so did many *English, French,* and *Dutch* [pray to Jesus], who had never turned to *God*, nor loved Him." He insists that it is not words but feeling, specifically love, that demonstrates sincerity. Williams's final lesson provokes a confession from Wequash in "broken English"—"*Me so big naughty Heart, m[e] heart all one stone!*"—followed by "*Savory expressions* using to breath *from compunct and broken Hearts,* and a sense of *inward hardnesse* and *unbrokenness.*"[7] It is a just-in-time injunction to love God that catapults Wequash across the final steps.[8]

By chastising Wequash for thinking language is how Christians speak to God, Williams implicitly admits that Native Christianity has never required fluency in English or any other European language.[9] Indeed, outward fluency—whether in terms of an uncomprehending rote delivery of Christian tenets or in terms of a European's well-spoken but unfeeling prayers—can be a sign of hypocrisy. Fluency may impede missionaries in effecting sincere and powerful conversions of Native peoples; colonists need only a basic vocabulary, perhaps like the one in *Key,* which resembles a kind of tourist phrasebook, to strip to the essentials of their theologies, appeal to feeling, and save the Indians.

Williams underscores this implication when he refers to Wequash's "broken English." But this phrase also recalls Stevens's insistence upon radical linguistic alterity. The quoted words undermine the presumed exactitude with which Wequash (and many other Native subjects of missionization) could have recalled Christian lessons. Wequash indicates that Williams's "*words . . . were never out of my heart,*" but if the two men were not fluent in each other's spoken and emotional languages, then the meaning of those words must differ from what Williams intended.[10] Even if he has memorized Williams's words exactly, his sense of the emotions he names—*enmity*, *wrath*, and later *love*—and their connections to the *heart* would necessarily differ. It begs the question: How does one translate Christianity into the heart?

If we take Williams's transcription of Wequash's words to be accurate, then Wequash's "broken English" not only questions the necessity of fluency for conversion but also suggests that Native peoples were agents of (mis)translation of the conversion of Christian belief and feeling. When he confesses that "me" heart is "naughty" and "all one stone," he is claiming to be more of a Christian, at least in his heart, because he is *not* fluent in English. Wequash doesn't need to recall theology or pray glibly. His heart simply needs to respond to a basic expectation that he love God, and the fact that he is unburdened by the English language adds to the intensity of his conversion. And only he knows what loving God means to him.

Or perhaps Wequash is tricking Williams. In *Key*, after this prefatory story, Williams offers collections of Narragansett phrases and ethnographic commentaries. Williams notes several times that, for Native peoples in the Northeast, truth in diplomatic and interpersonal conversation begins in the heart. To demonstrate that one is sincere and ready for peace, Narragansetts and the region's other Algonquin-speaking Native peoples would say, "Wunnêtu nittà [My Heart is good]" or "Wunnêtu ntá [My heart is true]."[11] If on his deathbed Wequash is saying his heart is "naughty," perhaps he is also denying that he wants peace with God or the English colonists in his final moments. Or maybe he is saying he has been lying about remembering Williams's words in his heart. His prayers might have been lies all along. In short, neither Wequash's gestures nor his broken English are sufficient for fully reading his religious affections. Wequash's confession seems to signal some kind of conversion, but of what kind? Toward Christianity and reconfirmation of his siding with the English and Narragansetts? Or repentance of his past actions and a desire to reconcile with the Pequot peoples he betrayed? Is his lack of fluency in English an impediment to or a weapon against European civility and Christianity?[12]

Here I am suspicioning that the illegibility of such moments is in part a refusal of Native peoples to have their religious affections known and translated. The illegibility is not wholly a result of colonial records under the control of settler colonists and their (mis)understandings.[13] In doing so, I am invoking two Native scholars, literary critic Craig Womack (Muscogee Creek) and anthropologist Audra Simpson (Kahnawà:ke Mohawk), both of whom foreground methods that celebrate uncertainty and incomplete knowledge. Womack posits that "the theoretical mode" he labels as "suspicioning" is "a kind of communal negotiation between arguments for doubt, certainty, and a middle position full of yearning . . . that dreams of resolution even when there is none to be found, even holds out the possibility of actually finding it whatever the unlikelihood might be of fulfilling expectations for conclusions."[14] In a similar vein, Simpson "refuse[s] to practice the type of ethnography that claims to tell the whole story and have all the answers" because such pretenses to omniscience inherently deny the asymmetrical and unethical formation of settler colonialist knowledge.[15] Illegibility makes Native converts' spiritual status, beliefs, and feelings difficult to pin down. Without verbal or emotional fluency, their religious affections elude stable meaning and easy translation. Under settler colonialism, colonizers historically hold interpretive authority. They decide, for example, when the words of a treaty and other European-language documents are unequivocal (and interpreted by colonialist courts and practice) and when context—such as the emotional and spiritual status of Native communities and leaders—must be taken into account.[16] By suspicioning that Wequash and other Native subjects of conversion and colonization knew what they meant when they expressed their religious affections even as they knew their communications with colonists were fraught with misunderstanding places contemporary scholars in Womack's "middle position full of yearning" between certainty and doubt. This yearning is productive because it reminds contemporary scholars that Native peoples of the past held agency over what they communicated, what they felt, what they believed, and how they interpreted the spiritual lessons of missionaries. In acknowledging that we are always suspicioning, at least in part, we refuse to impose a stance of mastery.

Approaching Wequash as an agent of unfluency places him in a longer tradition of northeastern Native men engaged in wit and wordplay to effect their visions of Christian community. Samson Occom (1723–1792), a Mohegan preacher and leader, is emblematic of this tradition.[17] Occom sought to translate Euro-American evangelical Christian theology to a Native context. In his writings about his own conversion and in his efforts to exhort his congregations, Occom resorted frequently to the language of feeling.[18] For example, in his narrative of his life, written in 1768, Occom connects learning the Word of God with feeling "uncommon Pity and Compassion to my Poor Brethren" and a calling to minister and teach his "poor Kindred."[19] For him, religious affections are something other than the submissive and artless filial love that Columbus fantasized about or the extralinguistic prayer of the heart suggested by Williams and Wequash. In Occom, the affections inspired by conversion are for his fellow Mohegans and his friends and congregants among the Native peoples of New England and Long Island. And it is in ministry to his own "Kindred" that the sincerity of his religious affections can be read.

Many of Occom's sermons, for example, explicate the connection between words, actions, and feeling. His most widely read sermon is the one he gave at the 1771 execution of Moses Paul, a Wampanoag man who was convicted of murdering a white man.[20] Quoting from the biblical New Testament book of James in this sermon, Occom asserts, "But the tongue can no man tame, it is an unruly evil, full of deadly poison." He then elaborates on James, but rather than focusing on the chapter's message of the ways that an entire body can be steered by something small, like the tongue, Occom shifts from James and asserts, "It is the heart that is in the first place full of deadly poison. The tongue is only an interpreter of the heart."[21] The sermon directly connects the heart and the tongue: if the tongue expresses "deadly poison" or is "an unruly evil," then the heart must be "full" of poison and evil.

Or perhaps, like Wequash, Occom is being a little tricky and offering an excuse for the tongue. It is *only* an interpreter. As Occom knew well as a Mohegan minister in eighteenth-century New England, interpreters and translators weren't neutral or perfect.[22] Sometimes they were inexpert or wrong; sometimes they took sides and skewed meanings; sometimes they lied. This alternative reading of Occom's elaboration partially accords with a verse earlier in James that says an unbridled tongue deceives the heart.[23] The inverse may hold true as well, with the heart deceiving the tongue. Even Occom's words are involved in a kind of deception. His inserted discussion about the heart comes between the direct quote from James and a subsequent quotation from Isaiah. Personally, I had to reread James to determine what was biblical quotation and what wasn't. Some editions of the sermon enclose the biblical verses in quotes; some do not. Would an audience listening to this sermon at Moses Paul's execution hear the distinction? Or would they hear Occom's elaboration as biblical verse? In this way, he supplements the New Testament and thereby alters its meaning. His words, according to his own reasoning, interpret his heart and yet again make clear the illegibility of Native religious affections to white colonists and even contemporary scholars.[24] In this way, his ambiguous preaching—what we might call tactical unfluency when it comes to quoting and interpreting the Bible—circumvents in part what Phillip Round considers to be the inescapable "ambivalence" that haunts the period's Indigenous literary expressions, including this sermon.[25]

For Occom, here and in his other writings, words and heart are uncertain, however true love for God, true religious *affection* for God, inspires affection for one's kindred and brethren. In his political writings, many of which are petitions to local and regional Euro-American governments, as well as his sermons for mixed audiences, he calls upon everyone, but especially those in power like colonial governments, to demonstrate their own true love for God through mercy and compassion for the Native peoples of the Northeast.[26] But Occom's grandest manifestation of his affection for God and brethren may have been his partnership in the effort to establish Brothertown, a separatist Native Christian nation in Haudenosaunee territory. In this way, we may suspicion that Occom's elusive interpretations of Christian feeling and language signal a refusal of legibility to white missionaries and colonists even as they offer instruction to them about Christianity. By connecting tongue and heart, interpretation and feeling, he suggests that he speaks a multiplicity of lessons to a multiplicity of audiences. His fellow Natives may be best positioned to translate and interpret his message because they communicate through a shared history of feeling.[27]

We might engage in a similar act of suspicioning when turning to Chief Joseph Brant's Mohawk-language book of Mark, based on the Protestant King James Bible. In a 2014 essay, Stevens discusses Brant's translation of *wilderness* and emphasizes that this word is a particularly thorny one for translation, in part because Mohawk language and culture do not have the same negative idea of wilderness, a word rooted in fear and lawlessness. Brant chooses *kah'rakon*, a word that Stevens points out refers to the forest, as distinguished from the village, *kanata*. *Kah'rakon* is wildness without the negativity.[28] It refuses colonialist legibility even as it evokes particular emotional valences from a Mohawk audience. "Wilderness"/*kah'rakon* appears five times in the King James and Brant translations of Mark, including four times in the first book, such as in this verse: "The voice of one crying in the wilderness, Prepare ye the way of the Lord, make his paths straight" / "Ne Oweana ouskagh yeweanodatye et-ho Karhàgouh [kah'rakon], wàdouh ne tsy'adearhàrah tsi-nondahawenohattye ne Royàner, senihah-hagwarighsyh ne Raohah-haògouh."[29] This verse announces the advent of Christ and calls upon those who have been waiting to prepare for his arrival. One would expect any Christian to have some sort of emotional response to this announcement, but Brant's Mohawk translation guides Mohawk speakers to a different feeling from the one available in the English-language version because the voice is crying in the *kah'rakon*, not the wilderness. When anticipating an arrival, Haudenosaunee peoples would often perform a ceremony at the border between the village and the woods, a ceremony known today to English-speaking historians as the Wood's Edge ceremony.[30] Steeped in such a tradition, wherein the "wilderness" is not negative but the home of one's village and wherein its edge is a place of ceremonial welcome, the feelings associated with Christian anticipation, preparation, and arrival would necessarily be different in Mohawk contexts. As with other non-scriptive Native forms of writing, Brant's translation suggests that the biblical text is similarly variable and renewable rather than static. As A. Zuercher Reichardt notes, Brant ends his version of the book of Mark with a signature that indicates the text was written ("wakhyadon"), not translated ("tekaweanadennyoh"), by him, "a concluding note made all the more striking in contrast to the empty space on the facing English page."[31] Like Wequash and Occom, Brant is not a transparent and passive transmitter of others' religious beliefs and emotions. He actively authored (mis)translations and (un)fluencies that counter those imposed by colonization. Whereas colonists often sought to foreclose meanings and alternative understandings so that the only ones remaining were their interpretations, these men's words proliferate possibilities and refusals at the juncture of heart and tongue and conversion.

It is here, I suspicion, in these Native men's "broken English," biblical alterations, and new translations, that we might find a response to Stevens's "challenge [to] the current revisionist emphasis on a supposed symmetry of influence during the Encounter." I agree with Stevens that we should not insist upon a symmetry of influence, because colonization was and remains devastating, genocidal, and ongoing.[32] Yet we can identify what the Anishinaabe scholar Gerald Vizenor terms "survivance." Survivance can be thought of as a combination of survival and resistance.[33] It thrives within simulation and play rather than dominance and static meaning and legibility. Religious affections, where the Indigenous convert mistranslates the language of Christian conversion, are a place for expressions of survivance. As the Muscogee Creek poet and musician Joy Harjo says in an introduction to an anthology of Native women's writing: "But to speak, at whatever the cost, is to become empowered rather than victimized by destruction. In our tribal cultures, the power of language to heal, to regenerate, and to create is understood. These colonizers' languages, which often usurped our own tribal languages or diminished them, now hand back emblems of our cultures, our own designs."[34] Columbus and other colonizers usurped the language of religious affections in addition to other languages, but Native Christians, like others, handed back emblems of their own designs that survived and resisted.

Notes

1. For more on the Taíno peoples, especially those who interacted with the colonists who established the colonial town La Isabela on the island of Hispaniola, see chap. 3 of Kathleen Deagan and José María Cruxent, *Columbus's Outpost among the Taínos: Spain and America at La Isabela, 1493–1498* (New Haven: Yale University Press, 2002). The Spanish playwright Lope de Vega imagines this encounter in act 2 of his ca. 1600 play *El Nuevo Mundo descubierto por Cristóbal Colón*. For an English translation, see Lope de Vega, *Discovery of the New World by Christopher Columbus*, trans. Frieda Fligelman (Berkeley: Gillick Press, 1950).
2. Christopher Columbus, "Journal of the First Voyage to America, 1492–1493," in *Heath Anthology of American Literature*, ed. Paul Lauter et al., 7th ed., vol. A (Boston: Houghton Mifflin, 2013), 131.
3. Perhaps crossing oneself and other gestures held particular meaning for the Taíno peoples. Indigenous peoples of the Americas were not strangers to sign-language systems. See, for example, Céline Carayon, "'The Gesture Speech of Mankind': Old and New Entanglements in the Histories of American Indian and European Sign Languages," *American Historical Review* 121, no. 2 (April 2016): 461–91. For Carayon's overview of the scholarly conversation about communication between Native and colonial peoples who spoke different languages, see Céline Carayon, *Embodied Eloquence: Nonverbal Communication among French and Indigenous Peoples in the Americas* (Chapel Hill: University of North Carolina Press, 2019), 1–6. Carayon insists on gesture's efficacy for communicating across cultures and languages, and argues that "colonial America was the site of rich intersections between effective traditions of embodied expressiveness." Carayon, *Embodied Eloquence*, 7. In my activity with students, we were attending to more superficial encounters than those discussed by Carayon.
4. Marie Balsey Taylor recovers Wequash's kinship ties throughout the region, including to the Narragansetts. Siding with the Narragansetts was as much with kin as against kin. See Marie Balsey Taylor, "Recovering Indigenous Kinship: Community, Conversion, and the Digital Turn," in *Afterlives of Indigenous Archives: Essays in Honor of the Occom Circle*, ed. Ivy Schweitzer and Gordon Henry (Hanover: Dartmouth College Press, 2019), 149.
5. See *New Englands First Fruits* (London: Henry Overton, 1643) and Roger Williams, *A Key into the Language of America: Or, An Help to the Language of the Natives in That Part of America, Called New-England* (London: Gregory Dexter, 1643). The authors of *First Fruits* were Thomas Weld and Hugh Peter.
6. Williams, *Key*, A3. For a discussion of Williams's *Key* and the relationship between civility, communication networks, and space, see chap. 3, "Forests of Gestures," in Matt Cohen, *The Networked Wilderness: Communicating in Early New England* (Minneapolis: University of Minnesota Press, 2009).
7. Williams, *Key*, [A6v–7].
8. *First Fruits* presents Wequash's conversion not as a break with that first conversation but as its culmination. During the single night he spent in the unnamed Williams's company, "as a Hart panting after the water Brookes he enquired after God with such incessant diligence that they were constrained constantly for his

satisfaction." Afterward, he apparently roamed among the English settlements, "complain[ing] sadly of his heart, saying it was *much machet* (that is, very evill)." Then, on his deathbed, that long-ago conversation and its lingering emotional effects at last took root, and he "yielded up his soule into *Christ* his hands." See *First Fruits,* 12–13. Drew Lopenzina speculates that Wequash's seeming grief is actually horror in the wake of the Mystic Massacre. See Drew Lopenzina, *Red Ink: Native Americans Picking Up the Pen in the Colonial Period* (Albany: SUNY Press, 2012), 80–84.

9. Something parallel happens in the quotes in note 9 from *First Fruits*, when the author makes a wordplay on "Hart" and "heart."
10. *First Fruits* says Wequash's initial interlocutors, including the unnamed Williams, were "well acquainted" with his language (12), but Stevens's essay indicates that these kinds of claims are necessarily suspect.
11. Williams, *Key,* 51, 181.
12. See Lopenzina, *Red Ink*, 80–84; Phillip H. Round, *By Nature and by Custom Cursed: Transatlantic Civil Discourse and New England Cultural Production, 1620–1660* (Hanover, NH: University Press of New England, 1999), 247; Kristina Bross, *Dry Bones and Indian Sermons: Praying Indians in Colonial America* (Ithaca: Cornell University Press, 2004), 190–92; Laura M. Stevens, *The Poor Indians: British Missionaries, Native Americans, and Colonial Sensibility* (Philadelphia: University of Pennsylvania Press, 2010), 185–86; Erik R. Seeman, *Death in the New World: Cross-Cultural Encounters, 1492–1800* (Philadelphia: University of Pennsylvania Press, 2010), 158–59; Taylor, "Recovering Indigenous Kinship," 143–48. These scholars don't even agree on whether Williams is presenting Wequash as a convert to or holdout against Christianity.
13. In her analysis of Native Christians' deathbed speeches like Wequash's, Bross insists that they have meanings beyond those ascribed to them by Puritans: "They used their dying speeches to assert the symbolic and lived value of their faith community." Kristina Bross, "Dying Saints, Vanishing Savages: 'Dying Indian Speeches' in Colonial New England Literature," *Early American Literature* 36, no. 3 (2001): 329.
14. Womack introduces suspicioning this way: "I would like to consider how suspicioning functions as an action, full of desire for a concrete resolution, a certainty it never achieves, an absence of closure that simply intensifies a hunger for verities. One suspicions when tackling subjects one feels unsure of, but risks a statement anyway. A suspicioner brings up taboos, secrets, impolite observations normally off-limits in states of self-assurance and control. Suspicioning takes advantage of doubt to go out on a limb and blurt out or whisper—a whooping ejaculation or sotto voce aside. Suspicioning foregrounds subjectivity and intuition, those things least empirical. A good suspicioner often has her neighbors in mind." See Craig Womack, "Suspicioning: Imagining a Debate between Those Who Get Confused, and Those Who Don't, When They Read Critical Responses to the Poems of Joy Harjo, or What's an Old-Timey Gay Boy Like Me to Do?," *GLQ: A Journal of Lesbian and Gay Studies* 16, no. 1 (February 17, 2010): 133–34. I thank Daniel Heath Justice for introducing me to Womack's concept.
15. Audra Simpson, *Mohawk Interruptus: Political Life on the Border of Settler States* (Durham: Duke University Press, 2014), 4.

16. See Chadwick Allen, *Blood Narrative: Indigenous Identity in American Indian and Maori Literary and Activist Texts* (Durham: Duke University Press, 2002), 18–22.
17. Occom was a lover of wordplay. It is present in his sermons, in which he was a master of biblical exegesis through close reading, but also his personal letters. In a 1771 letter about the shift at his mentor and former teacher's school from emphasizing the education of Native missionaries to the training of white missionaries, he angrily despairs that his "alma Mater" was at risk of becoming "too alba mater to Suckle the Tawnees." (Occom's anger was quite justified: he had raised scads and scads of money for the school during a long fundraising trip to Europe. His efforts made possible the founding of Dartmouth College, even as its founding betrayed its predecessor's Native graduates.) In a 1766 note to his wife, every sentence includes a play on the word "well." See Samson Occom, *The Collected Writings of Samson Occom, Mohegan: Leadership and Literature in Eighteenth-Century Native America*, ed. Joanna Brooks (New York: Oxford University Press, 2006), 98, 78.
18. For more on Occom's eloquence and its connection to Haudenosaunee rhetoric, see Angela Calcaterra, *Literary Indians: Aesthetics and Encounter in American Literature to 1920* (Chapel Hill: University of North Carolina Press, 2018), 47–82.
19. Occom, *Collected Writings*, 54.
20. For more on the sermon and its printing history—it appeared in many editions over the next few decades—see Phillip H. Round, *Removable Type: Histories of the Book in Indian Country, 1663–1880* (Chapel Hill: University of North Carolina Press, 2010), 67–69, 174–76. Michael Kelly, head of archives and special collections at Amherst College's Frost Library, has identified additional editions beyond the nineteen mentioned by Round. See Michael Kelly, "The Materiality of Native American Literature: Decolonizing the History of the Book," talk delivered at Northwestern University, March 3, 2020. Undergraduate students at Amherst College built a website that visualizes how information circulated regarding Moses Paul's crime and execution. It includes a map of many editions of Occom's sermon. See "Communication Networks in Early New England: A Story of Moses Paul and Samson Occom," https://arcg.is/1ST549 (accessed July 16, 2020).
21. Occom, *Collected Writings*, 180.
22. Throughout this essay, I have generally used *translation* rather than *interpretation* to name understanding the sense of words in another language. For those concerned, however, with precision in regard to interpretation versus translation, the former is for spoken contexts and the latter for written contexts.
23. "If any man among you seem to be religious and bridleth not his tongue, but deceiveth his own heart, this man's religion is vain" (James 1:26).
24. Katy Chiles argues that this sermon engages in the reinterpretation of racial categories, a process that "begins by stressing the universally transformative qualities of sin." See Katy Chiles, "Becoming Colored in Occom and Wheatley's Early America," *PMLA* 123, no. 5 (2008), 1401.
25. Phillip H. Round, "Early Native Literature as Social Practice," in *Oxford Handbook of Indigenous American Literature*, ed. James H. Cox and Daniel Heath Justice (New York: Oxford University Press, 2014), 66.
26. For more on Occom's legal interventions into the region's settler colonialist efforts to appropriate Native land and resources, see Lisa Brooks, *The Common Pot: The Recovery of Native Space in the Northeast* (Minneapolis: University of Minnesota

Press, 2008), 51–105; Caroline Wigginton, "Extending Root and Branch: Community Regeneration in the Petitions of Samson Occom," *Studies in American Indian Literatures* 20, no. 4 (2008): 24–55. For the role of Occom's work and writings in the Mohegan Nation's U.S. federal recognition process, see Melissa Fawcett-Sayet, "Sociocultural Authority: The Mohegan Land Case," in *Rooted Like the Ash Trees: New England Indians and the Land*, rev. ed., ed. Richard G. Carlson (Naugatuck, CT: Eagle Wing Press, 1987), 52–53.

27. Occom's sermon on Moses Paul directly addresses multiple audiences: Paul, non-Native peoples, and Native peoples. For more on Occom's sermons and audience, see Heather Bouwman, "Samson Occom and the Sermonic Tradition," in *Early Native Literacies in New England: A Documentary and Critical Anthology*, ed. Kristina Bross and Hilary E. Wyss (Amherst: University of Massachusetts Press, 2008), 63–71. For more on Occom and Brotherton, see Joanna Brooks's introduction to Occom, *Collected Writings*, 3–39, esp. 24–28.

28. Scott Manning Stevens, "'The Voice of One Crying in the Wilderness': The KJV and Ethno-Exegesis in Iroquoia," in *The King James Bible across Borders and Centuries*, ed. Angelica Duran (Pittsburgh: Duquesne University Press, 2014), 145–48.

29. *Book of Common Prayer/Ne yakawea yondereanayendaghkwa oghseragwegouh* (London: C. Buckton, 1787), 176–77. Brant also translates "desert place" as "kah'rakon" (184–85, 226–27). Brant's translation of the book of Mark is appended to this Mohawk translation of the Book of Common Prayer. English and Mohawk are printed on facing pages.

30. Much has been written on the Wood's Edge ceremony. See, for example, William Nelson Fenton, *The Great Law and the Longhouse: A Political History of the Iroquois Confederacy* (Norman: University of Oklahoma Press, 1998); Daniel K. Richter, *The Ordeal of the Longhouse: Peoples of the Iroquois League in the Era of Colonization* (Chapel Hill: University of North Carolina Press, 1992).

31. A. Zuercher Reichardt, "Translation," *Early American Studies* 16, no. 4 (2018): 806–7.

32. See Patrick Wolfe, "Settler Colonialism and the Elimination of the Native," *Journal of Genocide Research* 8, no. 4 (2006): 387–409.

33. Gerald Vizenor, *Fugitive Poses: Native American Indian Scenes of Absence and Presence* (Lincoln: University of Nebraska Press, 2000), 15.

34. Joy Harjo and Gloria Bird, introduction to *Reinventing the Enemy's Language: Contemporary Native Women's Writings of North America*, ed. Joy Harjo and Gloria Bird (New York: Norton, 1998), 21–22.

PART II
Mind, Body, and Experience

CHAPTER 5

This Seed Is God

Hallucinogenic Plants, Syncretism, and the Transformation of Religious Affections in Colonial Mexico

MELISSA FROST

In 1650 two Spanish women appeared before the Holy Office of the Inquisition in Mexico City to accuse their neighbor, a fellow Spanish woman named Ana Calderón, of engaging in illicit and heretical practices with an Indian medicine man. The basis of their accusation hinged on Ana's admission that her newfound health was the result of a mysterious "herb" that she drank under the care of an individual referred to simply as *un indio.* Under the influence of this herb, she entered a state of sleepless "suspension," in which she witnessed a series of visions that were deeply religious. She found herself in heaven and saw the Virgin Mary lying on her side cradling the baby Jesus in her arms. Turning her head, she then saw God surrounded by a multitude of "very beautiful and very plump" angels at play. A voice then spoke from within her breast; it was the voice of the herb telling her to rejoice, as she would now be cured of all her long-suffered ailments. Upon waking from her suspended state, Ana was so moved by her experience and feelings of well-being that she sat up and embraced the Indian medicine man at her bedside. Following the description of her curative hallucinogenic trance, the accusation against Ana goes on to cite a series of anecdotes identifying individuals who had also allegedly consumed the same herb under the Indian's care. Among the implicated were a number of notable Spaniards, including the wife of a high-ranking bureaucrat and several figures of religious significance: a sister of the Immaculate

Conception, an inquisitor of the Holy Office, an Augustinian friar, and a Franciscan. Of the individuals mentioned in the testimony, only Ana Calderón, Doña Michaela de la Mota, and an unnamed mulatto woman were formally accused in this process.[1]

The case against Ana Calderón—presented by Doña Lorenza Retíz de Arceniega and her daughter María—is a testament to the complex role that traditional hallucinogenic plants played during the colonial period in New Spain. Before 1519, Mesoamerican communities venerated hallucinogenic plants such as peyote, *ololiuqui* (morning glory seeds), *teonanácatl* (psilocybin mushrooms), and *picíetl* (a wild species of tobacco) as catalysts of the sacred. With the arrival of the Spanish conquistadors in the sixteenth century, the Catholic Church was slow to recognize the importance of these herbs, and would eventually come to associate them with inebriation, delusion, quackery, idolatry, and witchcraft. Despite mounting efforts at prohibition on behalf of the church throughout the sixteenth and seventeenth centuries, these controversial substances continued to shape the spiritual experiences of Native communities, while their use spread to non-Native segments of the population. Mesoamerican hallucinogens, far from being mere remnants of pre-Columbian practices, were adapted and incorporated into new forms of worship and came to shape the religious experiences—and, more specifically, the religious affections—of Native and non-Native colonial subjects alike. I define religious affections as powerful emotional experiences of the divine that affirm an individual's understanding of his or her identity as a Christian subject. Beyond the personal experience of the individual, this definition incorporates the greater context of seventeenth-century society in New Spain and the authority of secular and regular clergy over Catholic orthodoxy. The weight of church authority over the interpretation and categorization of religious affections shaped individual and communal responses to these experiences. Elizabeth Agnew Cochran writes of the moral dimension of religious affections and personal will through an analysis of Jonathan Edwards's *Treatise Concerning Religious Affections* (1746). As Cochran indicates, religious affections go beyond the scope of mere passions or emotions because they require the exercise of will; affections are emotions deliberately molded to bring the subject closer to the chief affection, which is love for God.[2] According to the Reformed tradition, religious affections are not spontaneous manifestations of divine light bestowed upon a passive subject; they must be exercised, fostered, perfected. Although the context of this essay is early modern Catholicism, a definition of religious affections that considers the importance of individual will and moral responsibility helps us understand the conflicting perspectives on hallucinogenic rituals as they developed in New Spain, where the people's appetite and appreciation for these substances clashed with the authority of the church. While individuals may have experienced impactful reinforcements of their faith through hallucinogen consumption, church officials categorized such experiences as heresy and idolatry.

To understand how hallucinogens came to mold religious experiences in the colony, I consider evidence of the syncretic role of hallucinogens based on Barbara H. Rosenwein's framework of emotional communities. She defines these as "groups in which people adhere to the same norms of emotional expression and value—or devalue—the same or related emotions."[3] As Rosenwein explains, many emotional communities coexist in any given society, and emotional communities shift and evolve. Within this framework, it becomes clear that traditional hallucinogen use transcended emotional communities otherwise bound by social position, creed, and ethnicity. The various emotional communities of New Spain valued hallucinogens very differently. In their capacity as religious leaders, a greater part of the clergy demonized these substances in line with the official stance of the church. Among the general population, individuals from all walks of life—including some regular and secular clergy—came to incorporate hallucinogens into their divinatory and medicinal practices, which in turn frequently included a dimension of religious experience, as was the case of Ana Calderón's alleged consumption. Hallucinogenic plants came to mold religious affections in both the individual experience of the consumer and the discourses that surrounded these substances among the common folk.

To understand the tension between Catholic orthodoxy and the power of hallucinogen-induced religious affections, this essay incorporates close readings of colonial texts as a way to explore the multiple facets of sacred hallucinogen use and the surrounding rhetoric. A close reading of the anti-idolatry treatises by the prominent clergymen Hernando Ruiz de Alarcón and Jacinto de la Serna exemplifies the stance of the church on the use of these herbs, while it also demonstrates how hallucinogenic practices spread to non-Indian castes. A visit back to Ana Calderón's sixteenth-century accusation before the Holy Office illustrates how official rhetoric against such plants dialogued with the habits and perspectives of the public. In combination, these texts allude to the gamut of discourses that surrounded hallucinogenic practices, from the erudite writings of idolatry extirpators to the gossip that circulated among members of the Spanish caste.

There is a substantial body of scholarly work that discusses the pervasive significance of sacred hallucinogenic plants in pre-Columbian societies. The fields of history, anthropology, and ethnobotany have produced significant work that sheds light on the use of these plants in the religious and medicinal practices of Mesoamerican peoples, and how they contributed to the resilience of rituals that have survived the test of time.[4] This essay contributes to such conversations by considering the spread of hallucinogenic consumption habits (both spiritual and medicinal) to non-Native communities in New Spain, and how such practices altered religious affections among Christian subjects, particularly those of the Spanish caste. In the broader field of early American studies, such a consideration supports a more nuanced understanding of the religious and medicinal exchange between European and Amerindian traditions in the colonial period. Through the consumption of these substances, individuals gained access to emotionally charged religious experiences that bypassed the mediation of the clergy.

Hernando Ruiz de Alarcón and Jacinto de la Serna were active participants in the campaigns for the extirpation of idolatry that took place throughout the seventeenth century. Their treatises are two of the most important sources on pre-Columbian Nahua hallucinogenic rituals that survived the colonial period, even if they did not circulate widely in their day.[5] The descriptions recorded by these two prominent religious figures reveal a great deal about how representatives of the church perceived the emotional dimensions of syncretic religious experiences. In both treatises, the authors describe sacred Nahua rituals involving hallucinogens with vocabulary related to satanic delusion and inebriation. This contrasts starkly with the perspective of Indian subjects who venerated these plants as embodiments of the divine and even came to associate them with Catholic symbols and figures. As evidenced by Ana Calderón's case, individuals beyond the Indian caste also adopted this perspective, suggesting that the profound psychological, emotional, and religious effects of hallucinogens may have contributed to the forging of new emotional communities that transcended caste. To understand the extent of the effect of these substances on religious affections, it is necessary first to establish the backdrop of New Spain and the function of hallucinogens in the context of seventeenth-century Roman Catholicism.

Hallucinogenic Plants in New Spain: Sacred Catalysts and Prohibited Idolatry

Current popular and scholarly discourses frequently refer to hallucinogen consumption as regarding the "psychological." Substances are defined according to their "mind-altering" powers; they affect human consciousness by stimulating the senses. With the conversation defaulting to the realm of the psychological, significant aspects of the emotional effects of these plants can sometimes fall by the wayside. Beneath the immediate correlation between hallucinogens and the mind is an equally substantial dimension of emotion. This can be appreciated in descriptions of hallucinogenic experiences, past and present. *Teonanácatl* mushrooms and peyote, for example, in addition to causing visual hallucinations, also tend to evoke emotions ranging from euphoria to anxiety.[6] The term "spiritual" often appears as a descriptor of hallucinogenic experiences as well. There have been a slew of recent studies by psychiatrists that measure the long-term impact of psilocybin mushrooms (*teonanácatl*) and possible uses of psychedelics as therapies for applications ranging from depression to end-of-life acceptance.[7]

The link between hallucinogens and emotional, spiritual, and physical well-being is ancient. The Nahua peoples of central Mexico located hallucinogenic plants at the very foundation of their religious and medicinal systems. Peyote, *ololiuqui*, *teonanácatl* mushrooms, *piciétl*, and *yautli* (Datura) are just a few of the dozens of hallucinogenic plants that Nahua *ticitls* (medicine men) used to heal ailing bodies and souls. In addition to their symbolic importance as catalysts of the sacred, the consumption of these plants play a vital role in the emotional experiences and personal identities of Indigenous peoples, past and present.[8]

Veneration of hallucinogenic substances stemmed from their ability to facilitate a direct connection to the sacred world.[9] In the context of the Nahua before first encounters, *ticitls* oversaw hallucinogenic rituals in private domestic spaces, while a network of priests incorporated sacred plants from across the Mesoamerican landscape into public rituals. While public intoxication involving hallucinogens was discouraged and punished in the urban context of the Triple Alliance of the Mexica, prohibition stemmed from an attempt to inhibit citizens from invoking the volatile sacred power of these substances and was not associated with a condemnation of the plants themselves. The unquestionable sacred nature of these plants suggests that the Nahua religious system was not structured to question or undermine the legitimacy of hallucinogenic experiences; the visions, emotions, and revelations brought on by the consumption of sacred herbs were part of the ambivalent sacred world.[10]

With the defeat of the Triple Alliance at the hands of Hernán Cortés in 1521, the Spanish crown established the heart of its expanding territory in the Valley of Mexico atop the rubble of the great city of Tenochtitlan. The sacred ambivalence that characterized pre-Columbian hallucinogens contrasted starkly with the perspective of the Catholic Church, which condemned all herb-induced revelations as witchcraft. The church frequently questioned the nature of religious experiences on the suspicion that even visions that appeared to be the product of divine forces could be the work of the devil, who had the power to delude the mind through manipulation of bodily humors.[11]

From its inception, the Spanish colonial enterprise included an intricate (and in many regards chaotic) network of institutions dedicated to the eradication of idolatrous and heretical practices of the many communities that cohabitated in New Spain.[12] Mendicant orders (Dominicans, Augustinians, Franciscans) in addition to the Jesuits—who arrived in 1572—would head the efforts of indoctrinating the Native populations throughout the sixteenth century and beyond. When the Holy Office of the Inquisition was formally established in New Spain in 1571, it retained jurisdiction over all non-Native subjects, while enforcing orthodoxy among Native communities became the task of the bishopric.[13] The missions of these institutions were guided by the effort to segregate Natives from non-Natives and establish a social hierarchy based on heritage, or "blood purity" (*limpieza de sangre*). The push for social order led to the development of a caste system that separated those of Spanish blood from Indians and Africans (*españoles, indios, negros*), while those of mixed ancestry (*mulatos, meztizos,* etc.) were organized along a very precise continuum based on their ancestral makeup and proximity to or distance from "Spanishness."[14]

On the surface, the caste system had clear demarcations establishing rank and position based on the blood purity of each colonial subject. Just below the surface of this seemingly organized structure was a much more intricate and compelling reality whereby people negotiated their positions of power based on a complex set of criteria that in many cases negated the rigidity of the caste system.[15] From the public spheres of the *zócalo* and the market to the seclusion of domestic spaces, individuals with wildly different views of the world engaged in bountiful exchanges on every conceivable level, from the most visible financial interactions to the less tangible exchange of beliefs and practices. Among these were forms of traditional medicine and knowledge of the supernatural. Laura Lewis explores the fluidity of the caste system and how these negotiations of power functioned in inter-caste relationships. The Spaniard, who sat at the apex of colonial society in both privilege and responsibility, was compelled to adhere to the norms of his position. Mixed castes operated on a fluid continuum, making individual status relational and malleable. Indians, who sat in opposition to Spaniards in this social structure, were the guardians of supernatural power and drew a particular form of social clout from their perceived intimacy with the unsanctioned world of witchcraft.[16] The value of supernatural knowledge meant that in many cases the prescribed power structure of the caste system was disrupted. The inherent power of Nahua sacred herbs was a significant part of that process. The wayward Spaniard, perhaps thwarted by the inefficacy of sanctioned means, might find himself at the mercy of an Indian or a mulatto who employed hallucinogenic herbs or other forms of magic.

To judge from surviving Inquisition records, the beginning of the seventeenth century saw a rise in accusations among mestizos and mulattos for use of peyote and *ololiuqui*. Surviving documents from Mexico City's General National Archive (AGN) indicate that the most common hallucinogen consumption by non-Indians during the colonial period was related to divinatory practices; the second most common was medicinal.[17]

The condemnation of Indigenous practices and their association with demonic forces did little to curb the Spanish and mixed-blood castes from engaging in unsanctioned Nahua ritual practices. Personal relationships fostered in domestic and public spaces led to significant inter-caste influence. This is the realm where the use of hallucinogenic sacred plants developed, shaping relationships and molding the religious experiences of subjects from across the social gamut.

By 1650, when Ana Calderón was accused, the Catholic Church had already waged a thirty-year battle against the use of Nahua sacred hallucinogenic herbs. A general prohibition on the consumption of "demonic plants" circulated in 1617, followed by a more specific edict prohibiting the use of peyote in 1620.[18] There are several reasons why these substances, as elements extracted from pre-Columbian practices, were problematic for the church. Their proliferation, as with any remnants of perceived idolatry, was evidence that conversion efforts had not been as successful as missionaries had hoped.[19] In addition to the association between hallucinogenic herbs and idolatrous practices, there was also the threat that these plants posed to church authority. Hallucinogenic trances that evoked strong emotions, visions, and feelings of ecstasy and euphoria interfered with the influence that the church exercised over the faithful.

The nature of unsanctioned forms of worship throughout New Spain, including hallucinogen use, presented challenges to a Catholic Church that struggled to maintain sway over Christian subjects. Oversight focused on quantitative behaviors and not emotional responses. As Helen Rawlings points out, the "good Catholic" of the early modern period was one who attended confession, observed traditional feast days, and had memorized the Ten Commandments.[20] With regard to emotion, it was specifically the delivered sermon that was meant to evoke emotional responses among the listeners.[21] Hallucinogenic plants disrupted this matrix of behavioral and emotional influence by circumventing this prescribed context for religious fervor and facilitating the experience of religious affections in contexts far removed from the pulpit.

While the Holy Office made efforts to thwart the use of hallucinogens, subjects from all walks of colonial society diversified and intensified their use of these substances while aligning their effects with the Catholic faith. During this time of intense social and cultural convergence, religious affections fueled by hallucinogenic experiences took syncretism beyond the symbolic to encompass the emotional and intellectual manifestations of faith, even for the Spanish caste. The use of hallucinogens would then pose a risk to religious authorities as they granted experiences of the divine to common subjects through Indigenous means, asserting the longevity of pre-Columbian practices and customs.

Emotion and Hallucinogens in Religious Treatises: Hernando Ruiz de Alarcón and Jacinto de la Serna

Historical accounts of hallucinogenic trances frequently employ vocabulary directly associated with emotional states. Even the earliest writings related to hallucinogenic rituals witnessed by Europeans are rich with the language of emotion.[22] Toribio de Benavente Motolinía, a Franciscan monk who was one of the earliest to document a *teonanácatl* ritual, described Natives as "cruel" and "rabid" under the "bestial inebriation" caused by these little mushrooms.[23] On the basis of his observations during his expedition in the 1570s, the royal physician and explorer Francisco Hernández noted that *ololiuqui* incited "lust" and turned Mexica priests "mad."[24] Bernardino de Sahagún, whose *General History of the Things of New Spain* offers the most complete and objective list of hallucinogenic herbs produced in the colonial period, included descriptions of peyote and *teonanácatl* rituals among the free-roaming Chichimeca peoples of northern Mexico. He describes rituals in which Native peoples consumed mushrooms that "caused inebriation like wine." These consisted of long nights of dancing and singing followed by bouts of abundant crying the morning after. Some who participated in these hallucinogenic rituals did not dance or cry but rather "sat, pensive, in their dwellings," while others "cleansed and washed their eyes and faces with their tears."[25] These early modern descriptions of behavior related to hallucinogenic rituals rely heavily on the language of emotion, inebriation, and the supernatural realm.

Juan de Cárdenas's *First Part of the Problems and Marvelous Secrets of the Indies* of 1591 was the first treatise to express concern about how these herbs affected colonial subjects beyond the Indian caste.[26] The beginning of the seventeenth century brought with it increasing conflicts regarding these substances and the threat they represented for the social order of New Spain. The church grew increasingly concerned with the remnants of traditional pre-Columbian rituals that persisted among converted Native communities. While each of the many groups responsible for maintaining and advancing the faith (inquisitors of the Holy Office, the mendicant orders) arguably represents an emotional community in itself, there were certain principles, experiences, and values that they shared. This included the rejection of Amerindian ritual forms such as the use of "demonic" herbs for medicine and divination.

Two of the prominent figures who participated in the extirpation of idolatry campaigns were Hernando Ruiz de Alarcón (1620s) and Jacinto de la Serna (1640s).[27] In their writings, both Ruiz de Alarcón and de la Serna recognized that traditional Nahua hallucinogens, particularly *ololiuqui*, peyote, and *picíetl*, were of primary concern. According to the official stance of the church, for the recently converted Indian caste, the continuation of hallucinogenic rituals highlighted the resilience of idolatrous Nahua customs. For non-Indian castes, including Spaniards, these "demonic" herbs had the potential to corrupt the soul, give leeway to the devil, and undermine the authority of church officials. Through dupery of the senses, these plants enabled the devil to manipulate the minds and hearts of men, making them particularly dangerous. A close reading of relevant fragments of these two treatises sheds light on the state of hallucinogen use in the seventeenth century. Their writings are also full of descriptive language that allows us to understand the stance of their emotional community, and how anti-hallucinogen discourse had developed in tandem with the extirpation of idolatry campaigns.

Hernando Ruiz de Alarcón, a member of the Order of Saint Augustine, wrote his *Treatise on the Superstitions and Heathen Customs That Today Live among the Indians of This New Spain* in 1629.[28] The Archbishop Don Francisco Manso de Zuñiga commissioned his intensive five-year study to aid in the detection and eradication of idolatrous practices.[29] In this sense, the purpose of Ruiz de Alarcón's work recalls that of Bernardino de Sahagún. Like Sahagún, Ruiz de Alarcón spent years chronicling the language and customs of the surviving Nahua peoples of central Mexico. His writings, however, were notably less objective in tone than those of his famed predecessor. While both shared the task of cataloging Native customs to facilitate their eradication, Ruiz de Alarcón's writings are more adept at giving voice to the anxieties of the mendicant missionaries and secular clergy who grappled with persistent and increasing evidence of syncretism.

Ruiz de Alarcón was ardent in his efforts to eradicate traces of pre-Columbian Nahua traditions among the surviving Indian populations of New Spain. In 1614 he was accused of subjecting Indians to acts of faith in the same manner as the Holy Office.[30] This was problematic because the Indian caste, at least on paper, was excluded from the jurisdiction of the Holy Office after 1571. Although the accusation was never pursued, it demonstrates that Ruiz de Alarcón's response to perceived acts of Indian idolatry was to hold recently baptized Natives to the same standards as non-Natives. It worried him that surviving Nahua practices would infiltrate the Spanish caste. His descriptions of Nahua rituals and herbs demonstrate that hallucinogens remained a vital component of the Nahua belief system well into the colonial period.

Unlike Sahagún, who listed the medicinal virtues of plants along with their inebriating effects in his catalogue of pre-Columbian knowledge, Ruiz de Alarcón focused solely on the idolatrous dimension of Nahua sacred herbs.[31] His writings on *ololiuqui*, peyote, and *picíetl* link these substances with rampant inebriation and conjuring the devil:

> The aforementioned things [peyote and *ololiuqui*] they hold and adore as a god; *ololiuqui* is a type of seed like lentils that is produced by a vine of this land, and when drunk this seed deprives one of judgment, because it is very warming; and through this medium they [*ticitls*] communicate with the devil, because he speaks to them when they are deprived of judgment by the aforementioned drink, and deceives them with different visions, and they attribute this to the deity that they say is in the seed called *ololiuqui* or *cuexpalli* that are one and the same.[32]

Elsewhere he writes: "The solicitor is out of his wits, in this state they believe that the *ololiuqui* or the peyote is revealing what they want to know; and when this inebriation or deprivation of judgment is upon them, they say countless nonsensical things, among which the devil tends to include some truths, which leads them to be deceived and duped in every sense."[33]

These excerpts illustrate the perspective of Ruiz de Alarcón's emotional community with regard to Nahua ritual forms and their effects on consumers of hallucinogens, as well as those who consult Nahua *ticitls*. Here his language emphasizes that Nahua medicine men are "deprived of judgment" (privados de juicio) under the influence of these plants, which opens the gateway to demonic control. He also describes the role of the devil in manipulating *ticitls* into thinking that their revelations are divine or true, denying the validity of any emotion that could result from the consumption of hallucinogenic plants.

Chapter 29, "Of the Cures and Fraud to Treat Fevers" ("De las curas y embuste para calenturas"), describes the use of different superstitious remedies, including *ololiuqui*, to cure illnesses. In this particular excerpt, Ruiz de Alarcón reveals the versatility of *ololiuqui* in Nahua medicine while also underscoring its association, from his point of view, with superstition and witchcraft: "Others [*ticitls*] use the superstitious *ololiuqui*, and not just for fevers, but for all manners of illness, and this is not surprising considering how established and accepted the abuse [of this seed] is among these heathen people, who almost all worship this seed, and believe it to be divine, and hence think it powerful against all illness.[34] In this passage he begins by underscoring the erroneous nature of Nahua customs with the statement that the Nahua attribute divinity to the *ololiuqui* seed. While acknowledging medicinal use, he dismisses this as a complete delusion orchestrated by the devil.

A notable aspect of this treatise is its specificity with regard to the hallucinogens listed. Although the Nahua pharmacopeia included dozens of different species of hallucinogens, Ruiz de Alarcón and Jacinto de la Serna reduced their focus to just three. There is an emphasis on *ololiuqui*. The little black morning glory seed is mentioned sixty times throughout Ruiz de Alarcón's treatise. Peyote appears twelve times, while tobacco/*picíetl*/*piciete* appears only seven times. In several entries that describe ritual use, these three plants are equal and interchangeable. The description of Nahua *ticitls* includes a reference to divinatory rituals that group these substances together in one category:

> If the question is about a lost or stolen thing, or due to a woman who has left her husband, or any similar case, here commences the practice of false prophecy and the act of divination as described in the preceding treatises, and divination was done in two ways: through sortilege or by drinking to this end peyote or *ololiuqui* or tobacco, or having another drink of it in one's place, and in every manner that such act requires, in all of this there is an illicit pact with the devil, who by the aforementioned brews appears many times before those who drink them and makes them believe that the one who speaks is the *ololiuqui* or the peyote or any other beverage that is drunk for this purpose, and the true shame is that it is in this way that many come to believe these charlatans, more than they believe evangelical preachers.[35]

The classification of these very different hallucinogens as a single cluster erases their identity as individual medicinal plants with very different effects. Unlike the chroniclers of the sixteenth century who were interested in monetizing medicinal discoveries from the New World, the seventeenth-century clergy who described these substances reduced them simply to "demonic herbs." In this fragment, Ruiz de Alarcón emphasizes the role of the devil in deluding gullible Christians through the use of these plants. There is also a reference to the personification of the *ololiuqui*, who takes a physical form and "speaks" to the consumer or *ticitl*. This quality recalls the case of Ana Calderón, who hears the voice of her mysterious herb speaking from her breast. Likewise, the incarnation of the *ololiuqui* is aligned—much to Ruiz de Alarcón's dismay—with Christian divinity throughout his treatise. In one fragment he describes the interaction between the embodied *ololiuqui* and an ailing man who is under the care of a Native Mazatec medicine woman: "[The sick man] was visited by a stranger who claimed to be the *ololiuqui*, and who consoled him, stating: 'Do not despair for you will be cured, for you have sought me. You did not seek me yesterday or the day before.' And with this story, this Indian woman legitimized her deception as if it were rooted in divine revelation."[36] As with the previous example, Ruiz de Alarcón's description highlights the convergence of Native rituals and Catholic forms. Here he underscores that the deception employed by the medicine woman depends on her usurpation of Christian language. The *ololiuqui* embodied as a stranger allegedly speaks to the ill man with soothing language that recalls that of Bible verses related to seeking God.[37]

Ruiz de Alarcón's treatise, with all its condemnation of hallucinogens, falls short of exploring the full extent to which the Spanish caste has been affected by pre-Columbian hallucinogenic customs. Spaniards appear only sporadically mentioned throughout his text. In chapter 7, section 1, he mentions the influence of Indian practices over non-Indian castes, specifically related to *ololiuqui*-drinking ceremonies. Here he makes a note of the ignorance of colonial subjects who believe the deceptions of *ticitls*. The example he offers is related to the use of *ololiuqui* to diagnose illnesses. In this case, if a *ticitl* is unable to find a physical reason for the malady, he takes *ololiuqui* to discover who might have put a curse on the afflicted. Ruiz de Alarcón notes: "Many cases of this kind have passed through my hands, some which require the intervention of the Holy Office because they involve other peoples such as Spaniards, mestizos, blacks, and mulattos, as in their suspicions [of the origins of a curse] they spare no one. And it is so that those who commune frequently with Indians, especially if they are ignorant people, are easily infected with their customs and superstitions."[38] This excerpt illustrates Ruiz de Alarcón's perspective on the moral decay of individuals from non-Indian castes who come to adopt superstitious customs. Although he repeatedly highlights and condemns the parallels that *ticitls* draw between divine Christian figures and hallucinogenic plants, he refrains from considering how those parallels may affect the religious experiences of Spaniards and mixed-blood castes. Ruiz de Alarcón equates the use of these substances with moral failure. Furthermore, any religious affection brought about by these substances would be classified as idolatry and heresy, regardless of how the individuals felt about their faith.

Hernando Ruiz de Alarcón's treatise inspired the work of Jacinto de la Serna. De la Serna built upon Ruiz de Alarcón's body of work through his investigations, producing an extensive treatise that expands the topic of Nahua idolatry and the threat it represented for non-Indian castes.[39] He completed his *Manual for Ministers of Indians to Aid in the Knowledge of Their Idolatries and Their Extirpation* sometime before 1656.[40]

A prominent figure in the church, de la Serna dedicated much of his life to the eradication of idolatry. After studying theology at the Colegio Mayor de Santa María de Todos Santos in Mexico City, he acted as parish priest of many principal cathedrals and institutions of the colony, including the University of Mexico.[41] In the prologue to his *Manual*, he suggests that the problem with Indian idolatry consisted of two components: the persistence of pre-Christian practices and the fact that baptized Indians were engaging in ancient traditions under the guise of the Christian faith.[42] In this sense, we see in de la Serna's writings a continuation of Ruiz de Alarcón's preoccupation with syncretism and the appropriation of Christian forms. De la Serna dedicates a considerable portion of his treatise to the many uses of hallucinogens among the Nahua. Like his predecessor, de la Serna focuses primarily on *ololiuqui*, peyote, and *picíetl*/tobacco. He puts a greater emphasis, however, on the role of Spaniards and other non-Indians in the propagation of idolatrous practices. For example, when discussing the use of *ololiuqui* for finding lost or stolen items, he states: "It is worthy of note that blacks and mulattos and even some Spaniards, having wandered from the Grace of God, seek out Indians to help them find lost things, whom they pay to discover what has gone missing: and it is very common that those of service warn those who they suspect have stolen these things, and threaten that they will have an Indian *ticitl* man or woman drink peyote to find out if they have, and in fact they do."[43] This segment is representative of how de la Serna positions non-Indian castes, including Spaniards, as important participants in the propagation of Indian idolatry. In chapter 4.2, "Los instrumentos de sus curaciones," de la Serna lists hallucinogens as one of the many treatment methods used by Nahua *ticitls*. While we can read this entry as an acknowledgment of the plurality of treatments mastered by the Nahua, it is framed purely as idolatry. Directly after describing hallucinogens as a treatment, de la Serna goes on to illustrate how delusion and quackery characterize all medicinal practices among the Nahua, precisely because they are so close to divinatory practices. *Ololiuqui* and peyote do not receive acknowledgment as cures for physical maladies; they are diagnostic tools that Nahua medicine men use to delude their patients into believing that they have discovered the cause of illness.

In addition to emphasizing the role of Spaniards in the idolatrous behavior of converted Indians, de la Serna reasserts Ruiz de Alarcón's preoccupation with the usurpation of Christian forms. He notes the syncretism in Nahua practices based on the personification of *ololiuqui* and its parallels to Christian divinity. In his description of the role of the *ticitl*, he underscores the blind faith that Indians have in these divinatory practices, particularly when they involve the wrath of both Christian and Nahua deities: "Because if [an ailment] is due to having angered our Lord, or the blessed Virgin, or any other saint, [the Indians] believe that [the *ticitl*] has the power to appease and placate them, and if it suits them, to say that the illness comes from having angered any of their gods to whom they attribute divinity, such as fire, the sun, water, or *ololiuqui*."[44] In his article on de la Serna's writings and the extirpation efforts in Mexico and Peru, José Luis González Martínez indicates that the preoccupation that led to the revitalized anti-idolatry efforts of the early seventeenth century stemmed from the degree of syncretism that was developing between ancient Nahua traditions and Christianity.[45] Baptized Indians seem to have had little trouble taking the sacrament and participating in church life while continuing to worship idols and engage in divinatory practices. Many of these methods depended on the continued use of hallucinogenic plants.

The texts of Ruiz de Alarcón and de la Serna illustrate the state of erudite discourse concerning hallucinogenic plants in New Spain in the first half of the seventeenth century. They demonstrate the preoccupations of the secular clergy, who attempted to eradicate behaviors related to hallucinogenic rituals. While these texts reveal a great deal about how the emotional community that worked toward extirpation viewed pre-Columbian hallucinogenic practices and their dangers, they are limited in their ability to illustrate the everyday experiences of colonial subjects. The diversity of peoples that came together in New Spain developed a complex culture of consumption deeply rooted in the traditions of the surviving Mesoamerican population. Since sacred hallucinogenic plants played a central role in the Mesoamerican religious system, it is not surprising that the customs and traditions surrounding these substances would be significant factors in the fluidity that characterized the shifting belief systems of the colony.

Ololiuqui and peyote, the two most notorious "demonic" herbs from the point of view of Ruiz de Alarcón and de la Serna, were also the substances at the heart of the organic syncretism that developed in New Spain. James Lockhart discusses the importance of these two plants in his study on post-conquest Nahua history. Both the inebriating black lentil-like seed and the little "white root" remained sacred and often appeared as offerings on Christian altars.[46] Noemí Quezada has demonstrated that hallucinogens were raised to the level of divine figures as made apparent in the writings of Ruiz de Alarcón and de la Serna. Each sacred Nahua plant had a corresponding Christian figure: peyote was the Holy Trinity and Jesus Christ; *ololiuqui* drew parallels with the Virgin Mary. It would then make sense that the powerful images experienced during hallucinogenic trances would impact the religious affections of the consumer.

Hernando Ruiz de Alarcón and Jacinto de la Serna recognized the inherent threat in the propagation of Nahua ritual forms, including the use of hallucinogens. Although both were aware of growing syncretism in the Indian caste, they do not seem to have understood the extent to which hallucinogens had come to influence non-Indians. Baptized Nahua peoples, even those who embraced Christianity, infused Catholic practices with pre-Columbian hallucinogenic traditions. As they did, their veneration of these plants spread to non-Indian castes, altering experiences of divinity even for European subjects. Although their point of view aligned with the principles of the Catholic faith, it was not the only perspective on these rituals or, perhaps, the most popular. As the accusation against Ana Calderón makes apparent, there was a full range of alternate sentiments and attitudes toward these substances throughout the general population, ranging from ambivalence among some to integration of these plants into religious life among others. Ana Calderón, a Spanish woman whose religious and healing experience depended on the consumption of a vision-inducing herb, is a micro-example of how hallucinogens caused shifts in emotional communities in the colony, and perhaps even the development of new emotional communities.

A Nahua Medicine Man, a Spanish Woman, a Mysterious Herb, and God

The accusation of 1650 against Ana Calderón offers ample evidence that Nahua hallucinogens were a vivid part of public discourse in the mid-seventeenth century. These were substances the church had prohibited, and their consumption was a point of contention with regard to the spiritual integrity and the moral rectitude of the individual. Any religious affections or revelations that might have derived from Nahua rituals would have automatically been condemned and classified as idolatry by the church. Ana Calderón's case suggests that the power of these plants to invoke religious images while inciting the emotional experience of the consumer made them powerful and desirable catalysts for the divine, even for Spanish Christian subjects.

Because of their capacity to shed light on the quotidian, inquisitorial documents are excellent sources for understanding traditional hallucinogen use during the colonial period. These records demonstrate that while traditional hallucinogens were a topic of interest among erudite clergymen preoccupied with idolatry, a culture of consumption among Nahua peoples expanded beyond the Indian caste, evolving with the demands of colonial subjects. The Inquisition records from the AGN demonstrate that there were fluctuations in patterns of behavior of non-Indian castes throughout the colonial period regarding hallucinogen consumption.

The black market for hallucinogens that developed throughout the seventeenth century in New Spain was a hybrid of European demands for divinatory aids and pre-Columbian religious and medicinal practices. True to its status as the most recognized and vilified hallucinogen of the colonial period, peyote appears in a comparatively large number of Inquisition transcripts. Most of the cases found in Inquisition records are related to divinatory use. The emphasis on the divinatory is more likely an indication of the anxieties of inquisitors rather than an accurate reflection of the consumption habits of the public. In addition to the number of divination-related cases, it becomes clear that peyote and other hallucinogens also played key roles in the religious experiences of colonial subjects, a prevalence mostly due to the pre-Columbian duality of medicinal and divinatory use associated with these plants.

As we saw with the writings of Ruiz de Alarcón and de la Serna, divinatory acts associated with the devil were of primary concern for the church, while medicinal use was secondary. The very first case concerning peyote in the surviving records dates from 1566, when a Spaniard by the name of Tomás de Lorrio was accused of discussing peyote and other heretical topics.[47] Following this early evidence of small-scale prohibition, there was only a small cluster of accusations, mostly presented against mulatto women for both consuming and administering peyote. After the publication of the edict against peyote in 1620, there was a notable increase in the breadth and scope of accusations, which include several confessions.[48] According to the 1650 accusations presented by Doña Lorenza and her daughter Maria, Ana Calderón's experience with the Nahua *ticitl* and his mysterious herb left profound impressions based on the weight of religious symbolism and his efficacy in curing her illness.

Ana Calderón's description of her visions is full of Christian imagery. There are no references to anything related to pre-Columbian symbols or deities other than the herb itself. Instead, her hallucinogenic experience was a complete affirmation of her Catholic faith. The images of heaven that appeared before her were deeply rooted in traditional Christian forms, and purportedly evoked powerful affections in the ailing woman. When her accusers allegedly warned Ana that she might have committed a violation in the eyes of the Holy Office, she reportedly defended her experience by stating that the herb she took "was not like peyote, which makes you see bad things. Everything that I saw was very good [todo lo que vide era muy lindo]."[49] It was enough for Ana that she had not consumed peyote to consider herself free from sin. The testimonies go on to claim that she further legitimized her experience by citing a slew of additional Spaniards who had also taken the herb. Among them was Doña Michaela de la Mota, whose experience is retold in detail in the testimonies. The wife of Secretario Cristobal de la Mota, she had purportedly entrusted the same Indian who treated Ana to help her solve a personal conundrum related to her many extramarital affairs. One of her rumored lovers was a parish priest.

When she took the mysterious herb to know the outcome of her illicit encounters, she saw her priest lover shackled and surrounded by flames and serpents. The voice of the herb then spoke from her breast, as it had with Ana Calderón. But instead of saying sweet heavenly things, it told her that her lover was in hell because he thought of her when celebrating Mass. This reference to the voice of the herb recalls the writings of Ruiz de Alarcón and de la Serna concerning the personification of *ololiuqui* and its ability to speak truths to those who drank it. Although there is no way to verify either Ana's experience or that of Michaela de la Mota, it is clear that both narratives suggest a profound correlation between the consumption of Nahua hallucinogens and the affirmation of Christian symbols and experiences. The hallucinatory treatments offered by the Indian medicine man circumvented the authority of the church while simultaneously affirming the religious identity of the consumer.

* * *

The powerful emotional and psychological effects of hallucinogenic plants made them particularly alluring for the diverse population of New Spain, whose daily lives were plagued by uncertainties. The spread of their use beyond the Indian caste challenged the authority of the Catholic Church and hindered efforts to identify and squelch idolatry in the colony. Despite church prohibition, hallucinogens affirmed Catholic symbols, rites, and experiences, even among the Spanish caste, while simultaneously ensuring the resilience of pre-Columbian beliefs and practices. The mendicant orders charged with preserving and propagating the Catholic faith recognized and rejected this syncretism in the seventeenth century but were unsuccessful in their efforts to eradicate the phenomenon. During the conquest and colonization of the Americas, it was precisely the fear of perceived demonic influence that led the mendicant orders entrusted with the conversion of Indian communities to reject ritual hallucinogens. The spread of African and Indigenous forms of worship, including hallucinogen consumption, increased throughout the seventeenth century. By the dawn of the eighteenth century, the persistent stream of cases involving peyote and *ololiuqui* demonstrates that non-Indian castes appropriated these herbs and utilized them for all manner of divinatory and healing purposes. While these cases have yet to be fully investigated, the persistence of Nahua traditions combined with evidence from the treatises by Hernando Ruiz de Alarcón and Jacinto de la Serna indicate that hallucinogens were particularly difficult to eradicate, in part because of their capacity to inspire religious affections in Christian subjects.

Notes

1. Inq. vol. 1602, exp. 1, 260 fols., 1650–1656, Archivo General de la Nación (AGN). Unfortunately there are no additional texts in the archive that describe the resolution of the case. It is unclear whether the Holy Office pursued the accusation or not, or whether the texts describing additional proceedings have been lost. All references to Inquisition cases are based on my research in the AGN, cross-referenced with Linda Arnold's "Inquisición (volúmenes y cajas), catálogo cronológico," Archivo General de la Nación, online catalogue, PDF, 2008.
2 Elizabeth Agnew Cochran, "The Moral Significance of Religious Affections: A Reformed Perspective on Emotions and Moral Formation," *Studies in Christian Ethics* 28, no. 2 (2015): 151.
3. Barbara Rosenwein, *Emotional Communities in the Early Middle Ages* (Ithaca: Cornell University Press, 2006), 2.
4. One prime example is the persistence of the peyote ceremony among the Huichol communities. See Peter Furst, "To Find Our Life: Peyote among the Huichol Indians of Mexico," in *Flesh of the Gods: The Ritual Use of Hallucinogens,* ed. Peter Furst (Prospect Heights, IL: Waveland Press, 1990), 136–184. For a historical perspective of peyote use based on Inquisition cases, see Angélica Morales-Sarabia, "The Culture of Peyote: Between Divination and Disease in Early Modern New Spain," in *Medical Cultures of the Early Modern Spanish Empire,* ed. John Slater et al. (Farnham, Surrey: Ashgate, 2014), 21–39.
5. David Eduardo Tavárez, *The Invisible War: Indigenous Devotions, Discipline, and Dissent in Colonial Mexico* (Stanford: Stanford University Press, 2011), 92.
6. See Mercedes de la Garza, *Sueño y éxtasis: Visión chamánica de los nahuas y los mayas* (Mexico City: Universidad Nacional Autónoma de México, 2012), 296; Richard Evans Schultes, Albert Hofmann, and Christian Rätsch, *Plants of the Gods: Their Sacred, Healing, and Hallucinogenic Powers,* 2nd ed. (Rochester, VT: Healing Arts Press, 2001), 47, 144–55; Michael Wink and Ben-Erik Van Wyk, *Mind-Altering and Poisonous Plants of the World* (Portland, OR: Timber Press, 2008).
7. Roland Griffiths et al., "Psilocybin Occasioned Mystical-Type Experiences: Immediate and Persisting Dose-Related Effects," *Psychopharmacology* 218, no. 4 (2011): 649–65; Thomas C. Swift et al., "Cancer at the Dinner Table: Experiences of Psilocybin-Assisted Psychotherapy for the Treatment of Cancer-Related Distress," *Journal of Humanistic Psychology* 57, no. 5 (September 2017): 488–519.
8. Peter Furst titled his 1966 article on the Huichol pilgrimage "To Find Our Life," basing it on the importance attributed to peyote and its role in helping individuals achieve personal fulfillment in their inner lives.
9. See de la Garza, *Sueño y éxtasis,* 68; Inga Clendinnen, *Aztecs: An Interpretation* (Cambridge: Cambridge University Press, 1991), 227.

10. For figures frequently associated with hallucinogenic plants, such as Xochipilli, "the ecstatic prince of flowers," as Tláloc, the rain god, see de la Garza, *Sueño y éxtasis*, 87.
11. *The Hammer of Witches* (*Malleus Maleficarum*, 1486) was the most important and influential treatise on witchcraft in the early modern period. The text references the writings of Thomas Aquinas regarding humors to explain how Satan manipulates the mind. See Christopher S. Mackay, *The Hammer of Witches: A Complete Translation of the Malleus Maleficarum* (Cambridge: Cambridge University Press, 2009), 197.
12. The Spanish governmental apparatus in New Spain consisted of five branches: Gobierno, Justicia, Militar, Hacienda, and Eclesiástico. In many cases these branches were intertwined with regard to authority. The last, Eclesiástico, dealt with church matters, including the Holy Office. See Peter Gerhard, *A Guide to the Historical Geography of New Spain*, rev. ed. (Norman: University of Oklahoma Press, 1993), 10, 17–22.
13. For a consideration of the jurisdictions of religious institutions in New Spain, see Richard E. Greenleaf, "The Inquisition and the Indians of New Spain: A Study in Jurisdictional Confusion," *The Americas* 22, no. 2 (1965): 141.
14. For a nuanced consideration of blood purity and the caste system, see Maria Elena Martinez, *Genealogical Fictions: Limpieza de Sangre, Religion, and Gender in Colonial Mexico* (Stanford: Stanford University Press, 2008).
15. Richard Greenleaf, in "The Inquisition and the Indians of New Spain," demonstrated that although declared jurisdictions were explicit in theory, the roles of the Holy Office and the bishopric overlapped, resulting in uneven and unpredictable enforcement. Mark Z. Christensen, *Nahua and Maya Catholicisms: Texts and Religion in Colonial Central Mexico and Yucatan* (Stanford: Stanford University Press, 2013), has demonstrated through the analysis of Native-language religious texts that there was not one but many "catholicisms" that developed in New Spain, depending on the priorities of those in charge of the indoctrination of Native peoples.
16. Laura Lewis, *Hall of Mirrors: Power, Witchcraft, and Caste in Colonial Mexico* (Durham: Duke University Press, 2003), 105.
17. Although Inquisition documents are notably problematic at establishing historical fact because of their reliance on secondhand accounts, they are very effective at communicating the trends in the preoccupations of the Holy Office and the quotidian patterns of behavior of colonial subjects. These cases frequently involved the search for missing items or persons. Peyote and *ololiuqui* were used to help locate lost or stolen items, mines or other treasures, and missing persons. Some examples include Cristobal de alzate hizo tomar el ololuique, para saber de unos animals perdidos, Atzcapotzalco (Inq. vol. 1552, exp. sn, F200, 1626); Testificación contra da. Maria de Castro, y un indio que tomo el oliuluque para adivinar en donde estaba la hija de la primera y asi lo adivino, Mexico (Inq. vol. 342, exp. 15, fol. 15, 1622); Carta de Antonio [Meneses] dando a conocer que dio la lectura y publicación del edicto de fe, y pregunta si el que un indio enfermo usara el peyote como remedio, estás faltando en algo, pues no lo hizo con intensión y sólo como medicamentos, San Johan Parangaricutio (Inq. vol. 1579 A, exp. 73, fol. 1, 1621); Consulta sobre si se puede tomar la raiz de peyote como medicina, michoacan (Inq. vol. 486, exp. 77, fol. 417, 1621).

18. For a transcript and translation of the edict against peyote, see Irving A. Leonard, "Peyote and the Mexican Inquisition, 1620," *American Anthropologist* 44, no. 2 (1942): 324–26. The 1617 prohibition is cited in Noemí Quezada, *Enfermedad y maléficio: El curandero en el México colonial* (Mexico City: Universidad Nacional Autónoma de México, 1989), 46.
19. For an example of failed conversion that led to violence, see Inga Clendinnen, "Disciplining the Indians: Franciscan Ideology and Missionary Violence in Sixteenth-Century Yucatán," *Past & Present* 94 (1982): 27–48.
20. Helen Rawlings, *Church, Religion and Society in Early Modern Spain* (New York: Palgrave, 2002), 80.
21. O. C. Edwards Jr. discusses the nature and composition of baroque Roman Catholic sermons in "Varieties of Sermon: A Survey of Preaching in the Long Eighteenth Century," in *Preaching, Sermon and Cultural Change in the Long Eighteenth Century*, ed. Joris van Eijnatten (Leiden: Brill, 2009), 4.
22. Toribio de Benavente Motolinía mentions *teonanácatl* (psilocybin mushrooms) in *Historia de los indios de la Nueva España escrita a mediados del siglo XVI* (Barcelona: Herederos de J. Gili, 1914), 21. Bernardino de Sahagún lists hallucinogens in *Historia general de las cosas de Nueva España,* 3 vols. (Mexico City: Impr. del ciudadano A. Valdés, 1829). The descriptions of these "inebriating herbs" include their potential medicinal and toxic properties as well as their suspected links to Nahua sorcery (3:241). Francisco Hernández's catalogue of the plants of New Spain, *Cuatro libros de la naturaleza y virtudes medicinales de las plantas y animales de la Nueva España*, was translated from Latin and published in 1615, nearly thirty years after his death in 1587. It contains references to *ololiuqui* and demonic influence. Juan de Cárdenas, a physician, published *Primera parte de los problemas y secretos maravillosos de las Indias* in 1591. This catalogue of American maladies and remedies illustrates the concerns of a young doctor as he confronted the particularities of treating patients in New Spain. The final chapter of his text, "En que se declara muy por entero si puede aver hechizos en las yervas, y que sean hechizos," employs the principles of humorism to explain how some plants, including peyote and *ololiuqui,* may facilitate demonic possession.
23. "Tenían otra manera de embriaguez que los hacía más crueles: era con unos hongos o setas pequeñas, que en esta tierra los hay como en Castilla; mas los de esta tierra son de tal calidad, que comidos crudos y por ser amargos, beben tras ellos o comen con ellos un poco de miel de abejas; y de allí a poco rato veían mil visiones, en especial culebras, y como salían fuera de todo sentido parecíales que las piernas y el cuerpo tenían llenos de gusanos que los comían vivos, y así medio rabiando se salían fuera de casa, deseando que alguno los matase; y con esta bestial embriaguez y trabajo que sentían, acontecía alguna vez ahorcarse, y también eran contra los otros más crueles. A estos hongos llaman en su lengua teonanacatl, que quiere decir carne de Dios, o del demonio que ellos adoraban: y de la dicha manera con aquel amargo manjar su cruel Dios los comulgaba." Toribio, *Historia de los indios de la Nueva España*, 21.
24. "Tambien [la planta] bevida provoca a luxuria, es de sabor y temperatura aguda y muy caliente. Antiguamente los sacerdotes de los ydolos que querian tratar con el demonio y tener respuestas de sus dudas comian desta planta para tornarse locos y para ver mil fantasmas." Francisco Hernández and Francisco Jiménez, *Cuatro*

libros de la naturaleza y virtudes medicinales de las plantas y animales de la Nueva España (Morelia: Escuela de Artes), 78.

25. *Historia general de las cosas de Nueva España* includes several examples that describe emotional behavior in hallucinogenic rituals: "Aquellos honguillos los comían con miel, y cuando ya se comenzaban a escalentar con ellos, comenzaban á bailar, algunos cantaban, otros lloraban porque ya estaban borrachos con los honguillos, y algunos no querían cantar, sino sentábanse en sus aposentos, y estábanse allí como pensativos" (2:366).

   "Ellos mismos descubrieron, y usaron primero la raíz que llaman *peiotl*, y los que la comían y tomaban, la usaban en lugar de vino, y lo mismo hacían de los que llaman *nanácatl* que son los hongos malos que emborrachan también como el vino; y se juntaban en un llano después de haberlo bebido, donde bailaban y cantaban de noche y de día á su placer, y esto el primer día, porque el siguiente, lloraban todos mucho, y decían que se limpiaban y lavaban los ojos y caras con sus lágrimas" (3:118).

26. Juan de Cárdenas published his *Primera parte de los problemas y secretos marauillosos de las Indias* in 1591.
27. José Luis González Martínez, "Sincretismo e identidades emergentes. El Manual de Jacinto de la Serna (1630)," *Dimensión Antropológica* 38 (September–December 2006), 89.
28. Hernando Ruiz de Alarcón, *Tratado de las supersticiones y costumbres gentilicias que hoy viven entre los indios naturales de esta Nueva España* (1629) (Barcelona, 2011).
29. Noemí Quezada, "Hernando Ruiz de Alarcón y su persecución de idolatrías," *Tlalocan* 8 (1980): 324.
30. Quezada, "Hernando Ruiz de Alarcón," 327.
31. Sahagún lists hallucinogens under "yerbas que emborrachan." *Historia general*, chap. 7, 3:241. His descriptions include both medicinal uses and intoxicating effects.
32. "Las sobredichas cosas tienen y adoran por dios, y el ololuhqui es un género de semilla como lantejas, que la produce un género de hiedra desta tierra, y bebida esta semilla priva del juicio, porque es muy vehemente; y por este medio comunican al demonio, porque les suele hablar cuando están privados del juicio con la dicha bebida, y engañarlos con diferentes apariencias, y ellos lo atribuyen a la deidad que dicen está en la dicha semilla llamada ololiuhqui o cuexpalli que es una misma cosa." *Tratado de las supersticiones*, 25.
33. "El consultor esta fuera de si, que entonces creen que el tal ololiuhqui o peyote les esta reuelando lo que desean saber; en pasandosele al tal la embriaguez o priuacion de juicio, sale contando dos mil patrañas, entre las quales el demonio suele reboluer algunas verdades, con que de todo punto los tiene engañados o embaucados." *Tratado de las supersticiones*, 39.
34. "Otros usan del supersticioso ololiuhqui, y no sólo para calenturas, sino para todo género de enfermedad, y no me admira supuesto el abuso tan recibido y asentado entre esta gente bárbara, que casi todos adoran esta semilla, y atribuyéndole divinidad, consiguientemente le atribuyen virtud contra todas las enfermedades." *Tratado de las supersticiones*, 186.
35. "Si la consulta es sobre cosa perdida o hurtada o por mujer que se ausentó de su marido, o cosa semejante, aquí entra el don de la falsa profecía, y el adivinar como queda apuntado en los tratados precedentes, y el adivinanza, se hace por

una de dos vías: o por sortilegio, o bebiendo para este fin el peyote o el ololiuhqui o el tabaco, o mandando que otro lo beba, y dando el orden que en ello se debe tener, y en todo ello va ilícito el pacto con el demonio, el cual por medio de las dichas bebidas muchas veces se les aparece y les habla haciéndoles entender que el que les habla es el ololiuhqui o peyote o cualquier otro brebaje que hubieren bebido para el dicho fin, y la lastima es que así a este como a los mismos embusteros los creen muchos, mejor que a los predicadores evangélicos." *Tratado de las supersticiones*, 147.

36. "Se le había aparecido una persona forastera que decía era el ololiuhqui y le había consolado diciéndole: 'no tengas pena que ahora mejorarás; que me has buscado: ayer ni anteayer no me buscabas.' Con esta historia tenía esta india acreditado su embuste como si fúndase en alguna revelación divina." *Tratado de las supersticiones*, 187.
37. For example, Matthew 7:7, Lamentations 3:25, Jeremiah 29:13.
38. "De este género han pasado por mis manos muchos casos, y en ellos ha sido necesaria intervención del Santo Oficio, por mezclarse en ellos otras naciones como españoles, mestizos, negros y mulatos, porque en tales sospechas a nadie perdonan. Y también los que comunican mucho los indios, especialmente siendo gente vil, fácilmente se inficionan con sus costumbres y supersticiones." *Tratado de las supersticiones*, 45.
39. Tavárez, *The Invisible War*, 90.
40. There are several transcriptions of Jacinto de la Serna's *Manual de ministros de Indios para el conocimiento de sus idolatrías y extirpación de ellas.* The version cited here was edited by Francisco del Paso y Troncoso as *Tratado de las idolatrías, supersticiones, hechicerías, y otras costumbres de las razas aborígenes de México,* 2nd ed. (Mexico City: Ediciones Fuente Cultural, 1953).
41. José Luis González Martínez, "Sincretismo e identidades emergentes," 89.
42. De la Serna, *Tratado de las idolatrías*, 53.
43. "Es digno de advertir, que negros, y mulatos, y algunos españoles, dejados de la mano de Dios, en cosas perdidas buscan indios, a quienes pagan, para que les descubran lo que faltó: y es muy ordinario en la gente de servicio amenazar a los que sospechan les han hurtado algunas cosas, con que harán, que beba un indio, o india Titzitl el peyote para saberlo, y de hecho lo hacen." *Tratado de las idolatrías*, 239.
44. "Porque si es falta de salud, le atribuyen el conocimiento de la enfermedad por grave, y oculta, y no conocida que sea, y que puede aplicar el remedio conveniente para curarla: si se trata de tener enojado a Nuestro Señor, o a la Virgen santísima o a otro cualquier santo, lo tienen por poderoso para desenojarlos, y aplacarlos y si les parece, que la enfermedad proviene de tener enojado a alguno de sus dioses, a quienes atribuyen Deidad, como son el Fuego, el Sol, el agua, el Ololiuhqui." *Tratado de las idolatrías*, 102.
45. José Luis González Martínez, "Sincretismo e identidades emergentes," 89.
46. James Lockhart, *The Nahuas after the Conquest: A Social and Cultural History of the Indians of Central Mexico, Sixteenth through Eighteenth Centuries* (Stanford: Stanford University Press, 1994), 259.

47. Inq. vol. 5, exp. 14, fol. 1, 1566, AGN.
48. The fact that three years after the original edict a more explicit edict was produced demonstrates the growing anxieties on behalf of the church regarding peyote. For one example of a confession of peyote use, see "Denuncia presentada por Francisco Moreno contra si mismo, por haber aconsejado a una persona que tomara peyote para adivinar." Inq. vol. 335, exp. 6, fol. 6, 1622, AGN.
49. Inq. vol. 1602, exp. 1, 260 fols. 1650–56, AGN.

CHAPTER 6

Local Devotions in New Spain

A Response to Melissa Frost

STEPHANIE KIRK

The case of Ana Calderón, brought before the Inquisition for consulting an Indigenous *curandero* and ingesting hallucinogenic substances, skillfully analyzed by Melissa Frost in her contribution to this volume, raises a series of questions that, when examined, permit us a wider understanding of local and unofficial New Spanish devotional practices and the religious affections they inspired in the faithful. Who made up the emotional communities that engaged in the ritualistic practices Frost discusses? Why did the church wish to silence them? And how can we understand the frowned-upon affective response that these practices stimulated in the religious subject? Non-institutional rituals and beliefs—such as those practiced by Ana Calderón—became ingrained in emotional communities because of the religious affections they inspired. These same religious affections were fed by the tension between resistance to the doctrine the church wished to impose via its institutional framework and the grounding these affections possessed in local communities and identities. These local practices offer us a privileged view of the experiences of marginal subjects whose knowledge and emotions were subjugated to a religious master narrative. James C. Scott famously dubbed this master narrative the "public transcript," identifying it as "the self-portrait of dominant elites" which they deployed to "affirm and naturalize" their power and "to conceal or euphemize the dirty linen of their rule."[1] Unorthodox colonial

Mexican religious practices, such as the consumption of hallucinogens, must be decoded from within these master narratives to reveal their "hidden transcript" (Scott) or their "subjugated knowledges" (Foucault).[2]

We can piece together the hidden transcript or excavate subjugated knowledges by reading between the lines of the extirpation manuals Frost describes, whose authors' detailing of the same Indigenous practices they wished to eradicate ironically helps to preserve them. We can also find the hidden transcript embedded in Inquisition documents like those that portray Ana Calderón's interrogation or in other official texts or printed matter that the powerful viceregal machine generated in its desire to control marginal communities. As Mary Giles eloquently explains, a deciphering of these records allows women, in particular, to "step forward like ghosts in a dream to claim existence and identity in the reader's imagination."[3] We must proceed with caution, however, when attempting to chart lived experiences and religious affections from official documents that were written with an entirely different goal in mind. Inquisition documents, for example, provide a valuable window onto the devotional culture of those for whom we would otherwise have no record. We need to recognize that the subjects' testimony was produced under coercive circumstances and acknowledge the mediation that occurred in the recording of their voices. The Inquisition, moreover, framed the experiences of women such as Ana Calderón in terms of religious deviancy—a category, as Nora Jaffary explains—the Holy Office itself created and promoted, and it is within this framework of perversion that the stories of women and other marginal subjects are told.[4] Official documents regulating such things as religious practices more often expressed the wishes of viceregal and imperial power brokers than the reality of the populace whose emotions and religious affections they sought to police.

The church's anxious desire to both reproduce and improve upon Old World religious models collided head-on with the realities that the imperial project confronted. This collision provided opportunities for marginal subjects to establish religious autonomy via the formation of emotional communities, the hybrid religious practices that connected them, and the religious affections these practices inspired. Frost gives compelling evidence of the importance of local religious practices in the forging of the emotional community she identifies. Her essay shows us the affective power of religious syncretism at work in colonial Mexico through the materialization of an emotional community based on the rites associated with the consumption of the sacred hallucinogens of the descendants of the Mexica. The affective power of these hallucinogens bound together a racially varied group, as we can see in Frost's essay, where she describes how, "upon waking from her suspended state, Ana was so moved by her experience and feelings of well-being that she sat up and embraced the Indian medicine man at her bedside." Calderón's response illustrates that the strictly defined caste culture with which the viceregal authorities attempted to impose order on a chaotic, racially diverse society—as exemplified in the *casta* paintings of the late seventeenth and early eighteenth centuries—existed more in theory than in practice in a variety of contexts, including the religious.[5] It also offered an opportunity for Indigenous *curanderos* to recoup some of the power and influence over the faithful and their religious affections that they had wielded in pre-Hispanic Mexico. Their administering of hallucinogens to a multiracial community furnished them with a meaningful and authoritative way to access the divine in the face of an official church that sought to portray them and their rituals as aberrant and heterodox in such texts as the extirpation manuals.

While the extirpation manuals Frost analyzes offer the reader invaluable information regarding the persistence of the use of hallucinogens among the Indigenous as well as their spread to the Creole and Spanish populations, these texts did not make the type of inroads against idolatry their authors had hoped. Frost points out, for example, that the manuals did not achieve wide circulation in their day. Viviana Díaz Balsera, furthermore, explains that the manuals and the extirpation of idolatry program that brought them into being represent the church's implicit acknowledgment that the great evangelization project upon which it had embarked in the sixteenth century had not been successful. In a painful irony, and despite their best efforts, the treatises offer proof of the continued presence of Indigenous subjectivities, the energetic and continued embrace by Native peoples of their ancestral religious practices as well as their possession of an uncanny and threatening ability to move seamlessly between their own spiritual world and that which the Spanish imposed.[6]

This rupture between the centralized and institutionalized view of the church and that of individual clergy and parishioners on a local level does not surprise us if we consider the tensions that existed in New Spanish Christianity between local religious customs and liturgical rituals that were enshrined in doctrine. William Christian, the foremost scholar of local religion in the Hispanic world, describes how evangelization itself "has generally allowed for an assimilation of local procedures and an accommodation to local holy places and time."[7] While the church as an institution used hierarchy, tradition, and priestly mediation to control the faithful, emotional communities engaged in unmediated and non-hierarchical affective experiences to bind themselves together. We see the failure of the church's attempt at total control of belief systems and their affective responses in the extirpation campaigns conducted in both New Spain and Peru in the seventeenth and eighteenth centuries. Although designed to reinvigorate unsuccessful assimilation of Indigenous believers, they "tended to run out of steam," allowing other issues to prevail and thus enabling the "targeted beliefs" to emerge from hiding and flourish again.[8] During the first two centuries of Spanish rule in New Spain, neither the church nor the crown was able to truly regulate even the activities of its own operatives, especially those in rural parishes and missions far from metropolitan centers of power. Factors such as geography, along with the dominance of the regular orders—beginning with the mendicants, principally the Franciscans, and later the Jesuits—allowed for variety in Christian practices and for the flourishing of local traditions in which Indigenous practices and beliefs played a big part. Emotional communities grew up around these local customs as worshipers became invested in the traditions, saints, and rituals connected to their everyday realities and developed religious affections that responded to them. Centralized church bureaucracies located in colonial cities and imperial metropoles could not challenge the rootedness of these traditions, nor could they police the local realities of inter-caste mixing on a variety of levels. These spiritual models were deeply permeated by peculiarly American issues of race, class, and gender, as were the emotional communities that grew around them.

The case of Ana Calderón demonstrates how Christianity itself was, by nature, a syncretic religion. Much has been discussed regarding the flexibility of Nahua devotional modalities and how they incorporated Christian practices into existing rituals following the Spanish conquest. As Frost notes: "Baptized Indians seem to have had little trouble taking the sacrament and participating in church life while continuing to worship idols and engage in divinatory practices. Many of these methods depended on the continued use of hallucinogenic plants." But, as she also points out, while the church and its extirpators concentrated their efforts on imperfect Indigenous assimilation of Christianity, they left a growing syncretism among Creoles and Spaniards unattended, unaware of the extent to which hallucinogens had come to influence non-Indians. Frost alludes to this when she describes how the consumption of hallucinogens in a religious setting cut across boundaries of class, race, and ethnicity and contributed significantly to what she terms "the fluidity that characterized the shifting belief systems of the colony." Christianity had weathered difficult periods in its ancient history by strategically engaging with syncretism, but the Renaissance along with both the Protestant and Catholic Reformations put an end to the dialectic between oppression and compromise that had characterized Christianity's reaction to religious hybridity.[9] New Spain, however, provided the perfect environment for syncretism to flourish and for the church's defenses to break down. Despite the great ambitions church and crown held for the transformation of the pagan land far from Europe with its schisms and religious wars, the reality proved to be radically different. In their introduction to their translation of Hernando Ruiz de Alarcón's seventeenth-century extirpation manual, J. Richard Andrews and Ross Hassig describe the religious panorama of seventeenth-century New Spain as one characterized by "poorly trained clergy, widespread indigenous practices, and multiple cross-cutting religious and inquisitional jurisdictions."[10] Orthodoxy could not flourish in such an environment. Clergy such as Ruiz de Alarcón and Jacinto de la Serna who set out to stamp out the persistence of Indigenous practices were poorly equipped for the challenge. Scholars have pointed out, for example, Ruiz de Alarcón's ignorance regarding the practices he describes and the tremendous misconceptions under which he labored.[11]

It is important to note that syncretism has been challenged as a concept for understanding the shifting patterns of both Christianity and Indigenous religion, with critics warning that it contains a "neocolonial substrate" which implies that the "third" product produced from the two cultures that meet and combine serves to create a whitening effect.[12] Solange Alberro explains, however, that while she uses the term "syncretism" to discuss the blending or meeting of religious beliefs and practices in New Spain, she understands this process as a negotiation rather than as a finished product. She terms it a "dynamic process resulting precisely from constant negotiations."[13] The daily interactions between people of different castes and traditions in both the marginalized neighborhoods of bustling cities and remote rural lands allowed these dynamic negotiations to occur. Despite the attempt to control the mixing of racial groups via a variety of exclusionary mechanisms such as the *traza*—an area of land in the center of the city exclusively for Spaniards—the realities of colonial society rendered such containment strategies impossible. Speaking specifically of women and the use of hallucinogenic substances within Indigenous rituals, Angélica Morales Sarabia describes the processes with which emotional communities were formed around the cultural and religious use of peyote and other hallucinogenic plants. While these traditions traced their origins to pre-Columbian traditions, they were also very much "alive in colonial homes" where women—"mothers, daughters, daughters-in-law, mulattoes, slaves, and domestic servants—lived in close-knit communities."[14]

The gendered component Morales Sarabia identifies in communities formed around the use of hallucinogenic substances, as well as the visions of the Virgin Mary and the infant Jesus that Ana Calderón experiences, recalls the similar experiences of visionary and mystical women who were often censured and persecuted for their unsupervised and supposedly extravagant relationship with the divine just as Calderón was. While women were not the only subjects whose piety took this form, they, more than men, found themselves singled out by Inquisition officials for heterodox practices. Following the Council of Trent, the church sought to rigorously curb women's visions by seeking to ascertain the theological basis of what these women claimed to have seen.[15] At issue was the question of authority. Women claimed authority for their connection with the divine as a consequence of these visions "and other extraordinary gifts."[16] Moreover, the church perceived these heterodox women and the affective communities they formed to be a threat to their rigid Tridentine model of Catholicism. These female embodied experiences challenged the church's controls over women predicated on the fear it had of their corporeality. Because of the extreme limits placed on their education, women's spirituality was often more connected to the body than the intellectualized worship that men such as the Jesuits practiced and which the church promoted as ideal.[17] The ecclesiastical authorities, however, placed women and other marginal subjects in a double bind since they excluded them from educational opportunities while at the same time frowning upon the practice of a more embodied piety. The church attempted to fashion a rigidly conceived model of female devotional practices that was primarily, although not exclusively, centered on the convent. Ecclesiastical authorities believed that the containment the convent seemingly afforded allowed them to better control and model female piety to conform to their exigencies. Other religious women lived a less controlled lifestyle, and through their visibility and the nature of their religiosity, they often found themselves contravening the church's control. Some of these women lived together in *beaterías*, which had some of the trappings of convents, but which allowed the *beatas* to enter and leave the secular world at will.

The unorthodox raptures experienced by women both within and without the convent could include, according to Nora Jaffary, "ecstasies, visions and locutions, bouts of diabolic possession and stigmata."[18] People of different classes and racial groups were drawn to these women, whom they considered to be holy, and would often consult them on spiritual matters or endeavor to witness their mystical transports, thus awarding them a visibility and fame that threatened the church's control.[19] Many of these women—almost all from the lower strata of society and many mulatta or mestiza—found themselves accused of faking their visions and of being false mystics.[20] In a seventeenth-century treatise on mysticism written for confessors, the Jesuit Miguel Godínez warns his readers to beware unstable women who eschew obedience to their confessor or other members of the religious hierarchy in favor of independent and unsupervised acts. He singles out as particularly prone to fakery "beatas melancólicas" (melancholic *beatas*) and "monjas principiantes de poco entendimiento" (young and foolish nuns). While he targets groups within both sexes for disapproval, according to the investigations of Antonio Rubial García and other historians,[21] most people accused of faking mystical experiences were indeed women, and thus Godínez's warnings speak to the gendered nature of these suspicions.[22]

While she herself was not a mystic—false or otherwise—the religious affections her vision inspired in her situate Ana Calderón outside the domain of the church's control and within a local emotional community. The specificity of her local, New Spanish reality is evidenced by the presence of the native *curandero*, and the description of the experience triggered by the hallucinogenic substance corresponds to the visionary transports of other women who "drew inspiration from local practices and from the lands and civilization in which they lived."[23] In her study of more than one hundred Inquisition trials of "false mystics" in seventeenth- and eighteenth-century Mexico, Jaffary shows how women accused of heterodoxy often employed Indigenous stimulants and mind-altering substances to induce what she terms "iluso paramysticism." She describes how several women were depicted as undergoing fits in which they vomited up objects including, in the case of Madre Paula Rosa de Jesús, pegs, wire pendants, and nails. Similar reactions occurred in the procedures used by *curanderas*, thus connecting the visions to products used in Indigenous remedies and healing. Other women's experiences involved visions incorporating New World content including angels dressed in Indigenous garments or subjects who described themselves as becoming a Black person during the throes of their mystical experience. It is difficult, however, to ascertain to just what degree visionary women were influenced by these hybrid practices drawn from Indigenous and Afro-Hispanic traditions.[24] What is apparent, however, is the suspicion and fear with which the church viewed possible connections between different racial groups facilitated by hybrid religious practices, as Frost clearly indicates in her discussion of the extirpation manuals and in the case of Ana Calderón before the Inquisition. If, as Barbara Rosenwein explains in *Emotional Communities in the Early Middle Ages*, emotional communities can be conceived of as a series of circles "none entirely concentric but rather distributed within the given space," we can see how the Inquisition endeavored, fruitlessly, to prevent intersections from occurring and to dismantle these communities of feeling through surveillance and punishment.[25]

Although visionary experiences brought many women—both nuns and laywomen—to the attention of the Inquisition, some scholars have viewed them as a vehicle for female agency. Rosalva Loreto López, for example, sees visionary nuns gaining subjectivity and a sense of self through this enhanced relationship with God and the path of virtue, prayer, and contemplation it offered.[26] The church did not want women to be singled out for special favors from God and wished to repress the religious affections their experiences afforded them. In this, women shared much with members of other marginalized communities, and so it is not surprising that local and non-liturgical devotional practices bound these groups together as we see in Ana Calderón's relationship with the Indigenous *curandero* as described by Frost. In navigating the restrictions their marginal status imposed, women and other subjugated subjects formed emotional communities from where they challenged the dominant narratives that attempted to circumscribe the character of their devotion and the religious affections these devotions inspired.

Notes

1. James C. Scott, "Domination and the Arts of Resistance," in *On Violence: A Reader*, ed. Bruce Lawrence and Aisha Karim (Durham: Duke University Press, 2007), 200.
2. Michel Foucault, "Two Lectures," in *Michel Foucault Power/Knowledge: Selected Interviews and Other Writings, 1972–1977*, ed. Colin Gordon (New York: Pantheon Books, 1980), 81–83.
3. Mary Giles, introduction to *Women in the Inquisition: Spain and the New World* (Baltimore: Johns Hopkins University Press, 1999), 1.
4. Nora Jaffary, *False Mystics: Deviant Orthodoxy in Colonial Mexico* (Lincoln: University of Nebraska Press, 2004), 16.
5. See María Elena Martínez's chapter "Changing Contours in the Age of Reform: 'Limpieza de sangre' in the Age of Reform" in her *Genealogical Fictions: Limpieza de Sangre, Religion, and Gender in Colonial Mexico* (Palo Alto: Stanford University Press, 2011), 227–64.
6. Viviana Díaz Balsera, "Atando dioses y humanos: Cipactónal y la cura por adivinación en el *Tratado sobre idolatrías* de Hernando Ruiz de Alarcón," in *Estudios coloniales latinoamericanos en el siglo XXI: Nuevos itinerarios*, ed. Stephanie Kirk (Pittsburgh: Instituto Internacional de Literatura Iberoamericana, 2011), 343.
7. William Christian Jr., "Catholicisms," in *Local Religion in Colonial Mexico*, ed. Martin Nesvig (Albuquerque: University of New Mexico Press, 2008), 260.
8. Christian, "Catholicisms," 260.
9. Carlos Eire, "The Concept of Popular Religion," in Nesvig, *Local Religion in Colonial Mexico*, 6–8.
10. James Richard Andrews and Ross Hassig, "Editor's Introduction," in Hernando Ruiz de Alarcón, *Treatise on the Heathen Superstitions: That Today Live Among the Indians Native to This New Spain* (1629), ed. James Richard Andrews and Ross Hassig (Norman: University of Oklahoma Press, 1987), 7.
11. Andrews and Hassig, "Editor's Introduction," 8.
12. Jossiana Arroyo, "Transculturation, Syncretism, and Hybridity," in *Critical Terms in Caribbean and Latin American Thought: Historical and Institutional Trajectories*, ed. Yolanda Martínez–San Miguel, Ben. Sifuentes-Jáuregui, and Marisa Belausteguigoitia (New York: Palgrave, 2016), 135.
13. Solange Alberro, *El águila y la cruz: orígenes religiosos de la conciencia criolla, México, siglos XVI–XVII* (Mexico City: Fondo de Cultura Económica, 2000), 29. Throughout the book, Alberro discusses how both the Franciscans and, most particularly, the Jesuits embraced a syncretic view of Christianity to better evangelize and incorporate the Indigenous neophytes into the church.

14. Angélica Morales Sarabia "The Culture of Peyote: Between Divination and Disease in Early Modern New Spain," in *Medical Cultures of the Early Modern Spanish Empire*, ed. John Slater, Maríaluz López-Terrada, and José Pardo-Tomás (Farnham: Ashgate, 2014), 22.
15. Giles, introduction, 6.
16. Giles, introduction, 13.
17. For a detailed discussion of the New Spanish church's fear of the female body as well as the historical genealogy of this emotion, see chapter 1 of my *Convent Life in Colonial Mexico: A Tale of Two Communities* (Gainesville: University of Florida Press, 2018).
18. Jaffary, *False Mystics*, 63.
19. Jaffary, *False Mystics*, 48–49.
20. In "Female Visionaries and Spirituality," in *Religion in New Spain*, ed. Susan Schroeder and Stafford Poole (Albuquerque: University of New Mexico Press, 2007), 163, Asunción Lavrin gives the most cogent explanation of the categories of mystic and visionary, which are often misused or conflated. She explains the relationship between the two identifying categories in the following terms: "Visionaries are in most cases mystics, and all mystics experienced visions." For Lavrin, then, a visionary implies someone who also follows a mystical path to achieve union with God. Mystics themselves strove to attain union with God. The chief or perhaps sole purpose of this union was the ineffable experience, but it could also provide a "venue whereby an important truth was communicated." A key difference between mystics and visionaries involved how the ecclesiastical authorities perceived their respective activities. Suspicion often fell on visionaries as priests raised doubts about the authenticity of their experiences or feared their visions might be the work of the devil, to whom women were most susceptible.
21. Antonio Rubial García, *La santidad controvertida: Hagiografía y conciencia criolla alrededor de los venerables no canonizados de Nueva España* (Mexico City: UNAM, Facultad de Filosofía y Letras/Fondo de Cultura Económica, 1999).
22. Miguel Godínez, *Práctica de la Theología Mystica* (Pamplona: En la Oficina de los Herederos de Martínez, 1761), 72.
23. Lavrin, "Female Visionaries and Spirituality," 161.
24. Jaffary, *False Mystics*, 103–4.
25. Barbara H. Rosenswein, *Emotional Communities in the Early Middle Ages* (Ithaca: Cornell University Press, 2006), 24.
26. Rosalva Loreto López, "Oír, ver y escribir: Los textos hagio-biográficos y espirituales del Padre Miguel Godínez. ca. 1630," in *Diálogos espirituales: Manuscritos femeninos hispanoamericanos siglos XVI–XIX*, ed. Asunción Lavrin and Rosalva Loreto López (Puebla: Instituto de Ciencias Sociales y Humanidades de la Benemérita Universidad Autónoma de Puebla, 2006), 157.

CHAPTER 7

Working Down a Bad Spirit

Slavery, Emotion, and the Inner Christ in the Early South

JON SENSBACH

Ailing and soul-weary, George Fox looked back on the founding years of Quaker struggle as a "cruel, bloody, persecuting time" when enemies ravened upon his followers like cannibals, "eating up the people like bread, and gnawing the flesh from their bones." Beatings, hangings, imprisonments, meetinghouse arson, and judicial intolerance from "the evil spirits of the world that warred against truth and Friends" had failed to quell the movement, but prophets were dead, survivors squabbled, and the Quakers' most militant days were already behind them. Still, though the world had failed to stay turned upside down, Fox remained a man of revelation, receiving in his despair a vision of New Jerusalem descending from heaven on one hand, and of the beast, the dragon, and the whore of Babylon drowning in the lake of fire on the other. Small wonder that, beset by the world's falseness and the tension of unresolved prophecy, and sensing another "violent storm of persecution coming suddenly on," he felt himself called across the ocean in 1671 to replenish a parched spirit: "It was upon me from the Lord to go beyond the seas to visit America." His destination: the satellite communities of believers who had fled persecution for North America and the West Indies.[1]

Wherever he went, God favored the battered evangelist with signs of approval for this emerging international fellowship of the heart. In Barbados, Fox was gratified to learn that an old enemy who had threatened to burn him alive was himself struck dead by a scorching fever—a "sad example" of divine justice, the Quaker leader noted without much sadness. In Virginia, where Governor William Berkeley had labeled the Friends "a pestilent sect" and the Assembly had denounced them as "an unreasonable and turbulent sort of people . . . teaching and publishing lies, miracles, false visions, prophesies and doctrines," Fox rallied his followers during "a heavenly meeting wherein the power of the Lord was so great that it struck a dread upon the assembly and chained all down." In the remote Albemarle region of northeastern Carolina, far from the control of Jamestown or Charles Towne, Quakers and other dissenters in the 1670s created egalitarian communities free to worship as they pleased. But during Fox's visit there, a physician challenged his claim that Native Americans contained the holy spirit. In rebuttal, Fox asked a Tuscarora chief whether he felt remorse for a wrong act, and the Indian's affirmative response proved that God dwelled in him, "sham[ing] the doctor before the governor and the people" so abjectly that he ran away, disavowing the scriptures. Finally, in Virginia, just before returning to England, Fox met with his flock to ensure that the important lessons stayed on, "sweeping away that which was to be swept out, and working down a bad spirit that was got up in some." With his soul restored, Fox left confident that God's prophetic word thrived among the Atlantic community of Friends.[2]

Though Fox did not elaborate on what sort of bad spirit needed "working down," it likely involved ordinary foibles like jealousy, anger, or selfishness, which he sought to purge for love, charity, humility, and harmony in the family of Christ. A good spirit, for Fox, was a spirit of agape, of sacred affections, the emotional glue that bound the Quakers together through a shared feeling of kinship with the Redeemer. Derived from the divine "inward light," that affinity—that friendship with Christ—could "sweep away that which was to be swept out." As the New England cleric Jonathan Edwards explained years later, "the first beginning and spring of holy affections" was found in "a love to divine things for the beauty and sweetness of their moral excellency." Infused with the "lamblike, dovelike spirit and temper of Jesus Christ," affections "naturally beget and promote such a spirit of love, meekness, quietness, mercy, and forgiveness as appeared in Christ." Edwards's taxonomy hews closely to the historian John Corrigan's description of religious affections as forms of "emotional knowledge" and "emotional relation to otherness" gained through perception and cognition. Anticipating Edwards, Fox exhorted the Quakers to venture far beyond any specific theology or practice to the interior realm of the heart; to gain emotional knowledge of one another and of Christ, they must be a Society of feeling.[3]

But Fox had not confronted every wayward impulse among Quakers in America, for his trip had put him in uneasy confrontation with their ownership of enslaved human beings. He had known about it for years, of course. In England during the 1650s, the group endured some of their most violent persecutions at the precise moment the African slave trade to the West Indies was accelerating, and Quakers began escaping to Barbados to take part in that colony's forest-decimating shift to sugarcane plantations. Though some went as indentured servants, and others as aspiring planters, so many bought enslaved persons that Fox struggled to reconcile the realization that his people—levelers, seekers, apostles of freedom, critics of power—were grafting a revolution of the spirit onto the revolution in sugar.

Expanded beyond a simple call to Christian fellowship, Fox's "working down a bad spirit" thus becomes a metaphor for the ethical lurching of Quakers and other Protestants cast adrift in the moral vacuum of Atlantic slavery. Christianity's complicity with, and often enthusiastic contributions to, the construction of hereditary slavery and early modern ideas of race needs little elaboration here. Emotions were a cornerstone of that project, because to enslave Africans, colonists claimed their heathenism made them incapable of Christian exaltation. New slave laws in the emerging British and Dutch colonies were the legal embodiment of an emotional force field that defined brown and black phenotypes as the outward reflection of inner monstrosity—loathsome, frightful, animalistic, devoid of affections, in need of permanent imprisonment.[4]

When the first antislavery protests stirred in the late seventeenth and early eighteenth centuries, therefore, they took place on the battleground of sentiment. Such few abolitionists as there were sought to convince white people that Africans could feel too—feel physical agony under the lash, emotional anguish in being unjustly spirited off into lifelong servitude, and psychic destruction at watching a child sold away forever. The "abolitionist insistence on black pathos," as Simon Gikandi has noted, affirmed a "black sensorium" of suffering and sorrow in contrast to the proslavery claim that enslaved workers were content. Slaveholders, the argument went, were damaging their own souls by manifestly not doing unto others. Historians have understood the appeal to sympathy and self-purification as an important chapter in the history of eighteenth-century emotions. Ethical knowledge and values, as scholars have argued and as the abolition movement demonstrated, can draw vital inspiration from emotions. But the emphasis on Black distress underplays the other side of the challenge to slavery: love, the kind of love shown by Black people themselves toward Christ. African Americans argued that they could give and receive spiritual love as only Jesus could. The souls of Black folk housed, or had the potential to house, Christ himself; how, then, could white people enslave their brothers and sisters in the spirit?[5]

Pathos and love converged in the remarkable epiphany of one ordinary white Quaker named George Walton during the American Revolution. Walton's radical imagination transcended the idea that African Americans embraced Jesus; he became convinced they actually represented the embodied Christ, thereby radiating the "beauty and sweetness of their moral excellency," as Jonathan Edwards might have said. Walton came to regard himself as formed by, and beholden to, the Black soul of Christ. As Walton saw it, enslaved Black people must save and sanctify whites; the Black Jesus's martyrdom would emancipate mankind from the sin of slavery. Walton's prophecy catalyzed North Carolina Quakers to emancipate enslaved persons and embroiled them in a years-long legal struggle with hostile state authorities over their right to do so. This essay argues that Walton's vision represents an extreme example of some white people's ability to imagine the emotional lives of African Americans with empathy rather than sympathy. At the same time, we fall short by limiting our focus to Anglo-American sensibilities in the eighteenth-century struggle against slavery. Rather, the "holy affections" of white and Black Americans became deeply enmeshed. The divine love that inundated Black and white alike promised to revolutionize humanity from within, or so it seemed. More than a plea for moral cleansing by white people, the pulsing heartbeat of abolition was the idea of African American godliness and moral superiority. On this emotional palette, the principal color was black.

* * *

God "hath made *all nations of one blood*," wrote George Fox in his 1657 letter "To Friends beyond the Sea that Have Blacks and Indian Slaves." Fox did not protest slaveholding by Quakers, but he urged them to teach Christianity to enslaved workers: "The gospel is preached to every creature under heaven; which is the power that giveth liberty and freedom, and is glad tidings to every captivated creature under the whole heaven." The indwelling Christ could reveal himself in the enslaved body as much as in anyone.[6]

Fox's appeal represents an early radical Protestant effort to smooth the ragged edge of slavery through humanitarian feeling for fellow human beings. His first sight of slavery after arriving in Barbados in 1671 strengthened his determination. Though appalled at the violence he saw, he was more concerned with the flourishing of what he considered barbaric African religions and polygamous mating practices. He accused colonial authorities and planters of tolerating this immorality by withholding Christianity from Africans. It was imperative for Quakers to "preach the everlasting Covenant, Christ Jesus, to the *Ethyopians,* the *Blacks* and the *Tawny-Moors* in your families." Fox invoked biblical precedent in encouraging Quakers to treat their enslaved persons gently and to liberate them after seven years, which may have been either a proto-abolitionist stance or simply a reflection of the fluid nature of West Indian slavery, which was in the process of becoming permanently heritable. At the same time, he vigorously refuted as "a most abominable untruth" the "slander" that Friends promoted slave rebellion, assuring the governor that Quakers urged enslaved persons to live with Christian humility and love for their enslavers. Unconvinced, authorities labeled the Friends subversive, though their preaching yielded only a few African Christians, and Barbadian legislators passed statutes explicitly stating that baptism could not be a pathway to emancipation. These laws became an influential template throughout the English Atlantic as emerging slave societies denied Africans freedom while prescribing when and how they could learn of Christianity. Still, here was a new Quaker spirit in America—a vague discomfort with the ownership of human property, a vow to garb it in gospel humanity and good intent, and resolute promises to uphold the tyrannical social order anyway.[7]

But it was Quakers, joined by Dutch and German Mennonites, in Germantown, Pennsylvania, who pushed further, lodging what is widely considered the first formal antislavery protest in colonial America, in 1688. No sooner had the Quakers settled in the colony than they began importing so many Africans for domestic and agricultural work that their fellow Quakers, led by Daniel Francis Pastorious, petitioned the monthly meeting: "Here is liberty of conscience which is right and reasonable; here ought to be liberty of ye body." It was unchristian to steal people and sell them into slavery. "Do consider, you who do it, if you would be done at this manner? And if it is done according to Christianity?" Their petition made little difference, but it forecast a standard antislavery rhetorical ploy in later decades: Imagine yourselves, slaveholders, as enslaved, and show kindly feeling toward those you claim as property.[8]

Among Euro-Americans, Christianity offered the only possible lexicon of dissent against the totalizing assertions that Africans were demons, that they had no souls, that they could not feel, or that they were not even people. Challenging the "Fiction of the Brutality of the *Negro's*," the Anglican minister Morgan Godwyn argued in 1680 that "God looks upon the Heart, not Colour." All men, he insisted, have "the natural right to the Privileges of Religion. . . . *Negro's* are Men, and therefore are invested with the same right, and to deprive them of this right is the highest injustice." Godwyn was no antislavery activist, and he meant the natural right to embrace Christianity, but in situating human essence in the heart rather than in superficial external markers like skin pigmentation, he was according fellowship in the most exalted kind of sentient community to Africans. Christianity alone gave Godwyn, Fox, Pastorious, and others the vision to see people of African descent, the imagination to recognize them as spiritual beings, the vocabulary to extend to them the not yet universally acclaimed idea of "natural rights," and the ability to feel kinship with damned and exploited people consigned to existential nothingness. The belief that African bodies and minds could also contain the inner Christ was the most powerful source of affective comradeship with the enslaved available to white people, when they acknowledged it. The realization that Africans could think, feel, love, and suffer as Christ did gave them an emotional visibility that legal codes and the machinery of the slave trade had erased.[9]

This fundamental recognition generated responses along a spectrum of sensibilities shading somewhere between pity, sympathy, compassion, and empathy: from a mild conviction that white Christians ought not to treat enslaved people inhumanely, to the notion that Black folk could sit in church, learn something about the Bible, and be baptized; and to the determined missionary outreach among enslaved plantation workers by the Moravians. Perhaps the most militant response of all came from the Quaker Benjamin Lay, a cave-dwelling vegetarian dwarf born in England in 1682, who emigrated to Pennsylvania in the 1730s. Radicalized by travels as a seaman to Barbados which exposed him to slavery's barbarism, he shunned all goods produced by slave labor, particularly sugar, and wrote a tract called *All Slave-Keepers That Keep the Innocent in Bondage, Apostates*. An abrasive, dogmatic character who tolerated no compromise with what he considered an evil institution, he attacked all slaveholders, including many of Philadelphia's wealthy Quaker elite, as infidels who would roast for eternity. Lay considered moderate solutions, gradual emancipation, and the like to be just as depraved. His stridency got him kicked out of Quaker meetings on both sides of the Atlantic, but his philosophy and methods laid the groundwork for the next generation of the more polished Quaker abolitionists John Woolman and Anthony Benezet, often considered the progenitors of the modern abolitionist movement.[10]

Just as critically, Black people themselves prized wide open a door that was partly ajar to assert a claim to equality in the family of Christ as the irrefutable basis of bodily liberty. This claim was explicit, for example, in the freedom petition and anti–slave trade protest of an enslaved parishioner named Greenwich in Canterbury, Connecticut, in 1754: "Some say that we are the seed of Canaan and some say that we are the Tribe of Ham but Let that be as it will Justise must Take Plase." It was written in the scriptures, he continued, that "non[e] should impose upon another nation" and that it was ungodly to supply arms to combatants in a "continual war amongst themselves" and "when you have don this you will steel as many of them and bring over Into your Contry to make slaves of them their soul and body." This was the logic that transformed Morgan Godwyn's belief in the "natural right to the Privileges of Religion" into what a group of enslaved petitioners in Boston in 1774 called "a natural right to our freedoms." For "how can the master and the slave," the petitioners asked, "be said to fulfill that command Live in love let Brotherly Love contuner and abound Beare yea one nothers Bordenes. How can the master be said to Beare my Borden when he Beares me down with the . . . chanes of slavery." This was the logic that fueled the genesis of Black evangelical Christianity in America.[11]

These protests suggest that religion lies at an important intersection of the history of Atlantic slavery and the history of emotions, and that at this junction are interwoven the tangled emotions of both enslaver and enslaved. After years of documenting, and occasionally celebrating, the resistance and agency of enslaved people, historians again remind us that the foundation of the system was violence—remorseless, boundless, grotesque violence, without pity or conscience, which aimed to terrorize and infantilize those who paid a catastrophic human cost in psychological damage. The slave ship, writes Stephanie Smallwood, "reduced African captives to an existence so physically atomized . . . so socially impoverished as to threaten annihilation of the self, the complete disintegration of personhood." Did that personhood survive in America? The dominant emotion for those trapped in the vast apparatus of auction block, whipping post, and countinghouse was terror. "In countries where slavery is established," declared the Jamaican planter Bryan Edwards in 1801, "the leading principle on which the government is supported is fear; or a sense of that absolute coercive necessity which, leaving no choice of action, supersedes all questions of right." And coercion, writes the historian Vincent Brown, rested not only on physical intimidation but also on elaborate attempts to "terrorize the spiritual imaginations of the enslaved." Because captive Africans often committed suicide in despair or defiance, and in the belief that their souls would return to Africa, planters decapitated and mutilated the bodies to convince the living that their spirits could not escape. Such were the tactics in the spiritual war against the African self—"soul murder" in Nell Painter's memorable phrase.[12]

Though Christianity played a fundamental part in this emotional assault, the concept of Christ within Africans also challenged the spiritual and social death of enslavement. This challenge unfolded in many places—in the West Indies, the northern colonies, in West Africa itself, and in the eighteenth-century southern British colonies, which were immersed in intersecting Protestant revival movements from northern Europe to the British Isles and North America. Welling up from diverse strands of Continental Pietism, evangelical Anglicanism, New England Congregationalism, and numerous dissenting traditions, these movements sought an urgent sense of emotional experience grounded in the individual's relationship with God. As Baptists, Methodists, Presbyterians, Moravians, and others took root from Virginia through the Carolinas and Georgia, their congregations coalesced around the sensory and linguistic vernaculars of the redeemed family: the touch of hands laid on shoulders, of lips kissing cheeks; the feel of water sprinkled on heads or poured in foot-washing tubs; the sound of kinship in the words "brother" and "sister"; the sight of fellow seekers gathered by the river; the quickening of Jesus in the heart. Evangelicals and African Americans reached out to enfold each other in such communities of the spirit. In 1740, after George Whitefield's visit to South Carolina, a "Moorish slave woman on a plantation" was overheard "singing a spiritual at the water's edge," and enslaved workers were said to be learning "a Parcel of Cant-Phrases, Trances, Dreams, Visions and revelations" and doing "nothing but pray and sing and thereby neglect their work." Such reports alarmed planters opposed to the dangers of spiritual equality.[13]

By the 1760s, however, white and Black congregants worshiped alongside each other in evangelical churches throughout the South, and explicitly conceived of themselves as forums for expressing and negotiating the emotions evoked by sacred experience, such as ecstasy, anxiety, gratitude, insecurity, and above all love. These "emotional communities," in the historian Barbara Rosenwein's phrase, became the most visible venues in eighteenth-century slave society for Black and white Christians to share and explore sentiments together, though of course the enslavement of Black worshipers meant these exchanges were inherently unequal. Some enslaved congregants, however, used the church "courts," where behavioral complaints were adjudicated, sometimes successfully, to bring charges of mistreatment against their own enslavers and win promises of more Christian treatment. African American lay preachers in Baptist, Methodist, and Presbyterian churches, many of whom were said to have extraordinary spiritual gifts, exhorted white and Black congregations, often in a charismatic, emotional style that drew upon both evangelical and African precedents. At the same time, while white appreciation for African spiritual sensibilities did not generally translate into respect for African religions themselves, African deities lived on in secrecy in southern slave quarters, kept alive by spiritual practitioners who often incorporated Christian idioms into traditional practices as complementary sources of sacred power.[14]

* * *

It was in the Quaker settlements of eastern North Carolina, the same region visited by George Fox in 1671, that the conviction of the indwelling Christ resonated perhaps as nowhere else in the eighteenth-century

South. Quakers in Perquimans and Pasquotank Counties enslaved people, but a hundred years after Fox's visit, as the colonies moved closer to rebellion, local Quakers linked the independence movement to the natural rights of Black people and began setting enslaved people free. Their emancipation movement represented a little-known southern front in the nascent transatlantic abolitionist movement, with principal nodes in Pennsylvania, London, and Manchester. This campaign derived its moral force by appealing to the sentiments of slaveholders to make them feel, not guilt, but an emotional identification with the enslaved. God's love was the wellspring of this imaginative spark. In North Carolina, that inspiration was filtered through the particular vision of George Walton, who located the divinity in people of African descent themselves, generating his and fellow Quakers' years-long antislavery crusade. A sea captain of modest learning who lacked the intellectual stature of John Woolman or Anthony Benezet, Walton is not known as a giant of abolition, but perhaps without fully realizing it, he followed their example, and his own experience shows the radical extent to which the revolution in affections could transform the self and ignite a desire to spread that transformation into the heart of southern slavery.[15]

Woolman himself had, in fact, been deeply influenced by his visits to the Quaker communities of remote "down east" North Carolina in 1746 and 1757, which exposed him, like Fox and Lay in Barbados, to the cruelties of a society in which anywhere from half to a majority of the population was enslaved. This realization fueled in Woolman a guilty purging of his own feelings of complicity in racism and slavery that led to the publication of his tract *Some Considerations on the Keeping of Negroes* in 1754. Woolman and Benezet, whose *Observations on the Inslaving, Importing, and Purchasing of Negroes* from 1759 was the other major Quaker antislavery manifesto from that decade, challenged the reigning intellectual and literary celebration of the passions as giving free rein to selfishness at the expense of others. For Woolman and Benezet, mankind's highest calling was to subordinate the self through God's love for the betterment of others. In this they both anticipated and echoed Adam Smith, who in his *Theory of Moral Sentiments* of 1759 argued: "To feel much for others and little for ourselves . . . to restrain our selfish, and to indulge our benevolent, affections, constitutes the perfection of human nature. . . . One great affection [should] take the place of all the others, the love of the Deity." In like vein, Benezet in 1759 pronounced himself prepared to "declare open War against the Kingdom of Self." The captivity of white colonists by Indians during the French and Indian War, he argued, ought to "teach us to feel for others" and renounce the trade in African captives: "While we feel for our own Flesh and Blood, let us extend our Thoughts to others . . . I mean . . . the poor Negroes." Critiquing the passions while praising feelings, he and Woolman argued that emotions were a fundamental element of natural equality and that enslavers owed it to God to imagine that Africans were capable of emotions too. This was the heart of "benevolent affections": the ability to imagine that opened the righteous pathway to self-discipline, moral purification, and a singular identity for Friends through abolition.[16]

Though religious antislavery drew upon natural rights philosophy, it also stood in stark contrast to the emerging racial science of the Enlightenment, which assigned people of African descent to humanity's bottom rung largely on the basis of a perceived lack of emotion. For Kant, Hume, Blumenbach, and Winckelmann, a dark-skinned phenotype reflected a phlegmatic soul ungraced by reason, sentiment, or beauty. "The Negroes of Africa have by nature no feeling that arises above the trifling," irrespective of whether they were enslaved or free, wrote Kant in *Observations on the Feeling of the Beautiful and the Sublime*, a judgment notoriously echoed by Jefferson, for whom the "eternal monotony [in] . . . that immoveable veil of black" shrouded all emotions in Black people. Africans' lack of emotion and reason excluded them from the embrace of modernity and the achievements of the enlightened self. Thus, if feeling—the ability to appreciate the sublime—undergirded the superiority of whiteness, then the Quaker insistence that Africans could feel as well undermined that very premise.[17]

There is no evidence that George Walton had read Woolman or Benezet or that his fellow Quakers in Perquimans County, North Carolina, were much influenced by Woolman's last visit among them in 1757, but their yearly meetings were part of the transatlantic circuit of both mailings and itinerant preachers, and so by the 1760s, Carolina Friends were certainly well attuned to the discussions about slavery. In 1768 the colony's yearly meeting declared that "the having of Negroes is become a Burthen to such as are in possession of them" and advised Friends to avoid the practice. In 1772 the meeting denounced the "great Evil and Abomination of the Importation of Negroes from Affica," by which "Iniquitious Practice Great

Numbers of our fellow Creatures with their Posterity are Doom'd to Perpetual and Cruel Bondage." The petition, however, fell back on the familiar refrain that the chief harm of slavery was its damage to white people: slaves "are become Nurseries to Pride, and Idleness, to our youth in such a manner that Morality and true Piety is much wounded." How much Walton knew of these protests is unclear; he enslaved people himself and was a recent convert to the faith, having been drawn to join in 1772 by a woman he wanted to marry. Whatever romantic calculus figured in that decision, it led him to a place in life he scarcely could have imagined.[18]

It started, as for many Quakers, with a dream. In 1772 Walton dreamed he was walking through a town looking for a meetinghouse.[19] He gave some clothes to a woman who greeted him deferentially, then continued up a "wet and Slippy" mountain, where he "overtook a Man which Appear'd to be a Gentleman, and I thought a Boy on his Right Hand which appear'd to be Black, I thought I did not like this Gentlemans Company and was going to run up the Hill, betwixt him and the Boy." Threatening him with a stick, the man tried to stop him, "saying I should not run in his Ground [because] I should make it rough and full of Holes so that others might come up also." At that point the boy, who Walton had assumed was a servant or enslaved, "gave me a stick that I might fight my way, it was all woolded or bound round So that it could not be Split." So armed, Walton made his way to the top of the mountain, where his adversary slipped and fell away.

After recording his dream in elaborate detail the next day, Walton interpreted it. His search for a meetinghouse, he believed, was a quest to "find truth amongst Gaity and Pleasures of this life." The woman who flattered him represented hypocritical Christians who masked their insincerity by posing as devout churchgoers; his own gift to her of clothes was a sign to "forsake all trade and the way of life I am now in." The slippery path up the mountain was his sojourn through the world—and the man who tried to block him, the devil. "The Small Black Boy at my right hand," he wrote, "is Christ Which was represented Black, to shew how much the Devil is exalted and Christ abased." The stick the boy handed him "was his Holy Spirit Bound round with truth So that it could not be Shaken by which I must fight against all the Slippery paths and wiles of Satan." To reach the summit was to enter the world for the first time; his enemy's tumble off the mountain was the fall of Satan.

Walton's dream revealed the catharsis of a sinner shedding a life of illusion and falsehood for a righteous path of absolution and purity. In describing their religious experiences, Quakers did not typically use the language of the "new birth" as evangelicals did, but Walton's dream essentially depicted the pangs of someone being born again. The midwife was Christ—not just any Christ, but a Black Christ, who defended him from Satan, guided him up the mountain, showed him a new way to live in the world. In a society beholden to the idea of a people's racial captivity, the dream was a jarring epiphany, a revelation steeped in biblical imagery, mystical elements, and prescriptions for sanctified living as though from an old prophet orating on a mountaintop. Whereas most Quakers of a previous generation, along with Pietists, evangelicals, and church people of various stripes, could acknowledge that Black people had emotions, had spirituality, had love and hope, had—or could have—Christ within them, in Walton's vision they *were* all of those things. Black people were Christ. They did more than simply evoke sympathy, pity, and remorse; they were the wellspring of emotion itself.

In this regard, the boy in Walton's dream represented what Mechal Sobel has called white people's "black alien other." In the eighteenth century, white narrators often described a tormented journey to a new self. Dreams revealed difficult turning points or life choices to be made on the way even as they gave guidance on how to make those choices. "Interior landscapes and dream actions," Sobel notes, "were often directly connected to social reality and future realization, and particularly to the changing perception of the nature of individuality and self-development." That change in self-awareness was often defined in opposition to, or projected upon, a Black figure who evoked a range of emotions—guilt, shame, revulsion, attraction—that demanded introspection and response. In Walton's case, Blackness itself was the purgative for an agonized conscience; the Black Christ took white people's sins upon himself. After all, as Walton pointed out in a letter to another Friend, Christ "came down among wicked men Suffering Persecutions, reviling, mocking, Scoffings, Spittings Buffetings Scourgings, and even the Painful, and Shamefull Death of the Cross, to Redeem Sinners and Do we so lightly regard his Sufferings that we cant follow the meek and humble example he set us." Deconstructing his own whiteness, Walton realized that he and other "white" people existed *because* of Black people, or more specifically, because of Black Christliness. The main problem with slavery, he understood, was no longer simply the harm it did to white people but the torment it inflicted on Christ. And if that was the case, the question became not whether Black people had the spirit within but whether whites did. Circuitously, Walton was coming to the conclusion Benjamin Lay had reached years earlier: no slaveholder could reasonably conceive of spending an afterlife anywhere other than in a lake of fire. Through his color-inverted dream, in which Black people became the source of life, Walton was working down a very bad spirit.[20]

There were precedents for imagining Christ as Black, or at least as a holy being who was not white. The statuary, crucifixes, and other iconography of African Catholics in seventeenth- and eighteenth-century Kongo portray Christ as African. Walton would not have known these images, but to dream of Christ as an enslaved, scourged person of African descent was partly the product of a restless colonial American culture that yearned to see Christ but did not envision him as having any particular complexion. Puritans had forbidden any depictions of Christ as idolatrous, and colonial Americans were largely unfamiliar with the representation of Christ as "white" in European artistic tradition. After the Great Awakening in the eighteenth century, ordinary people longing for a personal relationship with Christ visualized him not as phenotypically white but as a source of blinding light, of purity unconnected to color. The color white, in fact, did not necessarily represent purity, and might even have signaled the opposite. According to the *Universal Dream-Dictionary* of 1795, white or pale skin represented "a sign of trouble, poverty and death," whereas a "black face" meant "long life." "The lack of association between Jesus and whiteness," according to the historians Edward Blum and Paul Harvey, "left the spiritual terrain open to linking other colors and peoples to the sacred." In 1757, Quaker John Churchman dreamed of an "angelic apparition," seven feet tall, with the complexion of a Native American. "It was not unreasonable to conclude," Churchman reasoned, "that the Lord was in them [Native Americans] by his good Spirit, and that all colours were equal to him, who gave life and being to all mankind." There is no indication that George Walton knew of the dream experiences of other Quakers like Churchman, and he dreamed of the Black Christ twenty years before the *Universal Dream-Dictionary*'s positive interpretation of Black faces, but he was likely inspired in part by a long-standing openness to seeing the sacred in different appearances.[21]

Once seen, the Black specter of reproach kept haunting him. In another dream, "a Black man Seemingly one that had not been long from his own Country, who could Scarcely Speak English," chastised two Friends for supporting the slave trade. "The Black Seem'd to be Weeping, and told them he was very much troubled at those Wars, and fightings, and beg'd them to keep out of them." Less complex than his previous vision, the dream gave Walton an easy interpretation; he saw it as an indictment of Quakers, and white people generally, for pride, avarice, and abandoning God's word. "Be assured there is a day of firey tryall coming upon the Land, that the Children of God may be tried and purified." The dream also "has brought me under deep thought concerning the workings of divine providence, and my firm belief [that the] Blacks will become a People in which God will be Glorified, and Shew forth his Power, for the Knowledge of the Lord must cover the Earth as the Water's cover the sea." He described the dream as "Sweet and refreshing" because of its sense of assurance, its prescription for change, and its unambiguous moral lesson.[22]

Walton's accounts forge a strong connection between the rhetoric of feeling, bodily sensation, and the acquisition of knowledge. According to Ann Marie Plane and Leslie Tuttle, dreams, as emanations of our inner selves, "rely on a pictorial or metaphorical language" whose "content is guided 'by the emotions of the dreamer.'" Emotions, in turn, as another scholar argues, "emerge from bodily knowledge." A strong tradition in medieval and early modern Christianity considered dreams to be prophetic visitations, and Walton certainly regarded his own dreams in that way. His language was vividly pictorial and metaphorical: the Black Christ is mocked, beaten, and crucified, then, transfigured, he ascends, guides, triumphs, redeems. As the body of Christ represents the corporate Christian body, Walton evokes powerful images of both bodies enduring agonizing trials before being cleansed by the "hydraulic" flooding of divine emotional knowledge, as the oceanic comparison suggests. Walton's interpretation of what he had seen and experienced in his dreams thus confirms his own newfound bodily and emotional awareness. If Christ was life itself, and if Christ was Black, then he, Walton, must be Black too. Walton did not necessarily make that conceptual leap, but he now knew what Christ knew: the world must fall for it to rise again.[23]

Thus fortified, Walton began to see himself as an agent of providence to hasten the death of slavery. He wrote several long letters to Friends arguing "how contrary it is to truth and Holiness and the Spirit of Christ" that Black people were enslaved. "God has heard their cries and seen Affliction and will certainly deliver them from under the Yoke of Bondage," he predicted. To persist in the practice was to serve an "Enemy who . . . is as unwilling to let you out of Spiritual Bondage, as you are to let the Blacks out of outward Bondage." He appealed to the logic of natural law. "By birthright the Blacks are a free people as well as we, and God created all mankind for his honour, and glory, and to Shew forth his Power; therefore we are not to Judge them because [they] are Black, or to bring into Bondage those whom God created free." But his main appeal was to the conscience, to sentiment, to the inner light. "The Spirit of Christ opens the Prison Doors, and Sets the bond Servant free. . . . God searches the Heart and the veins; all outward shew or formal Cerimonies avail nothing if the Heart is not right with God." When Perquimans County appointed him to lead a slave patrol after fears of rebellion surfaced in 1775, he refused, citing Quaker pacifism as well as his opposition to slavery itself. Lamenting the "Spirit of AntiChrist that now rules in the hearts of many," he wrote in his journal that a patrol "most certainly can't proceed from the Spirit of Christ Jesus to Usurp the Liberty of our fellow creatures . . . to take them up and have them Whip'd without committing any other crime, but only walking peaceably along the Road, or being at Home with their Wives." Christ's spirit "is full of Mercy and Compassion, and tender Love to all Men," Walton wrote. Enslavers of Christ represented the inverse—Satan.[24]

Walton left little information about those he enslaved or how they and others of African origin might have influenced his dreams and epiphanies. On the eve of the American Revolution, about one-third of the enslaved population of eastern North Carolina had been born in Africa, and like earlier opponents of slavery such as Benjamin Lay, Walton likely saw regularly, and probably knew, survivors of the slave trade whose travails moved and galvanized him. Hoping to bring forth the inner Christ in them, Walton and other Quakers began holding religious meetings for Africans and African Americans, as George Fox had done a century earlier in Barbados, and in keeping with Anthony Benezet's school for Black people in Philadelphia. "Our Friend Sarah Metcalf Appointed a Meeting for the Blacks and desired that Moses Bundy & I would be there if we found freedom which Accordingly we both were," he wrote in his journal in 1777, "and it was a very tender time many good Cautions and Advices being given." A week later Quakers held another "Meeting for the Blacks at pineny Woods," where "many good Counsels & Exhortation[s] were deliver'd and I beleive Some of the Blacks were tender and I hope may Remmerber the good Advice given them." Whether such meetings persisted or generated a small community of Black Quakers is unclear, but African Americans might have found cognitive resonance between the Quaker inner light and the spirit visions and continuous revelations of African faith traditions.[25]

With pressure from Walton and others, North Carolina Friends denounced slavery all the louder. The 1775 yearly meeting called it "inconsistent with righteousness" and advised members who owned slaves to "cleanse their hands of them" quickly. The next year's meeting prohibited Friends from buying and selling slaves. Walton, who had not yet freed those he enslaved, did so that year along with thirteen other Friends; together they emancipated forty people. Forecasting "that awfull day" when "Earth shall disclose her Blood and no more cover Slain [Isaiah 26:21]," the meeting declared in 1777 that slave traders and masters were "partakers with Murtherers and Men stealers," and if "Men should be permitted to Reduce [such people] to a State of Bondage and Slavery, the guilt will be laid" to their account." Their manumission campaign, they contended, "hath the Sanction of Divine Approbation and ought to be Approved by all Reasonable Men."[26]

Walton was not the only slaveholding southerner in the late eighteenth century to receive emancipatory visions, nor were Quakers the only white southerners to call for an end to slavery. Religious fellowship with enslaved Christians prompted some planters to emancipate their siblings in Christ and some congregations to forbid enslavers among them. Soon after his conversion and entry into the Methodist Church in 1771, for example, Freeborn Garrettson of Maryland had a vision from God to free his slaves, which he promptly did, then embarked on a long career as a Methodist preacher and antislavery activist. Methodist leaders, including Garrettson, argued in 1780 that slavery was "contrary to the laws of God, man, and nature, and hurtful to society, contrary to the dictates of consciences and pure religion." Methodist slaveholders were given two years to free their slaves or leave the church. Baptists and Presbyterians made similar antislavery statements and likewise took measures to turn slaveholders out of fellowship. The wealthy planter Robert Carter III of

Westmoreland County, Virginia, converted to the Baptist faith in 1778 and came to believe that slavery was unlawful in the eyes of God. Inspired by the Swedish mystic Emanuel Swedenborg, he had a revelation he likened to a sort of spiritual death and declared that "the toleration of slavery indicates very great depravity of mind." He began manumitting those he had enslaved and eventually set some five hundred free. As such examples indicate, many slaveholders made a connection between religious experience and African American freedom, but George Walton's vision was perhaps singular in identifying a Black Christ figure as the source of eternal life, conflating the emotional worlds of white and Black alike.[27]

As defenders of slavery recoiled at the actions of people like Garrettson and Carter, they harassed antislavery evangelicals and passed laws making it more difficult to emancipate slaves. Authorities in North Carolina responded similarly to the Quaker emancipations. At a time when the British army was offering freedom to slaves of American rebels to help suppress their insurrection against the crown, the Quaker actions alarmed revolutionary state legislators. Through the Carolinas and Virginia, enslaved people tried to escape to find freedom with the British, and though there is no record that person enslaved by Quakers attempted to do so, the Quaker attack on slavery seemed further incitement to insubordination. Reiterating previous colonial statutes, the General Assembly of North Carolina in 1777 outlawed all manumissions (except for "meritorious service") as an "evil and pernicious Practice" and authorized the seizure and resale of freedpeople. In court, the Quakers argued that the law should not apply to those freed before its passage, but the court denied their appeal, and twenty-nine people were rounded up and jailed. The Quakers hired three lawyers to argue their case in court, but they lost, and the twenty-nine were sold at auction back into slavery. In its vindictiveness, the court even denied Quaker Thomas Newby's attempt to free his slave Hannah for meritorious service as a skilled midwife to both Black and white women.[28]

For the next twenty years the Quakers did legal battle with the state of North Carolina for the right to emancipate enslaved people. In 1778 a court of appeals overturned the state's authority to re-enslave those manumitted before 1777, but new legislation the next year reaffirmed the state's right to re-enslave. Asserting the rightness of restoring to "the much Injured Affricans . . . that Liberty and Freedom which is a Natural and Unalienable Right of all Mankind," the Quakers carried on quietly, and illegally, manumitting enslaved persons in defiance of a "cruel and barbarous human law." Many of these freedpeople continued to live on their former masters' property but were captured and re-enslaved, some after being betrayed by informers, whom the Quakers bitterly denounced. When Quakers tried to transport enslaved persons to Pennsylvania and manumit them there, North Carolina claimed the right to track them as escapees under the Constitution's Fugitive Slave Clause. "Instead of peace-makers," one congressman "looked upon the Quakers as warmakers, as they were continually endeavoring to stir up insurrections among the Negroes." A bill passed in 1797 asserted that because the "secret artifices of the Quakers" made it "difficult to discover and prove the actual emancipation of the Negroes," any African American "found to be going at large, or living in bye-places, or under the actual control and service of the owner" would be presumed to be emancipated and liable to arrest.[29]

In all, between 1777 and 1797 the state re-enslaved at least 134 people manumitted by the North Carolina Quakers. The Quakers kept a list of their names, several of which suggest African birth, such as Cuffee, Mingo, Cudgo, Sibba, Quea, and Zango. In sparse detail, the list describes the human costs of the state's punitive re-enslavement policy. "Glasgow and Jack carried a very considerable distance from their wives & children," according to one notation; "Tom and wife sold from their children," reads another. David was "parted from his wife & children," Jenny was "carried into the back country from her children," Hagar was "carried to South Carolina from her husband and children." There were others "that have been emancipated, sold as slaves again, and many instances of children born after their mothers were freed, sold with their mothers; in some cases sold and parted from their parents when small." The list reads like a catalogue of atrocities against Christ that the Quakers said would be punished with righteous fire. Among the re-enslaved was George Walton's own former slave Dinah. Was it she, or perhaps someone on the list, someone who infiltrated his consciousness, and his subconscious, inspiring him to dream of the Black Christ?[30]

Walton's own part in the story ended unhappily. During the 1780s, the Perquimans monthly meeting reprimanded him and his wife, Mary, repeatedly for alcoholism, finally "disowning" them for good in 1789. George Walton died later that year. But the chain reaction of events inspired by his dream played out long afterward. In 1797 the plight of manumitted people became public knowledge when four free men of color in Philadelphia petitioned the U.S. Congress for relief from persecution. Now recognized as the first Black petitioners to Congress, they were among those set free by North Carolina Quakers only to endure the terror of being "hunted day and night, like beasts of the forest, by armed men with dogs." After being emancipated, Jupiter Nicholson had been a sailor for two years, but on coming ashore was immediately chased by slave catchers. He escaped to Virginia, from where he made it to Philadelphia. Jacob Nicholson, "being pursued day and night . . . was obliged to leave [his] abode, sleep in the woods, and stacks in the fields to escape the hands of violent men who, induced by the profit afforded them by law, followed this course as a business." Job Albert and his wife "were night and day hunted by men armed with guns, swords, and pistols, accompanied with mastiff dogs," and were eventually seized, bound, and jailed. Aided by a white fellow prisoner, they escaped and fled to Philadelphia, but Albert's mother and sister were sold back into slavery after being set free. Thomas Pritchett cleared his own land and planted thirty barrels' worth of corn, but after a neighbor threatened to turn him in unless he came to work for him, Pritchett fled.[31]

Years later, such tales of harrowing flight from remorseless slave catchers became stock tropes in ex-slave narratives and abolitionist literature, but in 1797 they were not much in public discourse or awareness. Aided by Philadelphia Quakers and the African American religious leaders Richard Allen and Absalom Jones, the petitioners anticipated the later abolitionist strategy of appealing to the emotions of white audiences to convince them of the suffering of Black people who wanted only the "human right to freedom." They sought, among other things, to have the Fugitive Slave Act of 1793 repealed. They were convinced, they said, that congressmen were "men of liberal minds, susceptible of benevolent feelings . . . who can admit that black people (servile as their condition generally is throughout this Continent) have natural affections, social and domestic attachments and sensibilities; and that; therefore we may hope for a share in your sympathetic attention while we represent that the unconstitutional bondage in which multitudes of our fellows in complexion are held, is to us a subject sorrowfully affecting." They expressed faith in legislators, "who, under God, the sovereign Ruler of the Universe, are instructed with the distribution of justice." "Benevolent feelings," "natural affections," "social and domestic attachments and sensibilities," "sympathetic attention":

this vocabulary drawn from the well of religious sentiment also masked a harder-edged political purpose. The petitions represented, as one scholar notes, "hitherto unrecognized examples of interracial activism at the level of national politics" that would prove a model in the following decades. Though the petitioners hoped for a "liberal and benevolent reception," they met with mixed results. While rejecting the request to repeal the Fugitive Slave Act, Congress did strengthen a law restricting U.S. participation in the foreign slave trade. Some supportive legislators endorsed the idea of Black citizenship as well, though the argument was years away from gaining broad support.[32]

The petition articulated a crossing in the histories of religion, emotion, and slavery. Folded into larger revolutionary era debates about freedom and natural rights, the Quaker emancipation struggle in the American South yielded modest immediate effects beyond the troubled liberty of some small number of people. Those debates gathered strength as some white Americans realized that African-descended people contained—or, as George Walton saw it, embodied—the holy spirit. Credit them with trying to work up a good spirit. Refusing to acquiesce to the state's heavy-handedness, North Carolina Quakers found a way to give up their ownership of slaves legally and turn them over to trustees, who would treat them as virtually free. In subsequent decades, many antislavery Quakers left the state for Ohio and Indiana, while others who stayed behind helped African Americans to freedom through the Underground Railroad.[33]

But the backlash against them and other religious radicals was severe. Condemned by slaveholders for the interracial solidarity that fed their antislavery conviction, white Baptists, Methodists, Presbyterians, and other evangelicals in the late eighteenth and early nineteenth centuries bowed to external pressure by erecting new spiritual and spatial barriers between themselves and Black co-religionists. South and North, whites sequestered Black congregants at the back or in the balcony of churches, banned them from essential sacraments, or excluded them from fellowship altogether. Whereas white evangelicals had once engaged emotionally with Black worshipers, now they filed for emotional divorce.

In the Moravian community of North Carolina, for example, interracial spirituality long depended on the sharing of embodied space and physical contact. By touching and embracing each other, laying on hands, and exchanging the kiss of peace, Black and white Moravians reenacted the rituals of Christ and the disciples. "Not the slightest distinction between white and blacks can be made in matters of the spirit," church leaders insisted in 1797. But just a few years later, they elevated those distinctions. Enslaved brothers and sisters could now observe the foot-washing ceremony but were forbidden to take part. African American initiates were now received into fellowship privately, "as it would not be seemly to give Negroes the kiss of peace in a public service." Barred from once integrated graveyards, Black congregants were now buried in a separate graveyard. Black bodies became, once again, carriages of spiritual and social impurity. These gestures, part of a broader racial cordoning in the post-revolutionary United States, helped white evangelical southerners drop their objections to slavery and settle on a socially conservative proslavery religion.[34]

At the same time, alarmed by the tendency of African American and Native American Christians to identify a racially ambiguous Christ as a "suffering servant" ally in their liberation struggles, white Americans in the early nineteenth century increasingly coded Christ as white. As the white male citizen became "the embodied figure of civic inclusion," the "transformation of Jesus from light to white in the young United States made him a cultural icon of white power." In one Catholic church in the southwest Spanish borderlands, a dark brown Christ called "el Cristo negro de Imuris" (the Black Christ of Imuris) reportedly wielded "healing and magical powers that were linked to its blackness." But the days of an Anglo-American such as George Walton imagining Christ as a Black Redeemer faded from view, relegated as an antiquarian curiosity to a historically and culturally specific moment in the revolutionary history of a commercially aggressive nation committed to white supremacy.[35]

Years later, a formerly enslaved man saw Jesus in a vision. He wanted to speak to him but was ashamed to approach in front of other people. As he hesitated, another man gave a ticket through a window and passed through to a train platform. "My knees got weak, and I knelt to pray," he recalled. "As I knelt Jesus handed me a ticket. It was all signed with my name." Giving his ticket, he walked onto the platform. Unlike George Walton, the narrator did not describe Jesus as white, Black, or any color at all. It makes no difference. What matters is that Jesus protected him, steered him through a hostile world, and gave him entry into a select family. God promised another man he would "throw around [him] a strong arm of protection" and that his oppressors would be unable to "confound" him. God, one formerly enslaved person said, was a "time-God": "He don't come before time; he don't come after time. He comes just on time." For these and countless others who spoke of being "hooked in the heart," "barked at by the devil's hellhounds," or "struck dead" by God's might, sacred affections built an emotional wall against violent racism. Enslavement had not destroyed the self. It lived on in captivity and afterward; the inner light illuminated the darkness ahead.[36]

Notes

1. *Journal of George Fox*, ed. Wilson Armistead, 2 vols., 7th ed. (London, 1852), 2:85, 87, 91; Christopher Hill, *The World Turned Upside Down: Radical Ideas during the English Revolution* (New York: Penguin, 1972), 256.
2. *Journal of George Fox*, 2:120–23. On Quakerism in Virginia, North Carolina, and the West Indies, see James Horn, *Adapting to a New World: English Society in the Seventeenth-Century Chesapeake* (Chapel Hill: University of North Carolina Press, 1994), 394–99 (quote on 394); April Lee Hatfield, *Atlantic Virginia: Intercolonial Relations in the Seventeenth Century* (Philadelphia: University of Pennsylvania Press, 2004), 110–36; Noeleen McIlvenna, *A Very Mutinous People: The Struggle for North Carolina, 1660–1713* (Chapel Hill: University of North Carolina Press, 2009), 40–45. On the broader transmission of radical ideas to America during the mid-seventeenth century, see Carla Gardina Pestana, *The English Atlantic in an Age of Revolution, 1640–1661* (Cambridge: Harvard University Press, 2004); and John Donoghue, *Fire under the Ashes: An Atlantic History of the English Revolution* (Chicago: University of Chicago Press, 2013).
3. Jonathan Edwards, *A Treatise Concerning Religious Affections* (1746; repr., Glasgow, 1825), 317, 458; John Corrigan, ed., *Religion and Emotions: Approaches and Interpretations* (New York: Oxford University Press, 2004), 15.
4. Examinations of Protestantism' s cozy relationship with slaveholding and its contributions to ideas of race include Katharine Gerbner, *Christian Slavery: Conversion and Race in the Protestant Atlantic World* (Philadelphia: University of Pennsylvania Press, 2018); Rebecca Goetz, *The Baptism of Early Virginia: How Christianity Created Race* (Baltimore: Johns Hopkins University Press, 2012); Travis Glasson, *Mastering Christianity: Missionary Anglicanism and Slavery in the Atlantic World* (New York: Oxford University Press, 2012); Forrest Wood, *The Arrogance of Faith: Christianity and Race in America from the Colonial Era to the Twentieth Century* (Boston: Northeastern University Press, 1990).
5. Simon Gikandi, *Slavery and the Culture of Taste* (Princeton: Princeton University Press, 2011), 190–93; John Donoghue, "'Out of the Land of Bondage': The English Revolution and the Atlantic Origins of Abolition," *American Historical Review* 115 (October 2010): 943–74; Brycchan Carey, *From Peace to Freedom: Quaker Rhetoric and the Birth of American Antislavery, 1657–1761* (New Haven: Yale University Press, 2012); Karen Halttunen, "Humanitarianism and the Pornography of Pain in Anglo-American Culture," *American Historical Review* 100 (1995): 303–34. On the connection between emotion and ethical knowledge, see Michael Stocker, *Valuing*

Emotions (New York: Cambridge University Press, 1996), cited in Corrigan, *Religion and Emotions*, 15.

6. George Fox, "To Friends beyond the Sea That Have Blacks and Indian Slaves," in *The Works of George Fox*, vols. 7–8, *Epistles* (Philadelphia, 1831), no. 153, 1657.
7. *Journal of George Fox*, 2:102–3; George Fox, *Gospel Family-Order, Being a Short Discourse Concerning the Ordering of Families, Both of Whites, Blacks and Indians* (London, 1676). On Quaker slaveholding on Barbados, see Gerbner, *Christian Slavery*; Larry Gragg, *The Quaker Community on Barbados: Challenging the Culture of the Planter Class* (Columbia: University of Missouri Press, 2009); and Kristen Block, *Ordinary Lives in the Early Caribbean: Religion, Colonial Competition, and the Politics of Profit* (Athens: University of Georgia Press, 2012). On the rapid and influential expansion of sugar plantations on Barbados, see Simon P. Newman, *A New World of Labor: The Development of Plantation Slavery in the British Atlantic* (Philadelphia: University of Pennsylvania Press, 2016).
8. See Katharine Gerbner, "'We are against the traffick of mens-body': The Germantown Quaker Protest of 1688 and the Origins of American Abolitionism," *Pennsylvania History: A Journal of Mid-Atlantic Studies* 74, no. 2 (Spring 2007): 149–72.
9. Morgan Godwyn, *The Negro's and Indian's Advocate* (London, 1680), 9, 23, 27.
10. Marcus Rediker, *The Fearless Benjamin Lay: The Quaker Dwarf Who Became the First Revolutionary Abolitionist* (Boston: Beacon, 2017). See also Julie Holcomb, *Moral Commerce: Quakers and the Transatlantic Boycott of the Slave Labor Economy* (Ithaca: Cornell University Press, 2016).
11. Erik R. Seeman, "'Justise Must Take Plase': Three African Americans Speak of Religion in Eighteenth-Century New England," *William and Mary Quarterly*, 3rd ser., 56 (1999), 411–13; Sidney Kaplan and Emma Nogrady Kaplan, *The Black Presence in the Era of the American Revolution*, 2nd ed. (Amherst: University of Massachusetts Press, 1989), 13. On the broader spread of Black Atlantic Protestantism, see Sylvia R. Frey and Betty Wood, *Come Shouting to Zion: African American Protestantism in the American South and British Caribbean to 1830* (Chapel Hill: University of North Carolina Press, 1998); Jon Sensbach, *Rebecca's Revival: Creating Black Christianity in the Atlantic World* (Cambridge: Harvard University Press, 2005); John W. Catron, *Embracing Protestantism: Black Identities in the Atlantic World* (Gainesville: University Press of Florida, 2016); Mechal Sobel, *Trabelin' On: The Slave Journey to an Afro-Baptist Faith*, 2nd ed. (Princeton: Princeton University Press, 1988).
12. Stephanie Smallwood, *Saltwater Slavery: A Middle Passage from Africa to American Diaspora* (Cambridge: Harvard University Press, 2007), 125–26, 207; Vincent Brown, "Spiritual Terror and Sacred Authority in Jamaican Slave Society," *Slavery and Abolition* 24 (2003): 24–53 (Edwards quote on 24); Nell Irvin Painter, "Soul Murder and Slavery: Toward a Fully Loaded Cost Accounting," in *Southern History across the Color Line* (Chapel Hill: University of North Carolina Press, 2002), 15–39. See also Alex Bontemps, *The Punished Self: Surviving Slavery in the Colonial South* (Ithaca: Cornell University Press, 2001); and Saidiya Hartman, *Scenes of Subjection: Terror, Slavery, and Self-Making in Nineteenth-Century America* (New York: Oxford University Press, 1997).
13. Frey and Wood, *Come Shouting to Zion*, 91–95.
14. On the emergence of biracial fellowship in the eighteenth-century South, see Albert Raboteau, *Slave Religion: The "Invisible Institution" in the Antebellum South*

(New York: Oxford University Press, 1978); Margaret Washington Creel, *A Peculiar People: Slave Religion and Community-Culture Among the Gullahs* (New York: New York University Press, 1988); Mechal Sobel, *The World They Made Together: Black and White Values in Eighteenth-Century Virginia* (Princeton: Princeton University Press, 1988); Jon F. Sensbach, *A Separate Canaan: The Making of an Afro-Moravian World in North Carolina, 1763–1840* (Chapel Hill: University of North Carolina Press, 1998). Works exploring the centrality of emotions in these communities, especially through the idiom of kinship, include Janet Moore Lindman, *Bodies of Belief: Baptist Community in Early America* (Philadelphia: University of Pennsylvania Press, 2008); Anna M. Lawrence, *One Family Under God: Love, Belonging, and Authority in Early Transatlantic Methodism* (Philadelphia: University of Pennsylvania Press, 2011); Christine Heyrman, *Southern Cross: The Beginnings of the Bible Belt* (Chapel Hill: University of North Carolina Press, 1998); and Cynthia Lynn Lyerly, *Methodism and the Southern Mind, 1770–1810* (New York: Oxford University Press, 1998). On the idea of "emotional communities," see Barbara Rosenwein, "Worrying about Emotions in History," *American Historical Review* 107 (2002): 821–45, and Barbara Rosenwein, *Emotional Communities in the Early Middle Ages* (Ithaca: Cornell University Press, 2007).

15. Among the many works on Quaker abolitionism, see Christopher Brown, *Moral Capital: Foundations of British Abolitionism* (Chapel Hill: University of North Carolina Press, 2006); Maurice Jackson, *Let This Voice Be Heard: Anthony Benezet, Father of Atlantic Abolitionism* (Philadelphia: University of Pennsylvania Press, 2009); Jean R. Soderlund, *Quakers and Slavery: A Divided Spirit* (Princeton: Princeton University Press, 1985); Thomas P. Slaughter, *The Beautiful Soul of John Woolman, Apostle of Abolition* (New York: Hill & Wang, 2008).
16. Nicole Eustace, *Passion Is the Gale: Emotion, Power, and the Coming of the American Revolution* (Chapel Hill: University of North Carolina Press, 2008), 36–41. On the broader eighteenth-century revolution in sentiment of which the Quakers were part, see also David Brion Davis, *The Problem of Slavery in the Age of Revolution, 1770–1823* (New York: Oxford University Press, 1975), 45–48, 213–54.
17. For an overview of the emergence of racial science, see Ivan Hannaford, *Race: The History of an Idea in the West* (Baltimore: Johns Hopkins University Press, 1996). For discussion on the connections between race, emotion, and aesthetics, see Gikandi, *Slavery and the Culture of Taste*, 221–25.
18. Walton's story, from which my analysis draws, forms the basis of an excellent annotated edition of primary documents about Quaker antislavery in North Carolina: Michael J. Crawford, *The Having of Negroes Is Become a Burden: The Quaker Struggle to Free Slaves in Revolutionary North Carolina* (Gainesville: University Press of Florida, 2010), 76, 78 (quotes from minutes of the North Carolina yearly meeting).
19. This account is drawn from George Walton, "A Dream or Night Vision, 17th, 12th Mo, 1772," in Crawford, *The Having of Negroes*, 30–33.
20. Mechal Sobel, *Teach Me Dreams: The Search for Self in the Revolutionary Era* (Princeton: Princeton University Press, 2001), 9 (quote), 55–79. A similar argument is made by Carla Gerona in *Night Journeys: The Power of Dreams in Transatlantic Quaker Culture* (Charlottesville: University Press of Virginia, 2004), especially, with regard to African Americans in Quaker dreams, 21–27, 86–91, and 166–71. For

the quote from Walton's letter to Thomas Newby, n.d., see Crawford, *The Having of Negroes,* 43.

21. Cécile Fromont, *The Art of Conversion: Christian Visual Culture in the Kingdom of Kongo* (Chapel Hill: University of North Carolina Press, 2017); Edward J. Blum and Paul Harvey, *The Color of Christ: The Son of God and the Saga of Race in America* (Chapel Hill: University of North Carolina Press, 2012), 54–57.
22. Walton letter, August 18, 1774, in Crawford, *The Having of Negroes,* 47.
23. Ann Marie Plane and Leslie Tuttle, eds., *Dreams, Dreamers, and Visions: The Early Modern Atlantic* (Philadelphia: University of Pennsylvania Press, 2013), 6, drawing on Ernest Hartmann, *The Nature and Function of Dreaming* (New York: Oxford University Press, 2011); Monique Scheer, "Are Emotions a Kind of Practice (and Is That What Makes Them Have a History)? A Bourdieuian Approach to Understanding Emotion," *History and Theory* 51 (May 2012): 193–230 (quote on 204).
24. Walton, undated letter to Newby, in Crawford, *The Having of Negroes,* 40–45; George Walton journal, 1775–1777, in Crawford, *The Having of Negroes,* 51–52.
25. Walton journal, March 22 and 29, 1777, in Crawford, *The Having of Negroes,* 59.
26. Yearly meeting, 1775, and "A Just and Righteous Plea in Behalf of Liberty and Freedom," 1777, in Crawford, *The Having of Negroes,* 54, 121.
27. Lawrence, *One Family Under God,* 206–14; Lyerly, *Methodism and the Southern Mind;* Frey and Wood, *Come Shouting to Zion;* Andrew Levy, *The First Emancipator: The Forgotten Story of Robert Carter, the Founding Father Who Freed His Slaves* (New York: Random House, 2005).
28. Crawford, *The Having of Negroes,* 59, 64, 111–20. See Jeffrey J. Crow, *The Black Experience in Revolutionary North Carolina* (Raleigh: North Carolina Division of Archives and History, 1977).
29. Crawford, *The Having of Negroes,* 120–38 (quotes on 120, 138); Crow, *Black Experience,* 85.
30. Crawford, *The Having of Negroes,* 100–105.
31. Crawford, *The Having of Negroes,* 183; Freedmen's Petition to Congress, January 23, 1797, in Crawford, *The Having of Negroes,* 143–48. For a thorough discussion of the petitioners and their part in the antislavery movement, see Nicholas P. Wood, "A 'Class of Citizens': The Earliest Black Petitioners to Congress and Their Quaker Allies," *William and Mary Quarterly,* 3rd ser., 74 (2017): 109–44.
32. Freedmen's Petition to Congress, January 23, 1797; Wood, "A 'Class of Citizens,'" 114.
33. Crawford, *The Having of Negroes,* 184–90.
34. Sensbach, *A Separate Canaan,* 183–84, 201–4; Frey and Wood, *Come Shouting to Zion,* 149–81.
35. Blum and Harvey, *The Color of Christ,* 77–78, 88.
36. Clifton Johnson, ed., *God Struck Me Dead: Voices of Ex-Slaves,* 2nd ed. (Cleveland: Pilgrim Press), 1993), 147, 17, 170.

CHAPTER 8
Bad Spirits
Facing Fear on the Plantation
A Response to Jon Sensbach

KATHLEEN DONEGAN

Moving from the bad spirit of white slaveholding to the revelatory vision of a Black Christ, Jon Sensbach tells a riveting story that includes bondage and freedom, inhumanity and incarnation, laws and dreams. To tell this story, Sensbach works at the intersection of three fields of study: transatlantic slavery, the history of emotions, and the history of religion. In his configuration, transatlantic slavery begins with the enormous influx of enslaved Africans into the Caribbean and southern colonies during and after the mid-seventeenth century, the transformation of those colonies into planter societies with Black majorities, and the deepening racialization necessary to create and control this rapidly growing enslaved labor force.[1] Religion refers to the Quaker belief in the universal potential to receive the indwelling spirit of Christ, to live in and by its inner light, and to commune with others in "a fellowship of the heart." And emotion flows through the outpouring of compassion from the free toward the enslaved, the possibility of spiritual kinship, and the recognition of a common humanity given and protected by God. It is possible, however, to imagine this same trio of enslavement, emotion, and religion with different points of emphasis and, in doing so, to face another view of racial and spiritual relations on the plantation. In a shifted configuration, the transatlantic slave trade remains at the moment of its massive push forward in the creation of the plantation complex. But the operative emotion in play is the dominant emotion of those plantations: fear, along with its trail of terror, horror, mourning, fury, and threat. And the history of religion turns to the newly creolized form of an African spiritual inheritance: Obeah, adapted and responsive to the shocking realities of plantation life. At this intersection, a face of fear saw bad spirits at every turn, and looked upon even what good spirits might arise with a wary view.

Sensbach fully acknowledges the framework of plantation terror and its rampant destruction of bodies, societies, identities, psyches, and souls—in short, the willed destruction of the humanity of enslaved people. "The foundation of the system was violence," he writes, "remorseless, boundless, grotesque violence, without pity or conscience." I want to pursue this part of his treatment in more detail—first, because such systematic violence makes the possibility of spiritual identification even more extraordinary, and second, because keeping that violence in view recognizes that spiritual identification remains inextricable from the nexus of mass enslavement, terror, and the African spirit world in chains. This requires a deliberate return to the societies of the early Caribbean.

Sensbach refers to the planter Bryan Edwards's declaration that in slave societies, "the leading principle on which the government is supported is fear." Fear so pervasive is never of one sort, and its relations are always multiple. Primarily, enslaved people feared their masters. This was the very groundwork of the plantation—not only terror over the constant threat of extreme violence, but also horror at witnessing its daily enactment. Even at the start of the sugar revolution, when observers asked why the increasing slave majorities did not rise up against their overlords and take control of the island, Richard Ligon answered, "They are held in such awe and slavery, as they are fearful to appear in any daring act. . . . [T]heir spirits are subjugated to so low a condition, as they dare not look up to any bold attempt."[2] This awe and slavery was not only bodily; it was also spiritual, as Vincent Brown has shown. The sight of heads on stakes made the body quake, but they also caused the spiritual imagination to tremble.

But, in a much different way to be sure, enslavers also feared the people they owned. The possibility of rebellion was constant—from individuals who could poison food, to labor gangs with machetes in hand, to groups of fugitives who formed hostile and impenetrable communities in the caves and mountains, to large-scale collectives that conspired to revolt and sometimes attempted the same. The historian Michael Craton cites twenty-nine uprisings in Barbados and Jamaica alone by the turn of the nineteenth century.[3] Enslaved populations were perpetually restless, and because their bondage was total, enslavers treated any sort of resistance (performed or perceived) as an act of high treachery.[4] Fear of rebellion pervaded every aspect of planter rule, which is in part why it was so killing a thing. It was, in Brown's words, "a society in which domination, dissent, and the threat of incredible violence plagued every interaction."[5]

This much is clear. But when we bring Quakers into the conversation, we see that these relations of fear in the slave system of the Caribbean were not simply binary. Quakers and other whites also feared one another, even though many Quakers were enslavers themselves. Enslavers always feared that Christianizing the people they enslaved was a dangerous business and would lead perforce to manumission. Again, the early observer of Barbados, Ligon, tells the story of an ingenious enslaved man named Sambo who wishes to become a Christian. His owner refuses, saying that a Christian can never be made an enslaved person. But, Ligon protests, this would be making an enslaved person a Christian. There is no difference, the enslaver responds, for "being once a Christian, he would no more account him a Slave . . . and by that means should open such a gap, as all the Planters in the Island would curse him."[6] Planters' fears of the Quaker mission in the West Indies went even further. Given the Quaker message of spiritual empowerment, refusal of worldly hierarchy, equality of souls, and open meetings, enslavers were convinced that such things stoked the fires that led directly to revolt. It was clear to non-Quaker planters that encouraging conversion was tantamount to inviting rebellion.

In their turn, Quakers often feared for their own status on the island. Since their beginnings, Quakers' radicalism made them no strangers to protest and its repercussions. But on Barbados, the drastic accusations that they incited slave revolt threatened to strip legitimacy from a Society that was at that time striving for stability, recognition, and freedom to practice. Already Quakers were marginalized and vulnerable for their refusal to take oaths of loyalty or to serve in the militia—both crucial forms of control in a slave society. Nonetheless, Quakers were not fully marginalized from West Indian society because a great many were enslavers too, planters like their neighbors, whom they feared to cross on this of all principles. Of the approximately 1,200 Quakers who were on Barbados in 1680, more than 80 percent of their households held slaves.[7] One Quaker importer bought nearly 1,400 enslaved people from Africa in just four years.[8] "It is a slander and a lye that we should teach the Negars to Rebel," George Fox protested.[9] Rebellion was a concept Quakers abhorred for spiritual reasons, but it was also a real-time specter they feared alongside fellow planters. Their conflicted status as peacekeepers, religious radicals, and slaveholders all at once made them sit uneasily among the powerful whites.

But Quakers' fear *of* other masters seemed to pale in comparison to their fear *for* them. Eyes ever trained on Judgment Day, Quakers railed against corrupted planters' grievous sins and darkly warned that riches were of a day, but punishment was eternal. Writing in 1656 and addressing himself to those shameless "transgressors of the pure law of God," Quaker John Rous issued a blazing warning: "The cry of the oppressed is entered into the ears of the Lord of Sabbath, who will speedily come to pour forth his plagues upon you, you wicked ones, and execute his righteous Judgements upon you who live in fraud and deceit. . . . The day is come nigh wherein you shall have noe excuse for your filthiness, but the wrath of God shall be revealed in flames of fire against you, ye Earth-worms." In "the Lake which burns with fire and brimstone forever," he continued, surely they would "howl and lament for the wo and misery that shall come upon" them, a "misery that has no end.[10] Rous's condemnation of these godless libertines did not extend to the fact of slaveholding itself, however. While he raged against planters' vices, Rous was one of the wealthiest Quakers on Barbados, and the owner of 470 acres and enslaver of 204 people.[11] Thus, might the Day of Judgment visit Quakers themselves? "What then shall we do, when God rises up, and when he visiteth, what shall we Answer him?" asked John Woolman.[12] On Barbados, this was an ominous question.

If Quakers knew that the day of reckoning was nigh for all, there also existed in their writings hints that vengeance might come early to Barbados. Thomas Tryon, a religious radical with strong ties to the Quakers, predicted as much in his *Friendly Advice to the gentleman-planters of the East and West Indies* (1684), the first publication to use a fictionalized enslaved person to condemn slaveholding societies. Reflecting on the nominal Christians of Barbados, the enslaved character outlines both the superiority of the Christian faith and the deep hypocrisy of slaveholders who dare to profess it. But the judgment he forewarns near the end of the dialogue is of a bloodier type. Falling into "melancholy thoughts," he names what is in plain sight: all around those "houses cemented with blood" move people in bondage who are "intractable, sullen, morose, cruel and revengeful." Indeed, if the wrath of God awaited in the afterlife, "undoubtedly the cup of wrath" on the plantation was already "almost full," and "vengeance . . . must necessarily follow" those "Estates heap'd together by violence."[13] The realization was nothing new. Living on the Rous plantation during his stay in Barbados, George Fox saw things that in his words "burdened my life very much." He confessed, "Sorely was my spirit troubled."[14] Acknowledging the horror of slavery, the "cruel whippings" and "short allowances of food," even Quakers in Pennsylvania feared the enslaved would "rise up in rebellion and do as much mischief."[15] John Woolman, too, recognized that enslavers were perpetually at "Risque of their lives."[16]

All these many kinds of fear sat at the intersection of the transatlantic slave trade, religious history, and the history of emotion, forming a matrix of constant dread, extreme wariness, and pervasive threat that often erupted into violence (and did so daily in the lives of the enslaved). We can see then how stunning was the argument for common humanity and spiritual kinship in this atmosphere. When Quakers not only identified enslaved people as potential vessels for the indwelling spirit but also identified with them in a shared fellowship of love, it was a belief both religiously and socially radical. This fundamental recognition was, in Sensbach's words, a "powerful source of affective comradeship" that gave enslaved people "an emotional visibility" that slavery "had erased."

The dynamic of identification was not confined to proffering the Quaker's Christian fellowship, however. Even as enslaved Africans and Afro-Caribbean Creoles moved into the Quaker light, they were also bringing Africa and the Afro-Caribbean into the Quaker meetinghouse. In the Quaker mind, Africans and Afro-Caribbeans inherently had eternal souls, but they lived in a dangerous darkness. There is hardly a Quaker publication that does not pause over attributions of heathen beliefs and animalistic ways, what Fox referred to as "Debauchery, Whoredom, Fornication, and Uncleanliness."[17] These dark practices had to be thoroughly emptied before the soul could be filled. That was a Quaker belief. But returning to this triad of slavery, religion, and emotion, we must ask: What did the inner light look like to an enslaved person? What did it feel like to reveal a spirit indwelling in a condition of bondage? How did such a person hear the lesson of a broken heart healed? The answers are a matter of emotion, of mind, of body, of experience, and of practice. And all of these things are marked both by a creolized Afro-Caribbean spiritual world and by the brutality of slavery. Thus, with the influx of an enslaved population, plantation Quakerism itself becomes creolized and invested with the features of Obeah, a complex of spiritual and material practices through which enslaved people harnessed both the natural and supernatural worlds to heal their wounded condition. As Katherine Gerbner has claimed, Obeah "was the frame through which Afro-Caribbeans interpreted European religions."[18] In the creolizing world of the plantation complex, Quaker and Afro-Caribbean spiritual practices must have blended, despite their vast differences in relation to power. Shared access to the spiritual world created a crossroads, even if this synergy, by necessity, went unspoken.

Quakerism, wherein communing with the spirit within was a central belief, shared something with Obeah's "charismatic, shamanistic powers," whereby the "body [was] open to a world of invisible . . . forces."[19] The emotional and bodily displays, as well as the sensuous relation to Christ and to one another that marked Quakerism, resonated with elements that also underwrote Obeah's potency. When Quakers fell into trancelike states; when they quaked as a spirit moved in their bodies; when they poured out emotional speech in and through that inspiriting force; when they understood that this affective, transformative, and embodied religious experience bound them to one another, the Africans and Creoles in their fellowship must have recognized the signs of Obeah's spirit. When dreams brought revelations, they must have easily believed that the spirit's night travels disclosed deep truths. When an avowed enemy of George Fox fell down dead on the eve of that most prominent Quaker's arrival, they must have recognized the powers of their own spiritual specialists to slay through supernatural means.

Yet there were also important differences that Afro-Caribbeans might have taken as continuous but that Quakers would have called dangerous. In Obeah, spirit flowed in, but it also flowed out, most notably to imbue the Obeah fetish with inner life and thus with its fearsome power in the physical world. Spirits could also be stolen, as in the case of stealing someone's shadow and keeping it in a small coffin-like box. And spirits could linger, as in the case of the undying haunts at plantation sites of murder by torture or execution. These multiple understandings of spiritual mobility were barred at the meetinghouse door, but must have entered into it through the emotional experience of the newest converts, receiving spirit into their bodies and souls.

The affective history of enslaved people who became convinced of the inner Christ was also shaped by the experience of slavery itself. For how fervently would an enslaved person embrace the repudiation of worldly hierarchies? How would a person who knew, in his or her own body and agonized memory, that blood and wounds were no metaphor contemplate the blood and wounds of Christ crucified? Understanding of hell's miseries, visions of a day of justice—these were the lived experience of the plantation. They were religious affections written on the body as much as on the heart and soul. Even the creation of new kinship bonds with sisters and brothers in Christ would have been familiar, as chosen kinship also bound together the enslaved community, whose natal families were regularly and intentionally sundered. And the movement out of sin and into grace must have been understood as a reprieve from that frequent emotion of the enslaved that their owners called melancholy. The fatal condition came on mysteriously to the planters' minds, but in fact settled in when enslaved people—grieving, tormented, heartbroken—were convinced their souls were dead. The invitation into the light surely revived battered spirits as well as battered bodies.

Even before formal Christianization, inherently "Christian" emotions were sometimes recognized as already belonging to the enslaved. When Thomas Tryon ventriloquizes his enslaved character, the majority of the speech consists of revealing the "notorious" hypocrisy of enslavers who profess to be Christians. When the Christian "master" in the dialogue enumerates thirteen principles of Christianity, the enslaved speaker not only proves that each tenet is sorely lacking in the debased planters but, moreover, attests that such spirit is present in his own brethren. To avoid pride and ambition, to practice patience, to forbear, to implore a "great and mighty" spirit for succor and relief, to pray heartily, to show mercy and compassion to one another—if this was indeed what it meant to be a Christian, then the enslaved person was one.[20] Thus when Quakers proselytized, they were, in a sense, working up what was already a good spirit among those whom Fox called "the strangers that were within thy gates."[21] That is, if the bad spirit to be worked down seemed to be the heathenish darkness of Obeah, the good spirit to be worked up was also present in the enslaved community before the missionaries started their work.

As Sensbach demonstrates, and as I am emphasizing, good spirits and bad were not black and white. And what would work them up or down was equally variable. Bad spirit, of course, lived in the planters. You could tell by their emotional lives. There was found "Envy, Strife, Malice, Back-Biting and Slander," "Pride and Vainglory," "Violence, Fighting, Oppression, Cruelty," and more.[22] John Woolman claimed that planters' "insatiable Craving" led them into "a Maze" of "Dark Anxiety where all their Treasures are insufficient to quiet their Minds."[23] These were "Souls in perpetual Tumult"—bad spirits for sure.[24] Nonetheless, these bad spirits were convinced that Christianizing enslaved people would work up the worst spirit of all: the spirit of rebellion.

The particular "bad spirit" of rebellion is another place where Obeah and Quakerism meet. In 1675 on Barbados, a large-scale conspiracy to revolt was discovered two weeks before it was to be enacted, when one enslaved woman told her owner about a conversation she'd overheard. The plan included people from all across the island, and had been in the making for over three years. When the attempted rebellion was revealed, news spread quickly. According to the whites who learned of it, the strategy was for the enslaved to rise up, take the island, kill the masters, and set up a "Coramantee" man as king. This man, Cuffy, was likely an Obeah man, a powerful spiritual leader whose salves and fetishes—made of ingredients expertly chosen, ceremonially crafted, and ritually imbued with supernatural power—would protect the warriors and doom their captors. After sacred oaths were sworn, the uprising would have started with African-inspired "trumpets of elephants teeth and gourdes to be sounded on several hills."[25] This bad African spirit of Obeah, imported to and transformed by the colonies, was (in the stricken reports of white observers) the impetus and tool of rebellion.

But as much as this planned rebellion involved Obeah, planters were also convinced it involved Quakerism. Hadn't George Fox, who preached to scores of those enslaved, exhorted his own, "And therefore now you should preach Christ to your *Ethyopians* that are in your Families, that so they may be free Men indeed"?[26] Hadn't Quakers worshiped with the enslaved side by side and proclaimed their inner equality? Hadn't enslaved people had the temerity to speak inspired words, claiming they came from the spirit of God? And hadn't the Quakers set up separate meetings where enslaved people could gather on their own—open, free-form meetings that encouraged them to come out from "under their Oppression," outside of the eye of their overlords, or any white at all? Clearly, despite Fox's protestations, the effect of Quaker teachings was to "teach the Negars to rebel." Like Obeah, Quakerism also worked up a bad spirit, which was seen as the impetus and grounding of rebellion. Enslaved people attempting revolt were thus at once too heathen and too Christian, too backward in their superstitions and too forward in their belief, too monstrous in their demonic arts and too human in their God-given souls. The emotions that led to revolt were released by two religious traditions, each of which was seen to radicalize the enslaved.

Certainly Quakers saw themselves as good spirits stuck between the bad spirits of white devils and the bad spirits of Obeah gods. But when they looked at the people they owned, when they began to recognize these people as fellow spirits, what did they see? Sensbach tells the story of the Black Christ child, pointing George Walton's way to the mountaintop. But the early Caribbean was too haunted by specters for such visions to take hold. If the dominant emotion of the plantation was terror, one question had to be: What kind of terror would ultimately rain down? Was it always to be the terror of enslavers over the enslaved, the bad spirit of tyranny? Was there to be a terror of the enslaved over their owners, the bad spirit of rebellion? Or was it to be a holy terror, a divine retribution, the Great Good but Furious Spirit working down all the bad spirits in his merciless wrath? Some prayed for it, some prayed against it, but all conjured their way around this intersection of slavery, religion, and emotion, raising arms, and hands, and prayers, and voices, casting good spells and bad in an air so thick with terror that it came to look normal. Never was there such a need for revelation.

Notes

1. Kirsten Block, *Ordinary Lives in the Early Caribbean: Religion, Colonial Competition, and the Politics of Profit* (Athens: University of Georgia Press, 2012), 151. Block traces the growth of the African population in Barbados from reaching a slave majority in 1660 to achieving a two-to-one population ratio of Black people to white by 1670.
2. Richard Ligon, *A True & Exact History of the Island of Barbados*, ed. Karen Kupperman (Indianapolis: Hackett Publishing, 2011), 96–97.
3. Michael Craton, *Testing the Chains: Resistance to Slavery in the British West Indies* (1982; repr., Ithaca: Cornell University Press, 2009), 335–37.
4. See Vincent Brown, *The Reaper's Garden: Death and Power in the World of Atlantic Slavery* (Cambridge: Harvard University Press, 2008), 140.
5. Brown, *The Reaper's Garden*, 46.

6. Ligon, *History of Barbados*, 66.
7. Block, *Ordinary Lives*, 151.
8. Larry Dale Gragg, *The Quaker Community on Barbados: Challenging the Culture of the Planter Class* (Columbia: University of Missouri Press, 2009), 136.
9. Gragg, *Quaker Community* (quote on 136).
10. John Rous, *A Warning to the Inhabitants of Barbados* (London, 1656), 1, 3.
11. Block, *Ordinary Lives*, 276, n. 27.
12. John Woolman, *Some Considerations on the Keeping of Negroes* (Philadelphia: James Chattin, 1754), 20.
13. Thomas Tryon, *Friendly Advice to the gentleman-planters of the East and West Indies in three parts* (London: Andrew Sowle, 1684), 148 ("melancholy thoughts"), 209 ("cemented in blood"), 216 ("intractable, sullen, morose, cruel, and revengeful"), 208 ("cup of wrath" and "almost full"), 210 ("vengeance"), 211 ("Estates heap'd").
14. George Fox, *Gospel Family-Order, being a short discurse* [*sic*] *concerning the ordering of family, both of whites, blacks and Indians* (Philadelphia: Ranier Janson, 1701), 20.
15. Gragg, *Quaker Community*, 128.
16. Woolman, *Some Considerations*, 11.
17. Fox, *Gospel Family-Order*, 19.
18. Katharine Gerbner, "'They call me Obea': German Moravian Missionaries and Afro-Caribbean Religion in Jamaica, 1754–1760," *Atlantic Studies* 12, no. 2 (2015): 162.
19. Block, *Ordinary Lives*, 155; Justine S. Murison, "Obeah and Its Others: Buffered Selves in the Era of Tropical Medicine," *Atlantic Studies* 22, no. 2 (2015): 144.
20. Tryon, *Friendly Advice*, 174 ("notorious" hypocrisy), 151 ("great and mighty").
21. Fox, *Gospel Family-Order*, 6.
22. Tryon, *Friendly Advice*, 156.
23. Woolman, *Some Considerations*, 24.
24. Tryon, *Friendly Advice*, 178.
25. Katharine Gerbner, "The Ultimate Sin: Christian Slaves in Barbados in the Seventeenth Century," *Slavery and Abolition* 31, no. 1 (2010): 65. Gerbner's article gives a close account of the planned rebellion's aftermath, and especially of the Quaker Negro Act of 1676, which forbade Quakers from bringing enslaved people to their meetings.
26. Fox, *Gospel Family-Order*, 15.

AFTERWORD

Messy Entanglements

BARBARA H. ROSENWEIN

This is a pioneering book. If this is not obvious at first glance, it is because nowadays most historians agree that speaking of the Christian religion in early North America entails speaking about emotions as well. That is why Caroline Wigginton and Abram Van Engen introduce this book with a survey of the phases of the field of study called "the history of emotions."

What the editors do not say explicitly is how slow historians have been to realize that early modern *religious* affections belong within that history. Indeed, until recently many historians denied that early modern Christian groups (apart from the Catholic sort) expressed much affect at all. Even though Friedrich Schleiermacher, Rudolf Otto, and William James long ago outlined, in their various ways, some of the emotional elements involved in religion, their works were universalizing and not historical at all. Wigginton and Van Engen call the history of emotions a "relatively young subfield of historical studies," but it is positively ancient compared to the historical study of Christian emotions in the early modern period. Peter N. Stearns and Carol Zisowitz Stearns launched the idea of "emotionology" in 1985, opening the way to studies of changing standards of emotion over time. New approaches were added at the end of the 1990s. But studies of the religious emotions of Christians in Europe and North America picked up on little of this.

Instead, religious historians were mired in an older tradition that saw the Middle Ages as affective but the period thereafter as not. That idea began to take hold with the Dutch historian Johan Huizinga, who contrasted the colorful and violent passions of the Middle Ages to the drab rationality of the eras that followed.[1] It was much bolstered by the sociologist Norbert Elias, who, writing in the late 1930s, argued that European society underwent a "civilizing process" in the sixteenth and seventeenth centuries. During that period, he said, people learned to subdue their emotions. They developed a "super-ego" that worked "to control, transform or suppress" emotional impulses.[2] The immediate cause of this new affective economy was political; it was the result of the establishment of absolutist courts and their particular demands on individual comportment. The life at such absolutist courts offered a new social model that required behavioral and emotional self-restraint. More generally, Elias considered the crucial reason for the new self-control to be the increasing interdependency of people and institutions. Reliant on everyone else, people learned to suppress their affective upheavals.

Elias's argument was taken up in the 1960s by the historian Gerhard Oestreich, who, however, changed the terms by talking about social discipline rather than the civilizing process. Oestreich too assumed that emotions had been tamped down in the early modern period, but he considered the cause to be the regimen of early modern armies and the growth of the absolutist early modern state. Under these circumstances, the military practices of command and obedience were transferred very quickly to every social sector.[3] While Oestreich himself hardly touched on religion or religious institutions, his notion of social discipline was quickly adopted by historians of Protestantism, who saw in the processes of confessionalization that were taking place across all of Europe a new religious sensibility that stressed affective inhibition, whether imposed by fathers on their families, the ministers of Reformed churches on their congregations, or the consciences of individuals on themselves.[4]

This historiographical tradition was so strong that when Susan Karant-Nunn first began to talk about the emotions involved in confessionalization, she adopted the prevailing view, asserting that "along with the old religion [Catholic Christianity], emotion-oriented piety was at an end. . . . Indeed, princes, reformers, and magistrates sought to suppress strong emotion in all aspects of life."[5] It was only in 2010 that she recognized that there had been specifically Protestant emotions and undertook to explore how they had been both favored and cultivated.[6]

For historians of English and colonial North American Puritans, that reconsideration came even later, with Alec Ryrie's *Being Protestant in Reformation Britain*, published in 2013. There, Ryrie gently offered a truly revolutionary correction: "The emotional landscape of early modern Protestantism . . . is rather richer than is often assumed."[7] Only one chapter of Ryrie's book, however, was devoted to Puritan emotions. It was not until 2016 that a whole book of essays co-edited by him was devoted to the emotions of Puritanism on both sides of the Atlantic. As the editors remarked in their introduction to that book: "There was a time when the title 'Puritanism and Emotion' would have seemed like the set-up for a weak joke. . . . It no longer needs to be said that Puritans had emotions, nor indeed that their emotional range extended beyond lugubrious malice."[8]

Americanists' studies of religious emotions followed a similar timeline. When Nicole Eustace's book on the emotions of the American Revolution came out in 2011, it did not directly tie those emotions to religious feeling.[9] But soon thereafter came Abram Van Engen's study of the emotion of sympathy cultivated by colonial Puritans.[10] *Feeling Godly* adds to this historiography not only by ratifying the existence of religious affections of every sort but also by exploring how they were transformed (or remained intransigent) as various Christian communities came into contact with one another. The issue of change—emotional change—is thus at the heart of these essays.

* * *

How and why does emotional change take place? The scholars who forged the four "stages" of the historiography of the history of emotions outlined by Wigginton and Van Engen (and discussed at greater length in my and Riccardo Cristiani's survey) offer quite disparate answers.[11] Simplifying greatly, we may say that for "emotionologists," change occurs because emotions serve social functions; when socioeconomic transformations take place, they require new emotional standards to sustain them. Consider, for example, the new "service economy" that was coming into being in the United States in the 1920s. It required that "servers"—shop clerks, receptionists, salespeople, and the like—cultivate smiles, learn to be pleasant, and not show anger on the job. This represented a sea change from the acceptably angry factory worker of the industrial economy. The socioeconomic needs of service enterprises transformed the emotional standards of Americans.[12]

By contrast, William Reddy's idea of "emotional freedom" put the seeds of change in the enslaving nature of any emotional regime. Thus, explaining the birth of the French Revolution, Reddy argued that the constraints on feeling demanded by the court of the ancien régime spawned (as it were) their own antithesis—"emotional refuges" such as the eighteenth-century clubs, salons, and theaters where passionate emotional expression was given free rein. Those courtly alternatives themselves became the core of the early phases of the French Revolution until they too produced so demanding an emotional regime that new emotional refuges sprang up to counter it. In effect, rigid emotional regimes generate so much emotional suffering as to result in political and social—as well as emotional—change.[13]

Diverging from both of those paradigms of change is that offered by my idea of emotional communities. Again simplifying, I argue that, as new groups come to the fore for various reasons (political, religious, economic, intellectual, social), they bring with them their own emotional values, standards, modes of expression, and vocabulary. These ascendant groups influence the emotional communities "beneath" them, especially if those tangential or marginalized emotional communities strive to join the ranks of the more prestigious. But dominant emotional communities have far less impact (or even none at all) on groups willing to go their own way. Thus, for example, when the charismatic monk Saint Columbanus came from Ireland to the Continent at the very end of the sixth century, his particular brand of monasticism commanded so much prestige that he was able to reform the emotional style of a royal court. From cultivating emotions that emphasized love, sentiment, and family feeling, the court (in the next generation, and under Columbanus's influence) turned against all such familial expressions of affect. But other emotional communities of the time did not adopt this new style, as we may see from a cluster of writings to be dated toward the latter half of the seventh century.[14]

The newest phase of emotions history research emphasizes the practices of the body and the emotions connected with them. Indeed, as Monique Scheer puts it, emotions "emerge from bodily knowledge." She argues, on the one hand, that "the habitus must be static and binding to a certain extent, if it is to be more than just a loose cloak that can be thrown off on a whim." In short, it must be sustained and reinforced by frequent use.[15] By habitus she means bodily habits within a particular context: habitual kneeling to express humility and penance, for example. On the other hand, a habitus may change under the influence of new, ambient practices. She points to the ways in which nineteenth-century German Pietists reinforced but also transformed their own religious behaviors by adopting Methodist styles of worship under the tutelage of Christoph Gottlob Müller.[16]

* * *

Many of the chapters collected here, all focused on the religious emotions of early North America, offer excellent "test cases" for reinvigorating and refining these four explanations. Let us consider the major ways in which they do so.

Mark Valeri argues that eighteenth-century Calvinist evangelicals, far from clinging to the more traditional Puritan conviction that divine grace alone effected religious conversion, adopted the human-centered ideas of the English Enlightenment, which emphasized free will and choice. Although this would seem to be a highly intellectual and theoretical issue, in fact it was also (as Valeri shows) thoroughly emotional. Already in the Patristic period, Saint Augustine had argued that emotions were movements of the soul put into action by the will. Rather similarly, for Locke, the will determined the things that one loved (e.g., God, fellow man—or gambling and whoring) or the things that one hated (e.g., sin, lust—or Christ and neighbor). Drawing on the model of emotional communities, we might be tempted to say that the prestigious emotional community of the great English and Scottish Enlightenment philosophers exerted its emotional ideas on New Englanders.

But it is one thing to theorize and another to "feel." The spiritual diaries of the time occasionally incorporated the new "language of choice" exemplified by Jonathan Edwards. But they also revealed the older patterns, in which people experienced their emotions as coming from God. (Consider a somewhat similar situation today: most of us accept the scientific view that emotions are "in the brain," and yet we still "feel" them in our hearts and stomachs. Who would declare "I love you with all my brain"?) Valeri's chapter reveals the complexity of emotional change, the possibility of holding conflicting convictions at the same time, suggesting the sheer messiness and struggle that ensues when transformations are aborning.

Valeri's chapter alerts us to the fact that emotional and intellectual changes are in a sense incomplete; traditions, which include affective patterns, remain "under cover." One of the lessons of Scott Manning Stevens's essay on the religious conversion of the Haudenosaunee is that emotional traditions may act rather like recessive "genes," expressing themselves once again when the time is right.[17] Stevens emphasizes the huge linguistic and conceptual hurdles involved in preaching a theology (and the affects inextricably connected to it) to people with a language not just different from but even structurally alien to the languages spoken by the missionaries. There were, as well, cultural divides. In the case of the Haudenosaunee, it is Reddy's notion of emotional regimes that seems best to describe the situation, with the French and then (especially) the English playing the dominant role. Would it be right to say that the Iroquois experienced "emotional suffering"? Without question, they were bowing to the inevitable, made prisoners in their own land and subject to the rules of the colonizers. It certainly was the case that the Native Samson Occom declared in the mid-eighteenth century that he had been "awakened and converted" to the occupiers' religion. But was it by force? By example and conviction? By the three together? In any case, Native evangelism was not exactly the religion of the colonizers. Thus, perhaps ironically, the sense of "linguistic despair" that Stevens speaks of was that of the missionaries rather than the Indians. Their emotional regime, with its in-built ambition to reproduce itself fully because it was tied to God's truth, sometimes (as here) recognized and lamented its failures when it was unable to impose its norms perfectly on others. More pertinent to Reddy's point, however, is that the Native converts themselves suffered emotionally: Stevens speaks of their "anxiety" as they tried to work out their state of grace. Far happier were the Indians who lived where syncretism was permitted.

Thus, Reddy's explanation of emotional domination undoubtedly helps us understand the example of Haudenosaunee. But to understand their motivation in *adopting* the style of the regime (insofar as they did so), we must turn once again to the idea of emotional communities and also, in this instance, to emotionology. I would emphasize the prestige of Wheelock's Protestant school and the advantages that it promised to the

Indians: these were spurs to their religious—and perforce emotional—transformation. The Stearnses would no doubt also point out that the Haudenosaunee who converted to Christianity were adapting to the social and economic needs of the ambient ascendant society.

Then again, as Caroline Wigginton observes, the Haudenosaunee conversion entailed deliberate rebellion against (or unconscious deviation from, or the inevitable misunderstanding of) Protestant emotional norms. The examples of Wequash, Occom, and Joseph Brant thus provide other reasons—linguistic, political—for which emotional transformations might best be understood as messy and incomplete.

Melissa Frost's essay amplifies this point by suggesting that the religious practices of the body, too, may change in messy ways. While native Mexicans had been accustomed to venerate certain hallucinogenic plants "as catalysts of the sacred," this was not true of Spanish Catholics. Insofar as theirs was a religion of the body, it consisted in attending church, observing days of fasting, consuming wine, kneeling in penance, confessing, and so on. Furthermore, it included plenty of practices of which the clergy disapproved, such as the mingling of the sexes during church services and dancing on feast days. It could even involve using magical incantations and special herbs to ward off danger or enhance sexual potency and fertility.[18] But it did not involve hallucinogens. The fact that these were consumed by (some) Mexicans across the full spectrum of castes and classes does not in itself show *religious* emotional transformation. But when a Spanish woman like Ana Calderón claimed (after taking a hallucinogenic drug) to have seen the Virgin Mary, to have awakened with unwonted "feelings of well-being," and to be healed of terrible pain, this constitutes impressive evidence not only of religious syncretism but also of a profound transformation in her practices of the body and their emotional counterparts. She was still very much a Catholic (*pace* the views of the Inquisition) but a "messy" one, no longer fully a member of the emotional community of which she presumably had originally been a part. Or perhaps we might more correctly say, along with Stephanie Kirk, that Calderón's original emotional community had more flexibility than we would ordinarily surmise, for Ana Calderón was not alone in her willingness to open up to new religious experiences, practices, and feelings.

Finally, Jon Sensbach's chapter demonstrates how messy entanglements—among the enslaved, white enslavers, states with a vested interest in slavery, Quakers with the imagination to "feel kinship with damned and exploited people"—might lead to emotional, political, and religious transformations of so astonishing a variety that none of the paradigms of change that we have hitherto examined fully compass the phenomena on the ground. We are instead face-to-face with the irreducible individuality of responses to finely grained contexts that resist generalization. Here the anthropologist Andrew Beatty affords some guidance, helping us to jettison emotionologies, regimes, communities, and practices of the body in order to focus on "persons and particulars," on the precise narratives that constitute our lives and that underlie and generate our emotions.[19]

The essays in this book thus offer the seeds of some messy—and productive—entanglements of approaches and theories. And that is in addition to the important contributions they make to our understanding of early North American religious history.

Notes

1. Johan Huizinga, *The Autumn of the Middle Ages* (1919), trans. Rodney J. Payton and Ulrich Mammitzsch (Chicago: University of Chicago Press, 1996).
2. Norbert Elias, *The Civilizing Process: Sociogenetic and Psychogenetic Investigations*, trans. Edmund Jephcott, ed. Eric Dunning, Johan Goudsblom, and Stephen Mennell, rev. ed. (Oxford: Blackwell, 2000), 375.
3. Gerhard Oestreich, "Strukturprobleme des europäischen Absolutismus," *Vierteljahresschrift für Sozial- und Wirtschaftsgeschichte* 55 (1968): 329–47, translated as "The Structure of the Absolute State," in Gerhard Oestreich, *Neostoicism and the Early Modern State*, ed. Brigitta Oestreich and Helmut Georg Koenigsberger, trans. David McLintock (Cambridge: Cambridge University Press, 1982), 258–73.
4. See Susan R. Boettcher, "Confessionalization: Reformation, Religion, Absolutism, and Modernity," *History Compass* 2 (2004): 1–10; Thomas A. Brady Jr., "Confessionalization: The Career of a Concept," and Heinz Schilling, "Confessionalization: Historical and Scholarly Perspectives of a Comparative and Interdisciplinary Paradigm," both in *Confessionalization in Europe, 1555–1700: Essays in Honor and Memory of Bodo Nischan*, ed. John M. Headley, Hans J. Hillerbrand, and Anthony J. Papalas (Aldershot: Ashgate, 2004), 1–20 and 21–36.
5. Susan C. Karant-Nunn, "'Christians' Mourning and Lament Should not Be Like the Heathens': The Suppression of Religious Emotion in the Reformation," in Headley, Hillerbrand, and Papalas, *Confessionalization in Europe*, 111.
6. Susan C. Karant-Nunn, *The Reformation of Feeling: Shaping the Religious Emotions in Early Modern Germany* (New York: Oxford University Press, 2010).
7. Alec Ryrie, *Being Protestant in Reformation Britain* (Oxford: Oxford University Press, 2013), 3.
8. Alec Ryrie and Tom Schwanda, eds., *Puritanism and Emotion in the Early Modern World* (Houndmills: Palgrave Macmillan, 2016), 1.

9. Nicole Eustace, *Passion Is the Gale: Emotion, Power, and the Coming of the American Revolution* (Chapel Hill: University of North Carolina Press, 2008).
10. Abram C. Van Engen, *Sympathetic Puritans: Calvinist Fellow Feeling in Early New England* (New York: Oxford University Press, 2014).
11. Barbara H. Rosenwein and Riccardo Cristiani, *What Is the History of Emotions?* (Cambridge: Polity, 2018).
12. See Carol Zisowitz Stearns and Peter N. Stearns, *Anger: The Struggle for Emotional Control in America's History* (Chicago: University of Chicago Press, 1986), chap. 5.
13. William M. Reddy, *The Navigation of Feeling: A Framework for the History of Emotions* (Cambridge: Cambridge University Press, 2001).
14. Barbara H. Rosenwein, *Emotional Communities in the Early Middle Ages* (Ithaca: Cornell University Press, 2006), esp. chaps. 5 and 6. See also Barbara H. Rosenwein, *Generations of Feeling: A History of Emotions, 600–1700* (Cambridge: Cambridge University Press, 2016), chap. 2.
15. Monique Scheer, "Are Emotions a Kind of Practice (and Is That What Makes Them Have a History)? A Bourdieuian Approach to Understanding Emotions," *History and Theory* 51 (May 2012): 204.
16. Monique Scheer, "Feeling Faith: The Cultural Practice of Religious Emotions in Nineteenth-Century German Methodism," in *Out of the Tower: Essays on Culture and Everyday Life*, ed. Monique Scheer, Thomas Thiemeyer, Reinhard Johler, and Bernhard Tschofen (Tübingen: Tübinger Vereinigung für Volkskund, 2013), 217–47. On Müller's impact in Germany, see Friedemann Burkhardt, *Christoph Gottlob Müller und die Anfänge des Methodismus in Deutschland* (Göttingen: Vandenhoeck & Ruprecht, 2003).
17. See Rosenwein, *Generations of Feeling*, 318–20.
18. The religious practices of Spanish Catholics in the period, both those sanctioned and those not, are discussed in Allyson M. Poska, *Regulating the People: The Catholic Reformation in Seventeenth-Century Spain* (Leiden: Brill, 1998), esp. chap. 3.
19. Andrew Beatty, *Emotional Worlds: Beyond an Anthropology of Emotion* (Cambridge: Cambridge University Press, 2019), 125.

Contributors

JOANNA BROOKS is the award-winning author or editor of ten books on race, religion, gender, social movements, and American culture, including *Mormonism and White Supremacy: American Christianity and the Problem of Racial Innocence* (2020). She has appeared in global media outlets including the BBC, NPR, *The Daily Show*, CNN, MSNBC, and the *Washington Post*. In her day job as associate vice president for faculty advancement and student success at San Diego State University, she leads faculty development and student academic support efforts at a large public, research-intensive Hispanic-Serving Institution of higher education. She has also worked as a volunteer, activist, and organizer in the labor, feminist, anti-racist, LGBT equality, and migrant rights movements. She holds a Ph.D. in English from the University of California, Los Angeles, and is a proud fourth-generation southern Californian.

KATHLEEN DONEGAN is associate professor of English and Daniel E. Koshland Jr. Distinguished Chair in Writing at the University of California, Berkeley. She is the author of *Seasons of Misery: Catastrophe and Colonial Settlement in Early America* (2014)—honorable mention for the 2016 Early American Literature Book Prize—which investigates the relationship between suffering and violence in the colonial settlement period, and argues that the first forms of colonial subjectivity and literature were formed out of that catastrophe. She is at work on a project titled "The Spectral Plantation: The Other Worlds of Slavery," which traces modes of psychic departure enacted by people who physically remained within the colonial Caribbean plantation complex, following the pathways of haunting, madness, music, and the supernatural as they led to other worlds.

MELISSA FROST is an assistant dean with the University of Virginia College of Arts & Sciences and a scholar of Spanish languages and literatures. Her ongoing research focuses on the history of traditional hallucinogenic plant consumption in Mexico during the colonial period. She also studies how policies in the United States and Mexico affect the autonomy of present-day Indigenous communities.

STEPHANIE KIRK is professor of Hispanic studies at Washington University in St. Louis, where she holds affiliate appointments in women, gender, and sexuality studies and in religious studies. She is the author of two books, *Sor Juana Inés de la Cruz and the Gender Politics of Knowledge in Colonial Mexico* (2016) and *Convent Life in Colonial Mexico: A Tale of Two Communities* (2007 and 2018), and the editor of two volumes, *Religious Transformations in the Early Modern Americas* (2014, co-edited with Sarah Rivett) and *Estudios coloniales en el siglo XXI: Nuevos itinerarios* (2011). She has published numerous articles and essays on gender and religious culture in colonial Mexico and on the life and work of Sor Juana Inés de la Cruz. More recently she has been working on a monograph on transnational early modern Jesuit martyrdom and preparing a critical edition and translation into English of Carlos de Sigüenza y Góngora's convent chronicle *Paraíso occidental*.

BARBARA H. ROSENWEIN is professor emerita of history, Loyola University Chicago. She is the author of *Anger's Past: The Social Uses of an Emotion in the Middle Ages* (1998); *Emotional Communities in the Early Middle Ages* (2006); *Generations of Feeling: A History of Emotions, 600–1700* (2015); (with Riccardo Cristiani), *What Is the History of Emotions?* (2018); *Anger: The Conflicted History of an Emotion* (2020); and *Love: A History in Five Fantasies* will be published by Polity Press (2021).

JON SENSBACH is professor of history at the University of Florida. He is the author of *Rebecca's Revival: Creating Black Christianity in the Atlantic World* (2005) and *A Separate Canaan: The Making of an Afro-Moravian World in North Carolina, 1763–1840* (1998). More recently he has been at work on a study of religious awakenings in the early South and Atlantic world.

SCOTT MANNING STEVENS (Akwesasne Mohawk) is director of Native American and Indigenous Studies Program and associate professor of English with appointments in art and music history and religion at Syracuse University. His more recent publications include contributions to *The Oxford Handbook of American Indian History* (2016), *Why You Can't Teach United States History without American Indians* (2015), and co-author of *Art of the American West: The Haub Family Collection at the Tacoma Art Museum* (2014). His essays have appeared in such journals as *Early American Literature* and *Prose Studies*. He is the former director of the D'Arcy McNickle Center for American Indian and Indigenous Studies at the Newberry Library.

MARK VALERI is the Reverend Priscilla Wood Neaves Distinguished Professor of Religion and Politics in the John C. Danforth Center on Religion and Politics at Washington University in St. Louis. A historian of religion in early America, he has written about religious thought and the American Revolution and religion and commerce in New England from 1630 to 1760. He is the author of *Heavenly Merchandize: How Religion Shaped Commerce in Puritan America* (2010). He has more recently been working on a project that concerns conceptions of conversion, Protestant descriptions of other religions, and politics in Anglo-America from the English Civil War through the American Revolution.

ABRAM VAN ENGEN is associate professor of English at Washington University in St. Louis. He is the author of two books: *Sympathetic Puritans: Calvinist Fellow Feeling in Early New England* (2015), which looks at the influence of Puritan theology on the history of sympathy; and *City on a Hill: A History of American Exceptionalism* (2020), which examines the role Pilgrims and Puritans have played in origin stories of America from the 1600s to the present day. He is also the co-editor of *A History of American Puritan Literature* (2020). He has won a faculty fellowship and a Public Scholar Award from the National Endowment for the Humanities, as well as the Whitehill Prize in Early American History.

CAROLINE WIGGINTON is chair and associate professor of English at the University of Mississippi. She is the author of *In the Neighborhood: Women's Publication in Early America* (2016), which won the Early American Literature Book Prize, and the co-editor, with Joanna Brooks and Lisa Moore, of the anthology *Transatlantic Feminisms in the Age of Revolutions* (2012).

With Alyssa Mt. Pleasant and Kelly Wisecup, she co-edited an award-winning forum jointly published in *Early American Literature* and the *William and Mary Quarterly* on materials and methods in Native American and Indigenous studies. Her next book is *Indigenuity: Native Craftwork and the Art of American Literatures to 1900*.

Index